Quinn

Quinn

The Life of a Hockey Legend

DAN ROBSON

VIKING

VIKING

an imprint of Penguin Canada Books Inc., a Penguin Random House Company

Published by the Penguin Group
Penguin Canada Books Inc., 320 Front Street West, Suite 1400,
Toronto, Ontario M5V 3B6, Canada

Penguin Group (USA) LLC, 375 Hudson Street, New York, New York 10014, U.S.A.
Penguin Books Ltd, 80 Strand, London WC2R 0RL, England
Penguin Ireland, 25 St Stephen's Green, Dublin 2, Ireland
(a division of Penguin Books Ltd)
Penguin Group (Australia), 707 Collins Street, Melbourne, Victoria 3008, Australia
(a division of Pearson Australia Group Pty Ltd)
Penguin Books India Pvt Ltd, 11 Community Centre, Panchsheel Park,
New Delhi – 110 017, India
Penguin Group (NZ), 67 Apollo Drive, Rosedale, Auckland 0632, New Zealand
(a division of Pearson New Zealand Ltd)
Penguin Books (South Africa) (Pty) Ltd, 24 Sturdee Avenue, Rosebank,
Johannesburg 2196, South Africa

Penguin Books Ltd, Registered Offices: 80 Strand, London WC2R 0RL, England

First published 2015

1 2 3 4 5 6 7 8 9 10 (RRD)

Copyright © Dan Robson, 2015

Cover photo: David Cooper / Getty Images
Cover design: Lisa Jager
Author photograph: © Randy Risling, 2015

Manufactured in the U.S.A.

LIBRARY AND ARCHIVES CANADA CATALOGUING IN PUBLICATION

Robson, Dan, 1983–, author
Quinn : the life of a hockey legend / Dan Robson.

Includes index.
ISBN 978-0-670-06991-0 (bound)

1. Quinn, Pat, 1943-2014. 2. Hockey coaches—Canada—
Biography. 3. Hockey players—Canada—Biography. I. Title.

GV848.5.Q56R63 2015   796.962092   C2015-905154-1

eBook ISBN 978-0-14-319603-7

Visit the Penguin Canada website at **www.penguin.ca**

Special and corporate bulk purchase rates available; please see
www.penguin.ca/corporatesales or call 1-800-810-3104.

For my father, Rick Robson—a builder and a fixer.

With me, always.

Whoever came in took a lot of pride in their street.
They took a lot of pride in their lives. But that's what Hamilton is.
To me, it was always a city that was full of pride.
Pride in who they were. Pride in the work that they did.

—PAT QUINN IN *THE GLOBE AND MAIL*,
SHORTLY AFTER WINNING OLYMPIC
GOLD AT THE 2002 WINTER OLYMPICS
IN SALT LAKE

Contents

1

Glennie Avenue

The stories grew in time, distilled in early accounts then gaining flavor in the casks of their minds. Pat Quinn, the boy from east Hamilton—the boy they knew—became the man who laid out Bobby Orr, who steered the longest winning streak in the history of sports, who gave life to the game in Vancouver— the coach who ended the nation's fifty-year drought. The tales pour out, rich and full-bodied, varied slightly with each taste.

Here's one that has been told before, many times, in many ways. Pat Quinn—eight, maybe nine—was hiking home from St. Helen Catholic Elementary School one afternoon, past the white bungalows planted in the fields near the steel plants that sprouted industry in postwar Hamilton. His black hair, almost certainly, was combed and perfectly parted. His eyes punctuated by a wide brow. A steep nose, sharply cut, with a matching chin. His shirt tucked in, slacks neatly pressed. Shoes shined, as they always were. Trailing behind him, a pack of three older boys, tossing insults like darts.

Pat was big then. And that was the point the bullies hoped would prick him—that he was the boy too big for his age. He walked on for blocks, saying nothing, passing the white houses one by one, until he reached the corner of Glennie and Melvin Avenues, across from the kelly-green house with its matching fence.

Jack Quinn, the story goes, was working on his patch of lawn and saw his eldest son running from the jackals that snapped at his heels. He whistled. Just a curve of the lips, no fingers required. It was a mighty burst, piercing, and locally famous. The kind of beacon that reached tiny Quinns for blocks, announcing chores and bedtimes and sometimes this: Pat looked up at his father. Jack opened his hand wide and smacked his other fist into the flat palm, making a loud clap. Pat nodded. He spun around—*Always pick the biggest guy. He'll go down. The rest will run.* Eye contact. One, two. Boom, boom. The big one hit the sidewalk. The others ran like hell.

In the many lessons of Jack Quinn, fists were not necessarily the first option. But they were a tool, employed when needed. And they were often needed to settle differences on the scrappy streets and playgrounds near the bay in east-end Hamilton, where slate-colored stacks reached for smoky clouds.

If you were there today, you'd find the same tiny house on the corner of Glennie and Melvin, backing onto the old yellow-bricked Imperial Bank of Commerce. The house, now inhabited by Pat's younger sister Carol, has been revamped some—a few interior walls removed, the rooms redone, a potbelly stove long gone. The once-green panels are now white, matching the neigh-boring homes that line the streets like markers in a cemetery of soldiers. There are pieces of a past still lingering there, at

252 Glennie. Dusty tools in a workshop. Hockey sticks stacked in a basement corner. There are puck marks behind the drywall with the outline of a hockey net, painted black. The phone number is the same as it was when it was first assigned to the Quinns seven decades back.

Outside on the corner, above the sign for Glennie, another touts the street's new name: Pat Quinn Way. It's named for the boy whose story began here, building into legend—told, and retold—expanding, and perhaps embellished, with time. From the table in the narrow kitchen, you can still see the faint marks where the coal stove sat and picture the lounger where a grandpa slept and a yard with once-worn base paths. "There are plenty of ghosts in this house," says Carol.

The table is pretty much where it was then, when Jack Quinn sat in the same spot at its head, always. Pat, the oldest, was directly across from him. Jean Quinn loaded the table with a hot meal fresh from her stove. The bowls emptied quickly, but the family rule was strictly enforced: Take some, but always remember there's someone at this table behind you. That didn't mean you didn't have to keep your wits about you, though. Pat would tap Carol's shoulder and steal her milk when she looked the other way. Another Quinn family rule: Turn your head, and it's gone. And before the plates were cleared, always, Jack Quinn's quiz would begin: Addition. Subtraction. Multiplication. Division. Spelling, s.p.e.l.l.i.n.g., spelling. Each question geared to age and grade, ensuring that before the dinner plates were cleared Jack was certain his children were well on their way to a different kind of life.

The lessons of life were simple to Jack Quinn. It took everything he and his wife had to own the roof above them and put the food on those plates. Everything. If there was a different path to take, he knew it came with the education he'd never had the chance to earn. *Learn, learn, learn—never stop learning,* he'd preach. He carried a dictionary in his pocket, everywhere he went, looking up words he didn't recognize. Whenever a manual chore earned a groan from his kids, Jack was quick to remind them that they held the keys to their own futures. "That's why I say get an education," Jack told his eldest son, who grumbled about chiselling out a coal chute for the furnace. "You can pay somebody to do this."

A black-and-white photograph of Jack and Jean on their wedding day sits on the counter, wrapped around a candle, with a wick that burns into smoke and lingers. It represents a flame that started in 1940, in a dance hall perched at the top of a steep set of steps off Wentworth Street on Hamilton Mountain. There, with music spilling from the hall, falling over the city, Jean Ireland met a handsome young man named John Ernest Quinn. He was a terrific dancer. His friends called him Jack.

Jack was from the north side of town, the third of four kids, born on the kitchen table of Arthur and Mary Quinn's home on Ferry Street in 1916, in the midst of the War to End All Wars. (Arthur came to Canada from Liverpool in 1908. His father was a merchant seaman from Dublin. Mary was also Irish, but had been living in England. They were known as "the Scouse," what Irish people living in Liverpool were called. All of Mary's brothers were six-foot-four or -five—a gift that would be passed on to her eldest grandson.) At the start of the Great Depression, Jack graduated straight from the eighth grade at St. Joseph's to the TH&B rail yards. He didn't have much time to play sports when he was young—he and his brother delivered groceries or sold newspapers. He played the ukulele and loved to sing. He was a regular at local dances on Friday and Saturday evenings and was known to carry a couple of extra shirts because he'd sweat through them.

As Jack and Jean danced on Hamilton Mountain that night, the world around them was crumbling into another war. Shortly after they met, Jack walked down to the HMCS *Star* on Catharine Street on the Hamilton Harbour and signed up for the navy. He was immediately sent to Halifax, where he was assigned to sail the North Atlantic Run, guarding supply ships traveling to Great Britain. Jack would become the kind of war vet who was damn proud to have served, but never spoke much about life as a petty officer guarding rations and civilians from German U-boats as they snuck across the North Atlantic Sea.

The pair married two days after Christmas in 1941, while he was on leave. They traveled through Quebec on their honeymoon and visited the Basilica of Sainte-Anne-de-Beaupré on the St. Lawrence.

Once they were married, Jean made the trip to Halifax to visit her husband each time he returned safely to Canadian shores. Their first child was born on January 29, 1943, at St. Joseph's Hospital in Hamilton. Jack learned the news in a telegram while aboard the HMCS *Columbia*, a navy destroyer. The message came in four economical words: "It has a tassel." They named him John Brian Patrick Quinn—everyone called him Pat.

For a while, Jean moved out to Nova Scotia to be closer to her husband when he returned from his tours across the ocean.

In 1944, she rented an old converted chicken coop, overlooking Digby Bay in Clementsport, where she would be able to see Jack's ship return home. On those happy days of respite from worry, they would take Pat to the shore and dig for clams to bake on the beach. Jean and Jack had another son, Barry, in 1945. And then Carol, the only girl, was born in 1946.

When she wasn't in Nova Scotia, Jean lived with her parents in Hamilton on Wentworth Street. Jean's father, George Michael Ireland—better known as Snooze—was a local legend. The Ireland family settled in Canada in the early nineteenth century. George Michael was born in 1888 and grew up on the two-hundred-acre farm his parents owned in Burlington, Ontario. His father died when he was ten, and the family moved into the house on Wentworth. Snooze played hockey for the Hamilton Alerts in the Ontario Hockey Association, back when the game was played with seven per side and no substitutions. The team played on Burlington Bay until the Hamilton Hockey Arena was built. The thirty-eight-hundred capacity bunker-like building with wooden seats inside became known as the Barton Street Forum, but was affectionately dubbed "the barn." Snooze played in the first game there, on January 10, 1913, when he and the Alerts beat Welland 8–4. He also played baseball for the White Team—a local challenge team that took on, and generally beat, anyone looking for a match.

But Snooze had the most success with football. He was a center for the Hamilton Tigers and won the Grey Cup in 1915. (The rumor is that his nickname came from his propensity to fall asleep on the snap, something that became a family trait.) After winning the Grey Cup, Snooze used his local celebrity in the war effort, helping to form the 205th Battalion—known as the Tiger Battalion because several of the team's players joined. The *Hamilton Spectator* put his picture in the paper: "George Snooze Ireland joins the 205th," the caption read. Snooze would eventually end up on the front line in France, east of Vimy Ridge, where he was wounded by shrapnel in the right arm and left leg during a raid. After several months recovering, he returned to Canada in the spring of 1919 and that fall he married Irene Wade. They had five children and raised them in his own childhood home on Wentworth, next to the streetcar barn. He kept the shrapnel from his war wounds as a souvenir, and his grandkids would later frame the shards in his honor.

Snooze developed a close bond with his eldest grandson, Pat, whom he'd take to watch the Hamilton Tiger Cubs Junior A hockey team play down at the Barn. He often smoked Punch Margaritas and White Owl cigars, and sometimes let one of the Quinn kids spark the match. He gave Pat his maroon beret from his 1915 Grey Cup win, which Pat wore proudly throughout his youth.

When Jack Quinn finally returned from the war he found work selling men's clothing, until he discovered that he was color-blind. Shortly after that revelation, he joined the Hamilton Fire Service.

The young Quinn family rented a small house at 145 Vansitmart Avenue, in Hamilton's east end—a poor, working-class part of town, close to the factories and steel plants, where men spent their days moving molten iron with tongs and then punched out and replenished their fluids with a pint. It was a community built on hard work that yielded little pay, but offered high dividends in character and pride. The family lived in a two-bedroom bungalow heated by a coal stove in the living room, a temporary build for soldiers returning from the war. A few years later, in 1950, a fourth Quinn—Guy—was born, and Jack and Jean realized they had to move to a bigger home. Jack found a three-bedroom place just off of Barton Street, a white bungalow that was one of many issued by the government to house soldiers returning from war and ready to work in the factories. The row homes were initially intended to be temporary, as they were cheaply assembled with little room to grow. There were no sidewalks then, just trenches dug along the unpaved streets. But few families left.

The Quinns paid five thousand dollars for the house at 252 Glennie Avenue, on the corner of Barton Street (later renamed Melvin Avenue.) Principal, interest, and taxes came to fifty dollars a month. Proudly Irish, Jack painted the house kelly green. On the main level, the two original bedrooms and a washroom were rented out to help pay the mortgage. Jack found space for a master bedroom, the children's rooms, and a bathroom on the second floor, beneath a ceiling that angled sharply with the roof. He built a wooden bunk with shelves for the three boys just off the narrow stairs to the left. The beds sat above drawers, where the kids kept their belongings. Pat slept along the wall closest to the door. Barry's bed was on a right angle from the bottom of Pat's, along the wall. It connected to a third bed, along the wall across from Pat, where Guy slept. When Phillip was born in 1957, Jack added another bed to the bunks. Carol, the only girl, had a bed along the last wall all to herself and Jack and Jean slept across the hall.

When he was just seven, after a few years spent in the house, Pat helped his mother and father dig out the basement with shovels and picks. With the house hoisted up on blocks, they shovelled out barrels of concrete and dirt for days. In 1954, when the concrete floor was finally poured, the Quinns invited all the neighbors over to have a New Year's Eve party in the basement. The extra room served the family as a workshop, a boxing gym, and a hockey practice pad.

Jack built a makeshift washroom in the dug-out basement, where the kids bathed in a laundry tub until he put in a shower. He never got around to adding hot water, however. Next to the tub, there was a speed bag and a heavy bag made out of an old navy hammock sack filled with stuffing. Pat practiced his *one, two … boom, boom* on that bag, wearing gloves so he wouldn't skin his knuckles. Aside from bullies who had yet to learn the legend of Quinn, Pat developed a penchant for pounding on the Protestant punks who blocked his path on the grape field he and his friend cut through to get to St. Helen Elementary. His slacks, marked with faded purple spots from the splattered grapes, hung on the clothesline over worn-down basepaths and the limestone slab home plate where the Quinn children played ball.

Jean watched over the tornado of activity that swirled through and around the house. It was her domain—and she ruled with a stern, loving authority. Jean was the one the Quinn kids ran to, but also knew not to cross because she could have a temper. She was elegant, the kind of woman who would put on a dress and makeup to run errands at the grocery store. She was also the one who adventured through the woods with the kids, camping in the summers near Paris, Ontario. Jack would drive out to help them set up, stay for a couple of days, then head back to Hamilton to work while the kids spent their vacations swimming and practicing what they'd learned at the local Boy Scouts. While Jack was the one who pushed sports, Jean, a runner and swimmer who came from a family of athletes, understood the values inherent in them. If the kids started a league, they finished it. There was hardly ever an excuse to miss a practice.

Between his regular shifts as a firefighter, Jack picked up extra money driving a borrowed cab. On off days, he'd go door-to-door selling cans of Lustre Sheen, for workers to clean the grease off their hands. He made regular trips to the HMCS *Star* where he taught navy recruits and also tended bar. He would buy old cars then mine their cadavers to sell as parts.

Even with all the odd jobs, the hours spent to earn each nickel, Jack would make it home for dinner. And when his kids were young, plates cleared, he'd read them the daily comic about a rabbit named Uncle Wiggly in the *Hamilton Spectator*. And when it was time to teach knot tying to the Cubs over at the Normanhurst Community Centre, next to Mahoney, he was always there pulling his ropes. Jack smoked Buckingham cigarettes, which always reminded his kids of the story of his return from war on the HMCS *Buckingham*, a River-class frigate that bounced around on the rough Atlantic seas. At home in Hamilton, Pat and his younger siblings sang: "The Buckingham, the Buckingham, the Buck, Buck, Buck Buckingham."

There was no television in the Quinn house then. Pat would take his younger brother Barry on the streetcar down to the firehall where their father worked on John Street, just north of Barton.

They climbed a winding staircase to the second floor, where the crew watched TV. On Saturday mornings they watched cartoons, and when the shows were over, Jack would let Pat slide down the firepole. Jack became the first president of the firefighters' union in Hamilton. Eventually he'd be promoted to captain, and everyone would know him as Captain Jack. One night while Pat was playing ball hockey, the blare of sirens interrupted the game, and all the kids followed it down the street to a fish-and-chips shop with smoke coming out of it. A window on the second floor smashed open, and Jack Quinn stuck his head out. All of the kids cheered while Jack, who didn't have a mask back then, gasped for air.

Reflecting on those early years, Pat often recalled those trips to the firehall as among the happiest moments of his youth. On Saturday nights he'd make the trip on the streetcar and climb the winding stairs to watch NHL games on the tube. It was one of the few places he could see the games he'd listened to while sitting next to the woodstove in the living room, as Foster Hewitt described his dreams. (Years later, in 1968, he'd climb the stairs to the old gondola at Maple Leaf Gardens and find the man whose voice had captured his imagination so deeply.) Listening to those games he became a fan of Teeter Kennedy, his first hockey hero. He'd also become a young fan of the St. Catharines Teepees hockey team—the Chicago Black Hawks affiliate—where many future pros played their junior hockey.

When they weren't listening to hockey games, the Quinn kids often huddled around the radio in their parents' room listening to stories of Hopalong Cassidy, Inner Sanctum, and the Lone Ranger. Often, on those days, Jack and Jean would be down at the HMCS *Star*, dancing like they did when they first met. Snooze would watch the kids when they went. He'd doze in an armchair at the bottom of the stairs in the tiny living room with the black potbelly that heated the entire house. Upstairs in their bunks, Pat was in charge. He'd send his younger brother Barry down to get him a glass of water, using up his one trip downstairs allowed within the rights of grandkids sent to bed.

Once, when Barry had used up his trip downstairs for Pat, he found himself in need of relief. Afraid to wake Snooze, after much brotherly deliberation, he did the next logical thing and peed down through the floor grate into the woodstove. Snooze roared awake with a slur of words more suited to the gridiron, as the heat from the stove carried the distinctive scent of urine up to the boys in their beds and into the rooms rented out on the main floor.

There was trouble for that, most certainly. Jack was rigid with the rules—though loving and warm, he kept order in the house the same way he kept order as a petty officer in the navy. He wanted his kids to fend for themselves and be able to defend themselves. He wanted them to be respectful. And he wanted them to hang out with crowds that would take them in the right direction. Neither he nor Jean suffered foolish distractions. But within the rigid focus of home, there was always singing, always dancing. Always joy. Always love, Pat would grow up to say. And there was always a simple message: *Never stop learning.*

So around the kitchen table, they sat as a family, and learned, learned, learned. And when the plates were cleared and the quizzes answered to Jack's satisfaction, the Quinn kids would quickly be back outdoors, where life was mostly lived in those days. Pat would plan to head back to the outdoor rink at nearby Mahoney Park, just across Barton—where the floodlights were waiting for him to carve another story into his emerging local legend. But before he could sneak out through the enclosed front porch, the same lesson would catch him, every time: the father making sure his son knew that a bigger legend was waiting to be told, if only he'd put in the work to get there.

"Leave your stick here," Jack would say. "You go to that rink—and skate, skate, skate."

2

Mahoney

He was a giant, hitting balls clear across the fields to the factories, miles away—or so the stories go. The small tales grew to tall tales that grew to the legend of Pat Quinn at Mahoney Park. Just down from 252 Glennie, at the end of the block, a left on Barton and across the street, the park was named in honor of Thomas J. (TJ) Mahoney, a local member of the provincial parliament and member of the Quinns' church, St. Eugene Catholic Church. The Mahoney family land was used to build the wartime homes that the Quinn family and their neighbors lived in. Mahoney himself lived in a nearby house on Parkdale, where he would chase away the neighborhood kids (the Quinn boys included) who tried to knock chestnuts out of trees and onto his front lawn. When he died, TJ Mahoney was laid out in a coffin in his living room. The Quinn kids put on their Sunday best and shuffled in sheepishly to pay their respects.

Mahoney was a sacred place for kids back then—where baseball games were played in the evenings, sometimes under the lights. There was a tall backstop, dugouts, and rows of wooden bleachers. A caretaker raked the infield before each game, and nobody put their footprints in it until it came time to play. It was chalked and everything. The big time.

The Ed Hare Dodgers won the Bantam championships in 1955 on the back of Pat Quinn, who was twelve at the time. He often played games with teams several years older—the days of being picked on for his size now well behind him. On that Dodgers team, sponsored by a local insurance man who provided real wool sweaters, Little Bob Bratina had the misfortune of catching for his teammate Pat, who looked like a grown man to him. When Pat's fastball clapped into his mitt, it knocked Bratina onto his back. On the bench, the Dodgers leaned in to hear Pat's advice. When Puddles (a kid named Dennis Waters, who would go on to become pro wrestler Johnny Powers) was on the mound for the other team, Pat gave Bratina some words of wisdom: "He's scaring you off the plate with inside curve balls," Pat said. "Just hang in there." At his next at-bat, Puddles hit Bratina square between the eyes and smashed his glasses. Pat helped carry him to the "Mahoney medical facilities"—the nearby water fountain, where they dunked his head in hopes of stopping the bruising.

Through those summers, ball hockey battles would erupt on Glennie. It was always the same kids running the show, with Pat Quinn being the biggest and best of the bunch. There was Johnny Walker and Ronny Boles. Bobby Ibbott, a royal pain in the ass. Puddles was the only one close to Pat's size. And Bob Underhill, or Gotch. Bob Bernat, or Net. Richie Schaefer,

Donnie Kinch, and George Knill. Pat Quinn was better than them all, but he always played, building the stories that would become his legend. As a Catholic, he went to a different school than most of them, but it mattered little on Glennie when a game was being played. Justice was judged and decided quickly. A slash for a slash, a punch for a punch. A ball lost down the gutter was paid for with a mob of friends dipping your ass in the drinking fountain, leaving you with soaked bottoms.

As soon as the pegs went up in Mahoney each November, Gotch, who lived right across the street, would report to the boys that hockey was on its way. It was a full-sized rink, pegged out and lined with brown wooden boards before the snow would fall. When the ice was set, it was finished with carefully measured lines and regulation nets. Lights from the ball diamond lit the sheet at night. It sat next to another open ice pad, where families with young kids would come to practice skating, and teenage girls would work on their twirls and jumps. On long cold days, skaters and hockey players warmed up around the woodstove in the brown clubhouse nearby.

The Quinn kids knew that the moment they heard their father's shrill whistle coming from around the block, or as soon as the streetlights cast wide circles on Glennie, it was time to head home. Dinnertime. No arguments. Inside, around the table, it was another round of quizzes with the potatoes. And then Pat would try to sneak back out the door. The inevitable refrain would follow him, punctuated with the playful name his father often called him: *"John Brian Patrick Aloysius Quinn! Leave your stick! Skate. Skate! Skate!!"*

Pat might have been the best athlete in the Parkdale neighborhood, but stories of his talent on the ice were always told with a hushed footnote that big Pat Quinn wasn't the swiftest on his feet. Jack Quinn constantly reminded his son that being the best required a significant commitment to practicing the fundamental skills of the game. The game was played on skates, after all—you damn well better know how to use them.

If he couldn't sneak away before his father's reminder, Pat would dutifully leave his stick in the enclosed front porch and make his way up Glennie with just his skates in hand. It didn't matter. Pat always found a stick to use and a game to play in. No one was going to let a player like him waste time with stops and starts on the kiddie rink. He was always wanted at Mahoney, even for scrimmages with boys five and six years older. His younger siblings—Carol, Barry, and Guy (the fifth Quinn kid, Phillip, was still a few years from being born)—would sit in the stands and watch their brother play with the neighborhood's biggest and best. Despite his lagging feet, he had a knack for reading the game, and they admired the way their older brother played, even though none of them felt drawn to it the way he did. To the younger Quinns, the eldest outlined a blueprint for possibility. They also saw him work his ass off, whatever he did.

Each morning, Pat delivered the *Hamilton Daily Mail* and the *Globe and Mail*, which had a winding route with few subscribers spread across miles. If he had to leave early for a hockey practice with the local team, the route was picked up by Carol or Barry, or even Jean, who knew which fences to hop to speed up the trip.

Pat's entrepreneurial ambition didn't end there. He went door-to-door selling subscriptions for *Liberty* and *Life* magazines.

And well before Tim Hortons came on the scene, Pat took orders from neighbors for yeast donuts—honey dipped or jelly filled for twenty-five cents a dozen. Once he got the order, Jack would pick up the bakery confections and Pat would deliver them to the houses. He also got a part-time job at Pollock's grocery store, delivering groceries to the neighborhood in an old banana crate hitched to the front of his bike's handlebars. During the winters, Pat and Barry would hitchhike to the Bol-O-Drome on Parkdale Avenue to set up pins, earning five cents a game. Pat would run four lanes, while Barry did two. In the summers, they caddied at the Glendale Golf Club. Pat was always the first picked by golfers, who enjoyed his counsel on the game, and he often went out for a couple of rounds a day. (Later in life, the game would regularly end in choice words over missed shots. Pat excelled at a lot of sports, but golf was not one of them.)

The children's earnings went straight to Jean, who kept track of what was brought in and gave her kids their fair share. None would ever recall wanting for anything. Each kid found their sport. Carol was a ball player and Barry was a swimmer. Guy, then about five, would grow to be a football player—following the tradition laid out by Grandpa Snooze.

The Quinn basement was brimming with bats and baseballs, lacrosse sticks and India rubber balls, hockey sticks and well-worn hand-me-down skates. When they played hockey on the road or ice, Jean rolled magazines around their shins and held them in place with a cut-up inner tube. The kids who played ball hockey on still unpaved Glennie would sometimes play with frozen apples or droppings from the horses that pulled the wagons bringing milk, bread, or ice. (Pat would often tell the "horseshit puck" story in decades to come.) When the Quinn kids came in from a winter afternoon, they warmed up sitting next to the black stove in the family room, as they did on cold mornings before the block-and-a-half trek to St. Helen's.

Jack spent hours of the free time he managed to find tossing the lacrosse ball, playing baseball on their tiny backyard diamond, or perfecting the homemade backyard rink he'd make in the winter. Practice was everything. Pat hung tin cans from the ceiling in the basement in front of the net they'd painted on the wall. When he didn't have Carol donning the pads while he fired the puck, he tried to make each can ring.

Sundays were family days. After church, Jean sent her kids to the Sunshine Bakery, about three miles away, to pick up fresh loaves of bread for dinner. Pat's favorite was his mother's "hamburg stew," a made-from-scratch version of Hamburger Helper. And her famous grape ketchup—a secret recipe passed down through generations. After the family got their first television, Sunday evenings were spent sitting in the family room watching the *Ed Sullivan Show* in black and white. Pat sat up front, in the center of the room—the best spot—which came with the job of fixing the flip in the TV. He perfected the fix—two taps on the right or left, depending on the direction of the wave.

During summer visits to Grandpa Snooze's cabin at the Holy Family Camp in Cornwall on Lake Ontario, the kids measured their bravery by wading through the deep water to a pump, a round well casing, about fifty feet from the shore. Barry stood in the sand as Pat yelled to him, standing in his dripping bathing suit on top of the pump—"Come on, Barry! Come on!"—coaxing him out into the dark-blue water where only the big kids dared to go. After waiting and delaying, unsure and afraid, his brother's voice pulled Barry as he swam until he reached the edge of the pump. It was the same voice that told him to hurry as they picked raspberries, black currants, and peaches, making fifty cents a basket. The voice that supported his unfortunate decision to pee down the vent into the woodstove. It was the voice of an older brother, calling back and guiding him forward to all the places he would go.

On the first weekend of August in the summer of 1957, Jack Quinn managed to get some time away from work to take his kids camping. They drove up to Midland, Ontario—a couple of hours north of Hamilton, on the edge of Georgian Bay—and set up camp across the street from the Martyrs' Shrine, a gray Catholic church built in honor of eight Jesuit missionaries from the Sainte-Marie-among-the-Hurons settlement who were killed in the 1640s. They drove north from Midland to a park with a long sandy beach and a pool with a three-level diving board. Pat climbed up to the highest level, with Barry right behind him. Pat ran off the platform and dove into the water without hesitation, plummeting thirty feet. Barry watched his brother drop into the pool, looked down at the water from the platform, and promptly headed back to the ladder. Later that afternoon, as the Quinns lounged in the sand, they saw a boy wearing a mask and snorkel waving his arms about fifty feet off shore. At first they thought he was playing, but Barry swam out to make sure, with Pat following close behind. The boy was fighting to stay above the surface as Barry reached him and, panicking, he grabbed Barry and tried to pull himself up—instead pushing Barry under the water. Barry reached up for the shimmering light at the surface as the drowning boy put his weight on him. Pat arrived a few strokes behind and ripped the snorkeling mask from the boy's face, allowing him to breathe through his nose. He flipped the boy over onto his back and grabbed him under the chin to keep his head above water, pulling him back to shore, with Barry close behind.

Barry often found himself following his older brother, watching Pat push on, always striving to be more. The house on Glennie would always be home, but Pat wanted his life to take him much further than the blocks of wartime bungalows, where bills were paid with every nickel honest work could deliver. Pat didn't dream alone, though; it was a family commitment. As his potential on the ice became a possible path out of east Hamilton, the old beaten-down secondhand skates he wore just wouldn't do. Purchasing his first brand-new pair required sacrifice from everyone. Pat's many jobs helped with the bill. Carol had new fenders put on her bike, painted it up real nice, and sold it. The Quinns' beagle gave birth to five pups and each was sold. Grandpa Snooze chipped in, too.

When enough money was gathered, about fifty dollars, Pat dressed up in his best suit and tie. Barry did the same, and Carol wore her best Sunday dress. They climbed into Jack's green Studebaker and drove to Kenesky Sports and Cycle, while Jean stayed home with the youngest, Phil, just a baby then. Trips to Kenesky's were as memorable as Christmas mornings. Items purchased there became cherished family heirlooms, like the Cooper Black Diamond baseball glove Jack bought the kids the year Phil was born. Jack wrote the names of each of his kids in black marker along the brown leather padding of the fingers—five fingers for five children. They oiled it regularly with tea tree oil to keep it soft. And, on the day Pat got his first pair of new skates, the four Quinns walked proudly into Kenesky's. Carol and Barry sat across from Pat, eyes wide, as he pulled the brand-new skates out of the box. Pat pulled up the cuffs of his best church pants and slipped each one on, like a pair of enchanted slippers, making certain they fit just right.

3

Mentors and Toothpicks

"Skate, skate, skate...." It was the only way.

Jack Quinn knew it. Pat knew it. Sam Hart knew it, too. Hart lived just a couple of blocks away from the Quinns on Ivan Street and coached the local midget team of fifteen- and sixteen-year-olds in the Hamilton Police Minor Hockey League.

Over the years, Hart watched Pat develop as a young player on the ice at Mahoney or at the nearby Parkdale rink, where kids had to show up early to shovel snow off the uncovered ice.

Hart was a mentor to many young players in the area. Around the time Pat started junior high—about to sprout into an even taller, even more athletic young man—Hart saw his potential to carve out a future in the game. Pat's size was a benefit. He also had determination. There was only one problem: He was terrible on his skates. "If you can't skate, you can't make it," Hart told Pat. And so they set out to fix that.

Sam Hart, like Jack Quinn, knew the currency of hard work. One of the eldest of five brothers growing up in postwar and post-Depression Hamilton, his formal education took him as far as the eighth grade, when he had to drop out to help his family make ends meet. That leap from boyhood to manhood put a definitive end to his own hockey career, but Hart took up coaching in his twenties. He worked full-time at Hamilton's Westinghouse factory, where he started out as a laborer and eventually worked his way up to the engineering department. Like most of the guys working in the factories, he worked shifts—a week of nights, a few days' break, then afternoons, a few days' break, then a shift of days. It could be a punishing schedule that your body never really got accustomed to.

Pat and Hart would work around his factory shifts, meeting in the mornings or afternoons at Mahoney, between peak times when it would be just the two of them on the ice. Pat took on the one-on-one practices in addition to the ice time he had as a member of the Columbus Club peewee team.

"You look at the guys. You look them right in the chest," Hart instructed as Pat skated backward, focusing on his coach like he was a high-flying opponent. Up and down the ice, and back again, Hart would move forward, then side to side, making sure Pat's eyes didn't drift away from him as he defended. And then Hart would play the defenseman, firing intentionally inaccurate passes to Pat, so he'd understand what it felt like. Pat would stumble and strain to get the puck, left vulnerable to an open ice hit (if it wasn't just the two of them) as Hart stressed the importance of precision when defensemen advanced the puck. And the drills were always played at full speed because you never get to relax in the game. The lessons went on for hours, skating backward and forward, moving the puck quickly—or reversing it back around the net—understanding how to read the game, how to react, how to move with the flow, how to change it, how to know where the play is heading. Sam Hart taught Pat how to think the game, how to see it.

From time to time, Pat would drop by Hart's place, and the pair would chat about how Pat could improve his game as they sat on the veranda of Hart's white wartime bungalow where he lived with his wife. Years later, Pat would sign a picture of the two of them, which Hart kept tucked away, cherished, for the rest of his life. "Sam Hart. My mentor and best friend.—Pat," Quinn wrote.

When Pat was about fourteen, he was asked to play on a regional All-Star team organized by Bill Sherry, the coach of the Columbus Club peewee team that Pat played for. Sherry was a big supporter of Pat. The All-Star team would provide exposure and an opportunity for the young defenseman, who was already six feet tall and nearly 190 pounds. The All-Star team was affiliated with the Hamilton Tiger Cubs Junior B team (which Sherry had helped found in 1953). In those days, NHL teams had regional rights to players. Parents of junior players in Hamilton had to sign a form to allow their kids to play on the team. The form was considered to be an agreement that the player's rights belonged to an NHL team, and in Hamilton, regional rights belonged to the Detroit Red Wings. At the time, Jack Quinn didn't realize that the form he signed to allow his son to play on the regional All-Star team as a fourteen-year-old was the same form signed by the guardians of a junior player. That signature would serve to cause a conflict between Pat Quinn and the Detroit Red Wings that would never be fully resolved.

Pat was a jock who never turned away from a fight. He was also a bookworm, who worked tirelessly in school, and whose efforts were rewarded when he was named valedictorian of his eighth grade class at St. Eugene junior high. As a young teen, Pat was also a committed member of St. Eugene Catholic Church, a few blocks from Glennie, where he wore his best suits with those shined shoes and slicked hair. He sang in the choir and served as an altar boy. Pat considered dedicating his life to pursuing the wonder he found in faith, and the summer after eighth grade, he went to the Monastery of Mount Carmel in Niagara Falls. But he soon realized the rigid commitment to a chaste and viceless life—with no sports, specifically—just wasn't for him.

Instead, a priest at St. Eugene's, Father Cox, leveraged a connection at St. Michael's College School in Toronto and arranged an athletic scholarship that would give Pat a full education at the prestigious institution while he played hockey and football. It was the perfect unfolding of two dreams together. St. Mike's was affiliated with the Toronto Maple Leafs—the school had been a launching pad for NHL greats like Ted Lindsay and Red Kelly. When Pat arrived, the St. Michael's roster included future NHL stars like goalie Cesare Maniago and Leafs legend Dave Keon. And even if Pat didn't make it to the NHL, an education at St. Mike's, fully paid for, offered more possibility than the Quinns could imagine.

In the fall of 1958, Pat climbed onto a streetcar on St. Clair Avenue, in front of the St. Mike's campus just north of Toronto's downtown, with his friend Arnie Brown and a couple of their classmates. The streetcar took them east on St. Clair to Yonge

Street, and then they took the subway south to Carlton Street to the front gates of Maple Leaf Gardens. The school gave its players passes that got them in to see the Leafs play, standing in a section just behind the blue seats. The Gardens was a cathedral to the city and the Leafs had won nine Stanley Cups by that time.

Pat watched Dick Duff and George Armstrong star for the blue and white. He saw a young Frank Mahovlich and Bob Pulford skating up the ice. And back on the blue line, he watched the calm, measured play of twenty-seven-year-old Tim Horton—another St. Mike's alumnus. It was the first NHL game Pat saw in person, and it would be a decade before Pat attended another, this time as a player wearing a Leafs jersey in 1968.

Pat played football for the St. Mike's Kerry Blues that autumn, and planned to lace up for the school's hockey team, the Majors, as the season started. But the Red Wings intervened before he had the chance. Jack Adams, the fiery Detroit general manager who'd had Frank Mahovlich "stolen" from him by the Leafs, wasn't about to take it easy on anyone associated with the franchise. When he found out that his property was going to play for the St. Mike's Majors, the Red Wings demanded one thousand dollars from the Leafs for his rights. The Leafs didn't pay up. And while St. Mike's offered to honor Pat's scholarship to play football, he'd no longer be able to play hockey. Pat wasn't about to give up the game.

Furious, Jack and Jean Quinn went to a priest from St. Eugene's and asked him to speak with the Red Wings' representative in Hamilton, who coached the affiliated Tiger Cubs Junior A team. The Quinns believed they had been duped into signing the form that effectively made their son Red Wings property, and felt that

Detroit was sabotaging their son's opportunities. The meeting didn't end well. As the story is often told, Jean ended up grabbing the man by his tie and choking him a bit. *You're taking my son's life!* she is said to have shouted. However her rage truly manifested in that office, there is no dispute that Jean was a white-hot inferno. A full scholarship: a paid education for her son; his opportunity— stolen by the greed of a franchise that claimed a monopoly on his dreams. Jack and the priest had to pull her away—*Come on, Jean, come on*—leaving the stunned rep gasping for air.

Pat was crushed. He left St. Mike's after the fall semester and returned home to Glennie Avenue, finishing the school year at nearby Cathedral Catholic High School. The Burlington Industrials Junior B team gave him a spot on their roster, which was worth it for the ice time, but a big bump down from the St. Mike's squad he'd hoped to play for. Despite his slow feet he'd earned a reputation as a serviceable defenseman because of his size and strength and read for the game, and later that season, Pat was called up to the Junior A Hamilton Tiger Cubs—the top junior squad in the region. The Cubs were coached by Gerry Brown, a former NHL left-winger from Edmonton, who'd heard the stories of the young Quinn kid and his fists and was looking to add some grit to his lineup.

In Pat's first game with the junior club, Hamilton played the Toronto Marlies, which were coached by legendary Leafs goalie Turk Broda and ended up pounding the outmatched Cubs. Brown started to yell at Broda, over a perceived slight now long forgotten. The inciting action was an afterthought to the tale spun from the ensuing battle. In the heat of his rage,

Brown tapped the shoulder of his young call-up. Pat dutifully hopped the boards, skated across the ice, and dove into the Marlies' bench, battling any opponent he could find, especially Roger Cote—the Marlies tough guy who carried a toothpick between his teeth. "I wanted to shove it down his throat," Pat told Sam Hart later.

The performance helped earn Pat more time on the Tiger Cubs' regular roster the following season, while also playing Junior B hockey with the Hamilton Bees. All the Tiger Cubs players went to Hamilton's Central Secondary School, so Pat moved in with his grandparents, Snooze and Irene, at 32 Wentworth Street, just down the street from Central. Pat's home games were always at the Barton Street arena, where Snooze christened the ice years earlier.

When Pat was in twelfth grade, during a team party that year, he was introduced to Sandra Baker, a student at Westdale and a member of the CFL Tiger Cats Majorettes. They were set up by Sandra's friends. Pat was smitten, and soon Sandra sat at the kitchen table of the house on Glennie, meeting the Quinn family for the first time. She endured "the test" from Jack and the rest of the kids—"Oh look at that fly on the wall," one would say, while another drank Sandra's milk as she turned. Unfazed, she weathered the barrage of jokes and jabs, and as time passed, she became like a big sister, a new addition in the family—an honorary Quinn. After Pat's games, Sandra would come home with Pat and run upstairs, barging into the boys' room, startling Guy from his dreams. "Oh, sorry, did I wake you?" she'd laugh. When Pat was on the road playing hockey, Sandra was often at the Quinn house, helping Jean take care of the place.

As usual, Pat wasn't the fastest guy on the ice, but he worked as hard as or harder than anyone else on the roster. Pat quickly endeared himself to his teammates, with a sharp sense of humor and charismatic confidence. He was, if not *the* biggest, among the biggest players in the Ontario Hockey Association Junior A loop at the time. He didn't put up many points, but his impact was noticed. The *Toronto Daily Star*'s Gordon Campbell credited the 1959 arrival of Pat Quinn, goalie Dennis Jordan, and forward Bert Templeton with leading a resurgence for the Cubs. The team was sitting in the league cellar in November, but the call-ups had helped Hamilton push for a playoff spot by late January. The Cubs wouldn't make it, in the end, as they allowed fifty-nine shots against and lost 9–1 to the Guelph Biltmores in the final game of the regular season. Pat picked up two minutes for charging in the first period and a ten-minute misconduct in the second. Guelph was coached by Eddie Bush, who would move to take over the Hamilton team the next year.

Bush didn't see much potential in Pat, the oversized defenseman who offered little in the way of offense. Pat had recorded just two assists and no goals in the thirty-nine games he played with the Tiger Cubs over two seasons. He also served a ten-game suspension for swinging his stick at an opponent during a game. He was the definition of "stay at home." The Hamilton Tiger Cubs—who changed their name to the Hamilton Red Wings that year to help promote more ticket sales by showing their affiliation with their namesake in Detroit—had a lot of talent on their roster, including Paul Henderson. Henderson admired Pat's drive, despite the limitations he faced as a player. Pat always worked hard in practice and teammates noticed that his skating improved. He still wasn't swift, but he was steady. For a time Quinn even served as captain with the Hamilton Bees Junior B team. But he never won Eddie Bush's favor. He wanted a fast team with talented goal scorers. He wanted everything that Quinn would never be. When Bush took over the Hamilton team, he told Pat that he planned to send him to another Detroit Red Wings affiliate—in Melville, Saskatchewan, about ninety miles northeast of Regina. Pat found the tiny town on a map. It might as well have been Siberia. "Nah, I don't think so," he thought.

Uncertain of where his future in hockey was heading, Pat met with a friend from St. Mike's who was attending Michigan Tech. "They're looking for a defenseman here," he told Pat. "Why don't you call them?" The college was considered a rogue road to professional hockey at the time, as NHL teams mined their talent out of the junior players they controlled. Pat called John MacInnes, the head coach of the Michigan Tech Huskies. MacInnes offered him a full scholarship.

It was a new opportunity to pursue a life beyond the game, a chance to secure the education he'd hoped for. There was no way he or his parents could afford an education like this, but Pat wasn't sure what to do. The scholarship would likely diminish any hope he had of playing in the pros.

He went to Pinky Lewis, a long-time Hamilton amateur sports trainer, told him about the offer and asked for his advice. Lewis told Pat to go find Glen Sonmor.

4

"Go for the Education"

Glen Sonmor was a sporting legend in Hamilton—a kid from the east end who went on to play for the New York Rangers. Young boys smacked sticks at Mahoney and chased balls in road hockey games on unpaved streets like Glennie pretending to be him. If Sonmor could do it, they could do it, too. In the mid-1940s, Sonmor—five-foot-eleven and 160 pounds, with a long skinny face and dark-brown hair—had been a top basketball and football player at Delta Secondary School, and he had a shot at going pro in baseball. Sonmor chose hockey instead.

Years before he went pro, Sonmor had asked his basketball coach at Delta, a man he respected deeply, what he should do with his life after school. The coach told him to figure out whatever brought the most happiness, and then find the best way to make it happen. It didn't matter what you did, or how much money you made, as long as you didn't find yourself counting down the hours to the end of a day, or days to the end of a week. When Sonmor was playing in the minor league system for the

plum
rewards ™

Points Required	Reward Value
2,500	$5
4,500	$10
8,500	$20
20,000	$50
35,000	$100

Explore the benefits of plum rewards and become a member for free! Visit indigo.ca/plumrewards to learn more.

Chapters indigo COLES indigo.ca

Refunds or exchanges may be made within 14 days if item is returned in store-bought condition with a receipt. Items with a gift receipt may be exchanged or refunded onto a credit note for the value of the item at the time of purchase. We cannot provide an exchange or refund on magazines or newspapers.

plum
rewards ™

Refunds or exchanges may be made within 14 days if item is re
store-bought condition with a receipt. Items with a gift receipt may
or refunded onto a credit note for the value of the item at the time o
We cannot provide an exchange or refund on magazines or newsp

Chapters

Store# 00928 Chapters Surrey
12101 72nd Avenue, Suite 100
Surrey, BC V3W 2M1
Phone: (604) 501-2877

Tell us about your visit today
and enter to win a $500 giftcard!
Complete our survey at:
www.indigofeedback.com
See survey site for contest details.

Store# 00928 Term# 003 Trans# 418515
Operator: 923   11/21/2015 15:43
GIFT RECEIPT
****
QUINN   CFAA
9780670069910

****
A GIFT FOR YOU
****

It is with regret that we inform you
that this store will be closing on
January 23. We will be happy to continue
serving you at Indigo Grandview Corners
or on-line at www.chapters.indigo.ca.
Store# 00928 Term# 003 Trans# 418515
GST Registration # R897152666

009280030418515152

New York Rangers with the St. Paul Saints of the old United States Hockey League, he was one of the only players who had a high school diploma. "Kid, I've played pro hockey for ten years now," said his coach, John Mariucci, after finding out about the diploma. "You're the first one I've ever met who finished high school … You're going to college." And then he dragged Sonmor to the University of Minnesota, where he studied physical education through the springs and summers until he finished a master's degree. A short time later, Sonmor was playing left wing for a Rangers minor league team when he took a teammate's slap shot in the face and lost his left eye. With his hockey career over, Sonmor took the advice of his old basketball coach and did what he loved: He taught phys ed at Westdale Secondary School in Hamilton.

And so, that fall, Pat found himself reluctantly walking through the doors of a rival school in the city's west end. He made the trip to listen to Glen Sonmor—now a teacher with one glass eye—tell the story of his journey to a job where he never counted down the hours to the end of a day.

Eventually, Sonmor would take a different career path, though still linked to the things that made him happy. He remained a teacher, but as coach of the Minnesota North Stars. Years after their conversation at the high school in west Hamilton, the two local legends would meet again in 1980— each at the helm of a team battling in a Conference final for a chance to play for the Stanley Cup. The old mentor would fall to the young coach who'd once sought his counsel about an uncertain future.

But that was still a long way—many years, many lessons—from where he sat that day, listening to Sonmor, the basketball coach, echo a message he'd heard at the family dinner table for years. "Go for the education," Sonmor told him. "Take the scholarship."

Pat went to Michigan Tech—in Houghton, Michigan, on the shores of Lake Superior, a twelve-hour drive from Hamilton—for the fall term in 1960. He lived in barracks with all the athletes, including his pal Bob Pallante and a few other St. Mike's guys who'd gotten scholarships as well. He lasted one semester and never suited up for the Huskies—before the Red Wings stifled his education a second time. With the Tiger Cubs, Pat had been paid a stipend of forty dollars a week—a small sum that helped cover the player's food expenses. When Jack Adams, the Red Wings coach and GM, found out that one of the players in his organization was going to school, he again went out to stake claim on his property. Two other first recruits with the Michigan Tech Huskies had accepted similar stipends playing for different junior teams, but neither team made a fuss about it. However, the Red Wings sent the university stubs from the cheques that Pat had been given, proving that he'd accepted money to play junior with the Tiger Cubs. His scholarship was revoked before he had a chance to play a single game. It was St. Mike's all over again—and again, Pat was furious. It's all about control, Pat realized. The Red Wings—hockey itself—was sending a message: *Don't break ranks, kid.*

Pat would never forgive the Red Wings.

He returned to Hamilton after his semester in Michigan, hitch-hiking part of the seven hundred miles home, and decided he wasn't going to return to hockey that year. He picked up a job at the Dofasco Steel plant, not far from Mahoney. Pat's uncle,

Jack's brother Fred, worked there and helped get him in. He worked with big tongs, pulling steel around for half-hour shifts at a time. Pat worked the bull block—a machine that produced steel wire.

Working in that steel mill, Pat looked around at the men, hard at work in the heat and flames and molten elements, and knew this wasn't the life for him. He didn't want to punch a clock and slave away, counting down the hours to shift's end to hit a pub to replenish body and mind with fluids, just to repeat it all again the next day. It wasn't that Pat didn't respect the men who worked there. On the contrary: They were the men he grew up around, men he admired. They were a proud part of his life. But he couldn't stop there. He knew that those values— that ethic—could be applied anywhere. On the ice, certainly. And in the classroom. "Don't ever give it up," his dad always told him. Education was the *one* thing that would give him leverage in the workplace—whether with Dofasco or the Red Wings—and it didn't matter how long it took: He swore he'd get that degree.

But first, Pat was heading west.

The Edmonton Oil Kings were founded in 1950 by Jim Christiansen, the owner of a local Mercury car dealership. Christiansen also funded the Edmonton Mercurys Senior A hockey team that won gold at the 1952 Olympics in Oslo, Norway—a feat that no Canadian men's hockey team would accomplish for the next fifty years. The Oil Kings quickly became a junior hockey powerhouse, boasting future NHL stars like George Armstrong and Johnny Bucyk.

Edmonton was managed by Leo LeClerc, a colorful and very successful businessman who, like Glen Sonmor, had lost the use of one of his eyes—though LeClerc lost his at the age of two in an accident caused by the ashes of his grandfather's pipe. LeClerc, who refused to be paid for his job because he didn't want to be told what to do, had a knack for working the media and excelled at promoting his team. The Edmonton Gardens sat about six thousand people and nearly reached capacity for the team's regular Sunday afternoon games. The province didn't allow teams to charge for admission to games on Sundays, so between periods they took up a "silver collection," where fans tossed fifty-cent coins onto the ice. The Oil Kings were coached by Buster Brayshaw, who played briefly with the Chicago Black Hawks but spent most of his career in the minor leagues before pursuing a life behind the bench.

The Oil Kings had made the national final three years in a row but they had fallen short against bigger teams from Eastern Canada in the Memorial Cup each time. Brayshaw and LeClerc knew their team needed to add size and strength if it was going to win a national championship. They called Clarence Moher, the team's head scout, who was known for uncovering talent in unexpected places, just as he had with Norm Ullman.

Enter Pat Quinn—nineteen years old, six-foot-three, 230 pounds—sitting out in Hamilton, hoping for a new start. Like the Tiger Cubs, who had Pat's rights in junior, the Oil Kings were affiliated with the Detroit Red Wings. Moher knew about Pat's reputation as a bruising stay-at-home defenseman, and convinced the Red Wings to arrange a transfer.

Beyond his summer spent considering the priesthood, that brief time at St. Mike's, and his semester in Michigan, Pat hadn't strayed too far from home. Edmonton would be the farthest away he'd been, and for the longest time. Still, he readily accepted the chance to play for a high-profile, successful team like the Oil Kings. All the same, Quinn asked that the team pay for him to attend university, but it wouldn't commit the money for that.

For his part, education was important to LeClerc. He knew that very few of his players would turn pro and that a lot of junior players would slack off on their schooling thinking that hockey was all they needed. He pushed them to go to school while they played, making sure they kept up their high school grades or picked up correspondence college courses. A handful of the players took university courses. One studied dentistry. Another went to trade school to get experience with sheet metal.

When Pat first showed up at the Oil Kings practice, his teammates were shocked to find him as big as they'd been told. No one in the league—a loop that included mostly Senior A teams—was anywhere close to Pat's size. A sense of calm confidence came over them, as though an older brother had shown up on the playground after their seasons of being knocked around by bullies.

Like many a coach and mentor before him, Brayshaw knew that Pat's greatest challenge was skating. So he would keep him after practice and force him to do laps around the rink once, twice, ten times. Pat would get so pissed at his coach for not letting him off the ice that he'd throw his stick into the stands. Some rink rat would inevitably retrieve the heaved stick and bring it back. And Brayshaw would make Pat skate some more.

When he arrived in Edmonton, Pat moved in with the Knox family a couple of blocks from the Edmonton Gardens. Kay, or Mrs. Kay as Pat would come to call her, and her husband, Robert, lived in a two-story glass-and-stucco house with three sons and a young daughter (their eldest daughter having already left home). Swede Knox, their youngest son, was the Oil Kings' stick boy at the time, though he would go on to a thirty-year career as an NHL linesman. Mrs. Kay was a loving and spirited woman who took great pride in her family and community, and has been credited with starting the first neighborhood watch on their street. The Knox home was always open for visitors, and it wasn't unusual for a breakfast call to be answered by fifteen to twenty people. That season, it became a central hub for the Oil Kings, whose players would come over for weekend parties and home-cooked Sunday roasts. Pat lived in the basement with Don Hunt, the eldest son from Kay's first marriage (she remarried after Don's father passed away). The boys' room was a real disaster, with clothes and God knows what else strewn all over the floor. Although Pat was the billet, the Knoxes treated him as one of their own, and Mrs. Kay became a mom-away-from-mom for Pat. One night when he and a teammate stayed out past curfew, Kay covered for her billet when the coach called to check in. When Pat got home, however, he could tell she was disappointed in him. He didn't sleep well that night, and the next morning, sitting at the kitchen table, he apologized for letting her down. "You didn't let me down, you let your teammates down," Kay responded. "The ones who were counting on you."

Pat never forgot those words.

Decades later at her funeral, Pat, then coaching in Vancouver, would talk about what the family matriarch gave him and other teenage boys who came to stay with her each September, leaving their own families in hopes of chasing the Canadian dream to make it to the NHL. "Many people think that discipline is the most important part of competition and that you learn it at the rink. You don't learn it at the rink; you practice it there. You learn it in a family environment," he said. During that eulogy, Pat also credited Kay Knox with imparting wisdom that would help to sustain his decades-long marriage.

On Saturday morning, December 1, 1962, Pat woke up early and crawled out of bed in the basement room he shared with Don Hunt. He flicked on the television set in the Knoxes' basement rec room and sat down on their chesterfield as the dark screen wobbled into an image. It was foggy in Toronto. He had to strain, but he found Sandra through the gray, flipping her baton as she led the Tiger Cats Majorettes down Yonge Street in a parade for the Fiftieth Grey Cup, between the Hamilton Tiger Cats and the Winnipeg Blue Bombers.

Ever since Pat had gone out west, Sandra would spend time—between dance classes she taught and the hours of practice with the Majorettes—at the Quinn house on Glennie. She would help Jean in the kitchen, or with chores around the house. She'd playfully pick on Guy, then twelve, and help take care of Phillip—Pat's five-year-old brother, with whom she'd develop a close bond through the years. Although it felt like they had lost a brother, the Quinn kids warmly welcomed Sandra as a sister. Sandra and Pat would talk on the phone every few weeks but they mostly wrote letters to one another. Every so often, on her lunch hours, Sandra would stop by the offices of the local newspaper, the *Hamilton Spectator*, which had a room filled with publications from all over the world. The editor at the time let her check the Edmonton papers so she could read about Pat and report back to his family.

Sandra flew to Edmonton to visit Pat that Christmas. She watched him play at the Edmonton Gardens, where he had become one of the most popular players to the thousands of fans packed into the arena for each game. The Oil Kings were the hottest ticket in town—and the players became something of local celebrities. While some players certainly took full advantage of the benefits that come with municipal fame—hanging around the pool hall, partying hard, and picking up girls—Pat took on a leadership role as one of the older guys on the team. The Oil Kings' raucous gatherings overflowed with booze and philandering possibilities. But Pat was committed to his love back in Hamilton, to finding a future in the game, and to the education he'd never stop pursuing.

Though he didn't wear a letter, Pat became a pseudo captain on the ice, working in tandem with the veteran captain Roger Bourbonnais, with whom he'd become close friends through life. Pat gathered the players for team meetings and was one of the most outspoken veterans in the bunch. Younger teammates, like Glen Sather, looked up to Pat. Rumbling through cold Alberta nights on the Oil Kings' Greyhound to towns like Drumheller, Moose Jaw, and Flin Flon, Sather and Quinn often played chess on a board they set up between the seats. Pat taught his western teammates how to play euchre, a game far more popular back east. When he wasn't moving pawns or teaching cards, Pat spent those long trips reading. Books on history. Books about leaders. Books on economics. Pat had missed the deadline to sign up for classes when he got to Edmonton, but he was still keen on going back to school and often quizzed Bourbonnais about the classes he was taking through the University of Alberta. They'd roll past snow-covered wheat fields, mountains rising just beyond, stretching for specks of light in the endless black sky.

In May 1963, the Edmonton Oil Kings reached the Memorial Cup final for the fourth consecutive season. (It was the team's seventh appearance in the national final since 1950.) Leo LeClerc wanted his players to think only of getting that cup. There were to be no distractions. Or, only one: Pat Quinn was getting married.

Before the Niagara Falls Flyers arrived from Ontario for the seven-game series at the Gardens, each member of the Oil Kings put on his best tie and the players walked to a nearby Catholic church together. Sandra Baker had returned, and this time, Jean Quinn came, too. LeClerc had made all the arrangements. The Knox family sat in the wooden rows among the players. Don Hunt was best man. Pat Quinn—now twenty—stood tall at the altar, his black hair neatly parted, shoes polished, with soft eyes and a sharp smile. Sandra, dressed in white, walked slowly toward him.

And they left that church to walk through life together as Pat and Sandra Quinn. At that moment, though, there was little time for further celebration. The Oil Kings had practice in an hour.

5

"They're Not Tough ...
They're Just Dirty"

The packed Edmonton Gardens was dead silent as Gary Dornhoefer lay flat at center ice. The Niagara Flyers' star right-winger hadn't seen it coming. Pat Quinn had been in the penalty box as the Flyers broke out of their zone—then the gate opened, and the bull charged out. Dornhoefer had cut across center ice with the puck, avoiding another Oil Kings player— blind to what was barreling toward him. He can't recall what happened next; his brain spared him the memory. Dornhoefer's stick and gloves flew into the air while his body went the other way. He crashed to the ice in a crumpled heap. Nearly seven thousand Edmonton fans went quiet.

To get to the 1963 Memorial Cup, the Oil Kings played in a loop that included tough senior teams in the Central Alberta Hockey League, made up of more experienced players. They beat the Estevan Bruins in six games and won the regional title, the Abbott Memorial Cup, in a five-game series against the Brandon,

Manitoba, Wheat Kings, a junior team. Their eastern rivals, the Flyers, had a stacked team, boasting future NHL talent like Dornhoefer, Ron Schock, and Terry Crisp. They had knocked off Eddie Bush's Hamilton Red Wings, the Montreal Junior Canadiens, the Neil McNeil Maroons (the St. Mike's Majors transferred to Neil McNeil Secondary School in Scarborough that season), and the Espanola Eagles to earn their spot in the Memorial Cup. They were favored to win.

The Flyers arrived in Edmonton by train, set to play the entire series as the visiting team. Despite that disadvantage, Niagara Falls was cocksure and yappy. They routed the Oil Kings 8–0 in the first game, while fans in the Gardens sneered and cursed, clutching at the Flyers' jerseys over the boards (this was before glass dividers were common in hockey arenas). The Edmonton players slunk, demoralized, into the locker room.

By this time, the Oil Kings were in their fourth consecutive Memorial Cup final, a record. For captain Roger Bourbonnais, in his final season as a junior, this was his third kick at the can. And again, it looked like his team would fall short. In fact, the Edmonton Oil Kings had been to the Memorial Cup six times in the team's brief history—and six times, they had lost. The previous season they had fallen to the Hamilton Red Wings, whose coach, Eddie Bush, had cast Pat Quinn off as a player who could barely play Junior B hockey, let alone perform at the game's highest levels. The year before that, in 1961, the Oil Kings lost the series at home to the St. Mike's Majors—the other team the Red Wings had prevented Quinn from playing for.

Oil Kings coach Buster Brayshaw believed this to be the best team he'd brought to the championship. They were bigger and he'd been pushing them to play like the eastern clubs, which he felt had come out on top in the past by "clutching and grabbing, playing the man and shooting the puck a lot." The Oil Kings could play as tough as anybody, he said.

In the locker room, as media and fans were already writing the team off, yet again, Brayshaw was adamant that the lopsided score meant little. "We just had a bad game," he assured his dejected players. Leo LeClerc, the cerebral manager, also showed little concern: "We're going to turn this thing around," he said.

Sure enough, the team roared back, taking the second game 5–2 to even the series. Butch Paul, an eighteen-year-old center from Red Willow, Alberta, scored twice and set up an additional three goals.

But it was Pat whom teammates would credit with turning the series around. In the final period of the third game, as his siblings listened to the broadcast over the radio back home on Glennie Avenue and his mother and Sandra watched from their seats in the corners, he stepped out of the penalty box and caught Dornhoefer looking the other way. It was a clean hit, a solid boneshaker—or, rather, bonebreaker. Dornhoefer was carried off the ice on a stretcher and taken to the hospital, where he was put in a cast from his ankle to his groin to hold his fractured right femur in place. Quinn was given a five-minute penalty for charging. Hockey code dictates that if you want to change the momentum of a game with a hit like Quinn's, you'd better be ready to drop your gloves. But no one on the Flyers challenged him. Niagara Falls didn't have a player remotely equal to the task. Clarence Moher had been right when he picked up the afterthought defenseman, Pat Quinn, working in the

Hamilton steel mill: No team could push the Oil Kings around with Quinn on the roster.

The hush that fell after Quinn's hit was brief. The Edmonton fans were fired up and the noise in the Gardens seemed to cow the Flyers, who never managed to get back into the series. The Oil Kings took game three 5–2 and didn't shy away from the rough stuff. The local papers loved it. The other side saw it differently. Toronto's *Globe and Mail* sports columnist Dick Beddoes—an Edmonton native—criticized the Oil Kings for playing with "manners peculiar to a slaughterhouse." And he had a point. Through the series, nine of Niagara Falls' nineteen players were injured. "Some of them deliberately," Beddoes wrote, adding that the media praise of the rough play served to "ignite young athletes who check everything, including their brains."

Leo LeClerc, whose lifelong ambition was to bring Edmonton its first Memorial Cup, kept his thoughts to himself as the series went on, but the Flyers' owner and coach Hap Emms didn't hold back. "They're not tough," he told the press. "They're just dirty." And he had little praise for the fiery crowds: "I'd never like to bring a club team back to Edmonton again," he said. The series even prompted the *Edmonton Journal* to print an editorial lamenting the violence, with the headline: "Is This Sport?" But no one doubted that if the Flyers could respond, they would.

The Oil Kings were up three games to two, heading into the sixth game of the series. They finished the first period leading 1–0 off a goal from Doug Fox, who netted a rebound off a shot by captain Roger Bourbonnais. Glen Sather, Max Mestinsek, and Butch Paul—known as the best line in junior hockey at the time—pulled Edmonton further ahead in the second. Sather tapped in a goalmouth pass from Mestinsek. A few minutes later he was stopped point-blank by Flyers goalie George Gardner, but Paul tapped in the rebound. The team had received an extra jolt at the beginning of the second period when the crowd jumped to its feet to cheer the return of Pat Quinn to the ice, after he fell hard into the boards in the first. In his single season with the Oil Kings, he'd already become one of the most popular players on the team—never more, though, than on that day.

Gregg Pilling, the Oil Kings' fiery winger, scored only one goal in the series, four minutes into the third period. But it gave the team a lead that seemed insurmountable. It looked like those three straight losses in championships would finally be redeemed. It looked like the Memorial Cup would be won by a team west of Manitoba for the first time since the Regina Pats won in 1930. The Edmonton Oil Kings would be the first club from Alberta to win it since the Calgary Canadians beat Kingston in the 1926 final. The crowd went nuts, hurling exuberance down on the beaten Flyers, crushing them.

But it wasn't over. Every hockey player knows the feeling: the harder you cling to a lead, the quicker it seems to slip away. The Flyers' Bill Glashan broke goalie Russ Kirk's shutout with eleven minutes remaining—just enough time for hope to survive. Ron Schock scored for the Flyers three minutes later. Then, with just two minutes remaining, Terry Crisp scored another Flyers goal to make it 4–3.

Play-by-play announcer Wes Montgomery called it "one of the most heart-stopping comebacks of all time." The Oil Kings were on the brink of collapse. The Flyers pulled goalie George Gardner with thirty-five seconds left for an extra attacker.

Montgomery howled disjointed phrases into his microphone:

> In the Oil King end ... it goes in the corner ... Crisp picks it up ...
> flips it in front ... he fires! ... HITS THE GOALPOST! ...
> Here's Crisp! ... He hits the side of the net ... back in the
> corner ... THE GAME IS OVER! ... The Oil Kings have won
> the Memorial Cup ... And the fans are out on the ice ...
> THERE ARE FANS ON THE ICE! ... As the Oil Kings
> defeat the Niagara Falls Flyers four to three and bring Edmonton
> its first Memorial Cup in history.

The fans on the ice lifted Quinn, Roger Bourbonnais, and
goalie Russ Kirk onto their shoulders and carried them around
the rink. A novelty crown was put on Bourbonnais's head and a
royal-blue-and-gold jacket was draped over his shoulders. It was
terribly embarrassing for the twenty-year-old, who didn't relish
the limelight the way Quinn did. (Despite their different personalities, Bourbonnais and the Big Irishman remained lifelong
friends.) With the captain hoisted, the bravest Oil Kings fans
managed to get the 230-pound Quinn up on their shoulders too.
It was the proudest moment of their young careers.

Three straight trips to the Memorial Cup, and now Edmonton
had the crown. Tears welled in the corners of Buster Brayshaw's
eyes as he spoke to the press while the players celebrated around
him. Manager Leo LeClerc, who'd been silent up until then
throughout the series marred by near "donnybrooks in the first
five games" as the *Edmonton Journal* described it, said simply:
"I'll let my players do the talking on the ice." One of the reporters suggested that the prim and proper LeClerc would be

thrown in the shower to celebrate the Oil Kings winning the Cup. LeClerc straightened up and informed the scrum that the club had respect and would never stoop to such degrading depths. But later, in the Oil Kings locker room, a puddle pooled around LeClerc as he stood drenched to his knickers after an unceremonious, but probably not unwelcome, involuntary shower. The smile of a champion was, finally, wide across his face.

With Pat's junior hockey career over, the newlywed Quinns stayed in Edmonton through the summer of 1963, wondering where the first adventure of their life together would take them. Quinn picked up work doing security for the Edmonton Exhibition Association, which ran the city fair and racetrack, and owned the Oil Kings. He was a celebrity employee. Everyone knew who he was. Quinn spent more time signing autographs that summer than he did tossing unruly gamblers out of the racetrack. Roger Bourbonnais noticed something about Quinn shortly after he arrived in Edmonton—he loved to talk to people. "And he talked *to* you, he didn't talk *at* you," Bourbonnais noted. "It was like you were the only person. He'd focus on you." Kids would run up to him on the streets of Edmonton and ask for his autograph. Quinn stopped each time. He never rushed away and would often comment on something unique about them, or start asking questions. "What's your name?" and "What's your team?" he'd ask. "He enjoys this," Bourbonnais thought. "He really does."

Once the whirlwind had subsided, the newlyweds could finally have their honeymoon—a weekend in Banff. But the couple had no car and no money—and no place to stay. Roger Bourbonnais, however, had a '57 Ford and his girlfriend (and future wife), Jeanette, owned a tent. So the four of them piled into the old car. And with one tent and several cases of beer, they drove for the mountains to sleep under the stars. Pat and Sandra joked that they were "chaperones" for their unwed friends. A few days later, with several empty bottles and a story they'd share for decades, the Quinns felt there couldn't be a finer way to spend a honeymoon.

6

The Policeman

He was nameless to them. Faceless. Just one unknown among more than a hundred, trying to get noticed. Hoping for a chance. Two years before the Memorial Cup win, Pat Quinn, then eighteen and playing for Hamilton, was invited to his first NHL training camp. He made the trip down from Hamilton to Detroit and carried his bag into the Olympia, the magnificent red barn on Grand River Avenue. The Quinns were a Leafs family, despite Hamilton's regional connection to the Red Wings. But loyalty could be overlooked, of course, if one day the Quinn name were to appear in a Red Wings program at the Olympia. Past slights could be forgiven, if not forgotten, if the Red Wings brass found some way to make the Quinn kid part of their future.

Quinn was nervous, knowing that the odds were set against him. He knew he'd been invited just to fill a sweater at practice. But it was a rare opportunity and one that he didn't intend to let slip past him. He remembered the hours on the ice at Glennie under the guidance of Sam Hart, with his father's words pushed up behind him: *skate ... skate ... skate....* And so Quinn did, staying on the ice long after the other nameless and hopeful had returned to the locker room. He circled the ice alone, trying to will his feet on, quicker and quicker, though his quickest would never be enough. Still, he kept on, kept at it, until another pair of skates carved into the ice behind him.

They belonged to Gordie Howe.

Mr. Hockey hit the ice with the lowly, oversized junior, imparting a few tips on the game that he'd learned while becoming the best player in the world under those same lights at the Olympia. We swear memories to immortality, only to have them fade through time and inevitably drift from the halls of our minds. But for Pat Quinn, this moment—this brief, generous gesture from a living legend—would be framed and well lit, revisited over and over as he'd go through the decades trying to explain just what the small act of kindness had meant to him.

Three summers later, in 1963, Quinn made another trip to the Detroit Red Wings training camp. He was, again, among more than a hundred hopefuls, but he thought that this time, his appearance in the Memorial Cup and a full week of national press might have given him an identity.

The players were divided into four teams, which played against each other through the camp. Contracts were offered up throughout the week, but not to Quinn, who became convinced that no one from the Red Wings organization even realized he was there.

That might have been true, but in the seats of the near-empty Olympia, at least one person was focused on Quinn. Ray Miron had never watched Quinn play before, but he'd learned enough about his bone-breaking intimidation to know that Quinn was the right player to add some protection to the lineup of his Knoxville Knights, the minor pro team he ran in Tennessee that played in the Eastern Professional Hockey League. Miron operated the Cornwall Falcons out of his hometown in eastern Ontario, before moving up the ranks of hockey management and decamping south to Tennessee. He'd developed relationships with key figures in the game, like Toronto Maple Leafs coach and general manager Punch Imlach.

The Knights were independent, with no affiliation to any NHL team. Miron wouldn't get any players from the NHL pro teams unless he signed them on his own. So, to build his roster, he scoured NHL training camps looking for talent that wasn't quite ready to play in the six-team show. During the Leafs training camp that year, he had told Imlach that he was looking to add some muscle to his Knoxville team.

"Listen," Miron told Imlach. "I need one tough guy back on defense."

"Well, if you want a good, tough guy," Imlach replied, "Pat Quinn's the guy you should try to get."

The Leafs had Quinn on their list of players to watch, knowing that the league was getting exponentially more physical. The need for big, tough players with the unique talent of intimidation was growing. The "policeman," as the position would come to be known in the sport, was just forming in the early 1960s. It would grow into one of the game's most controversial parts, lauded and vilified in equal measure, as the "tough guy" or "goon" who sends gloves, sticks, and fists flying to right wrongs and settle disputes, real or imagined. The cop's reputation alone would protect his team from opposition assaults. Fighting had always been banned from the game, but still openly celebrated. And a mere five minutes in the box served more as a rest than a deterrent.

After watching a single scrimmage at the Olympia, Miron saw the qualities he was looking for in Quinn. He sought out the Red Wings afterthought and invited him to come and play for his team in Knoxville, Tennessee.

The "C form" Quinn signed with Detroit committed him to play with the Red Wings if he was going to play in the NHL; however, because the Eastern League was independent, Quinn was able to sign a contract without violating his terms as a player owned by the Red Wings. (The Eastern League was founded in 1933, and was officially classified as an amateur league, even though players were paid. As amateurs, its players were not bound by their professional commitments.) Knowing his chances with Detroit were limited, if not nonexistent, Quinn agreed to sign with Knoxville.

During the next skate, Red Wings assistant Jimmy Skinner spotted Miron sitting in the stands. Skinner was known as general manager Jack Adams's right-hand man—the guy who did a lot of the dirty work that went with managing an NHL team. He was someone players didn't want to see, because his visits rarely brought good news. "What are you doing here?" Skinner asked Miron. "I just signed Quinn to come and play in the Eastern League," Miron told him.

Skinner threw Miron out of the Olympia. Then he hauled Quinn off the ice in the middle of a skate and into Detroit coach Sid Abel's office. As Quinn would later remember it, Abel sat behind the desk, silent, while Skinner did all the talking. "Who do you think you are?" he charged.

But Quinn was thinking the same thing. He wasn't going to let the Red Wings decide where he would play. Knoxville had given him control—a chance to make a bit of money to support his family and play hockey on his own terms. The Red Wings had meddled with his life enough. They had yanked him out of St. Mike's and cost him a scholarship to Michigan Tech.

He knew that going against the system would be costly. He knew the NHL brass was suspicious of players who stepped out of line. And he knew that going rogue in an unaffiliated league would be viewed as a betrayal. So he wasn't surprised when Skinner told him he'd make sure Quinn never played hockey again and threw him out of training camp.

Having finally met the Red Wings bosses nose-to-nose, Quinn packed up his gear and hitchhiked home to Hamilton.

It wouldn't take long, in the fall of 1963, for Quinn to prove his utility during training camp for the Knoxville Knights. At the time, all of the teams had camps and exhibition games in southern Ontario, and Knoxville was based in Welland. During the Knights' first exhibition game, against the Nashville Dixie Flyers in Port Colborne, Quinn surprised his teammates by jumping off the bench and taking on two of Nashville's players at once, tossing them to the ice. Later in the off-season, against the Johnstown Jets—the team that served as inspiration for the movie *Slap Shot*—Quinn got into a fight on the ice and then, after it was broken up, jumped into the opposing penalty box to continue the melee. Johnstown general manager John Mitchell wasn't impressed. "What are you doing, Ray, bringing guys like that into the league?" he asked Miron. "Look, you run your team and I'll run my team," Ray replied.

Many of the Knights lived at the Black Oak Motel, a cluster of cabins that sat on the side of Broadway Street, in the Tennessee Valley, with the Great Smoky Mountains rising up to the west. The motel was about thirteen miles from the city center, where the Knights played in a new seven-thousand-seat arena called the Knoxville Coliseum. Each unit had a kitchen, a living room, and one bedroom, and the players got a deal to stay at the Black Oak through the winter season, when tourism was low.

It was a humble place to start a family. Pat and Sandra Quinn were young, barely twenty years old, living off an independent-league salary and expecting their first child. Most of the players were in their early twenties and made around $125 a week. On top of their weekly salary, the Knights were given two dollars a day for meals, which barely covered the cost of the six-pack the players downed with burgers from White Castle after games and practices.

"You had to love the game," says Wayne Clairmont, a member of the Knights that season. "It was a survivor league." The six-team NHL was a long way from Knoxville. The town wasn't a stepping-stone to loftier goals; it was a low plateau. For some, it was a brief stop before the dream became too far out of reach. For others, it was an extended stay—delaying the transition to life beyond the blue-collar industry of the game. Quinn realized that many of the players were clinging to the sport, unwilling to let go, as beyond it, the world was a difficult, uncertain place. The thought worried him. Yet here he was, living in a motel off a highway in Tennessee. He'd resolved never to fully rely on the game.

The Eastern League was made up of nine teams, divided between south and north divisions. Seventy-two games were jammed into a six-month season. And there were only thirteen players on the roster because the "league was run by a bunch of morons" who wanted to keep the costs low, says Don Labelle, the Knights' player coach. (Bench coaches were an unneeded expense.) The team drew a little more than three thousand fans a game at the Coliseum. Just as he had with the Edmonton Oil Kings, Quinn became a fan favorite in Knoxville.

The Knights' closest rivals were three hours away in Nashville. The other two south division rivals were Charlotte and Greensboro in North Carolina, a seven-hour bus ride away. Those were the close games. In addition, the Knights took regular trips to Philadelphia and Johnstown in Pennsylvania, New Haven in Connecticut, and widely separated destinations in New York state from Long Island on the coast to Clinton upstate—thirteen hours from Knoxville.

The team traveled in a silver-domed bus from the late 1930s, akin to a Silverstream trailer. Because the road trips were so long and teams were so cheap, the players slept in open bunks, head-to-toe, down the middle of the bus, with the odd stop at a motel during long hauls up north. At the front, there were seats for lounging, where players would chat with the driver, Swan Seymour, a round man with a big sense of humor. Seymour also owned the bus, which might explain why he drove it slowly: "There's a dog pissing on the back wheel, Swanny. Get this thing going!" But Seymour's light foot was a welcome comfort when players relieved themselves out the front door as they rolled down the highway, because the bus wasn't equipped with a toilet.

During the season, Quinn and a few of the Knights went hunting with the president of the University of Tennessee, Andrew Holt. Quinn told Holt how he started his college education at Michigan Tech, but was forced to leave his scholarship because he had played junior hockey and accepted a small amount of expense money. Holt was impressed by Quinn's passion to earn a degree, and arranged for him to start taking classes.

Sandra gave birth to their first child on Valentine's Day, 1964. The Knoxville Knights were playing Charlotte that night, and with a nod to the date and the circumstances surrounding her emergence into the world, the new parents named their daughter Valerie Charlotte Quinn (Val for short). The hockey schedule was unbending, and despite Pat's undoubted preference to spend time with his wife and tiny daughter, the Knights went on another long road trip the day after Valerie was born. Sandra didn't drive at the time, and while Pat was away she was confined alone with the brand-new baby in that old motel at the side of the road. Rowena Miron, Ray's wife, refused to let Sandra navigate the unsure first days of motherhood alone at the Black Oak motel, however, and moved Sandra and the baby in with her while Quinn was bunking in the old silver bus with the Knoxville Knights. Rowena Miron and Knights player Wayne Clairmont would become Val's godparents. During spring break that year, the entire Quinn family—Jack and Jean, Barry, Carol, Guy, and Phillip—drove down to see Pat and Sandra and the new baby.

Quinn played all seventy-two games with the Knights that 1963–64 season. He scored six goals and thirty-seven points, while leading the team with 217 penalty minutes—almost a hundred more than the next most-penalized Knight, Don Labelle. To his teammates, Quinn was more than a tough guy— he was a friend and protector. Labelle was a decade older and a career minor leaguer. As a playing coach, he paired himself with the hulking young defenseman. At six-foot-two and 205 pounds, Labelle was big for the era and often played protector of his teammates. With Quinn by his side—at six-foot-three and 220 pounds—Labelle didn't have to worry about saving anyone else's neck. The Irishman had it covered. "Nobody wanted to mess with him," Labelle says.

Quinn wasn't entirely invincible, however. During a mid-season game against the Johnstown Jets, Quinn went hard into the corner after Danny Patrick, a five-foot-ten-inch, 150-pound forward. The outcome seemed like it'd be as ugly as it was inevitable. But with Quinn charging in furiously, Patrick jumped into the boards with both skates and shot himself backward, catching Quinn off balance and knocking him back onto his ass. There was a learning curve, even for a scrappy giant like Quinn.

Late in the 1963–64 season, Ray Miron received a call from John Mitchell, the general manager of the Johnstown Jets who had chastised him for putting a player like Quinn on his roster at the start of the season. Mitchell "lollygagged" around the question, says Miron, before explaining that he wanted to make a deal. "Who's the player?" Miron asked him. Mitchell replied: "Pat Quinn." But Ray Miron had no intention of losing the defenseman he'd swiped from the Red Wings.

Miron was doing something right. NHL teams may have hated him, but they also respected him. After that season, Punch Imlach hired the ambitious hockey executive to run the Tulsa Oilers, the Toronto Maple Leafs' farm team in the recently developed Central Professional Hockey League (which was shortened in 1968 to Central Hockey League, or CHL). The CHL was a minor professional league founded by Jack Adams and owned and operated by the NHL. Along with the Toronto Maple Leafs' Tulsa Oilers, the Chicago Black Hawks had the St. Louis Braves, the Boston Bruins had the Minneapolis Bruins, the Montreal Canadiens had the Omaha Knights, the Detroit Red Wings had the Indianapolis Capitals, and the New York Rangers had the St. Paul Rangers.

After accepting the job, Miron told Imlach he wanted Quinn on his team. But even though he hadn't signed a pro contract with Detroit, Quinn still technically belonged to the Red Wings.

Sid Abel and Jimmy Skinner now realized he was a decent prospect to hang on to. So there was a problem. The Red Wings wouldn't give him up. But for once they didn't stand in his way. They loaned Quinn to Tulsa, while maintaining his rights.

Tulsa, Oklahoma, would be a home base for the Quinns through the next four years, as Quinn shuffled from team to team, packing his family into a beat-up Oldsmobile Cutlass with the belongings they'd need towed behind them in a wooden trailer fastened on a metal chassis. The family rented a furnished apartment, and Quinn, who'd spent the summer studying at the University of Tennessee, enrolled at the University of Tulsa, continuing to inch toward an economics degree.

That November, the Oilers played a match against the Canadian national team in Winnipeg. The national team was run by legendary coach Father David Bauer, and was considered an alternative to pro hockey for players who wanted to pursue an education. The team represented Canada at the Olympics and world championship tournaments. Quinn's old teammate and friend Roger Bourbonnais was on the team. The Oilers beat the Nats 3–0 at the Winnipeg Arena on November 23, 1964. But the real action happened after the game.

The Oilers went downtown to celebrate their win at the Town and Country nightclub, where a brawl broke out between the Oilers and some other patrons. The *Winnipeg Free Press* reported that Quinn had kicked a man who was on the ground, spent the night in jail, and pleaded guilty to an assault charge. But the paper's story isn't quite true, according to Roger Bourbonnais, who was there that night. He says Quinn was sitting with him when the fight broke out at the other end of the bar. Quinn went over to help out his teammates. But Bourbonnais saw a bartender call the police, and pulled Quinn out of the bar. He dropped him off at his hotel. And that was it—that is, until the police showed up at Quinn's door. They were with a man who said he had stolen his jacket. Quinn didn't know what he was talking about. But the officers took him in. At the station several other detained Oilers were drunk and acting belligerent. Quinn refused to sign a confession to the theft charges and spent the night in jail. But in the end, it was Ray Miron who faced the real heat. He had to write a lengthy letter to Punch Imlach explaining why the Leafs' farm team was behind bars in Winnipeg. The Oilers rebounded from the brawl in Winnipeg and put together a decent season, free of jail time.

Tulsa faced the Omaha Knights in the playoffs, but the series was cut short for Quinn. It wasn't an opponent who brought him down, though. He was engaged in his familiar rough stuff in front of the net when a linesman piled in to make peace. He tackled Quinn, and toppled him backward. Quinn couldn't twist his leg around quickly enough and his ankle snapped, an experience that marked the beginning of his lifelong disdain for officials.

The next season, in 1965, the young Quinn family was on the road again. The Red Wings, starting to see more value in their oversized man, wanted to keep him directly in the team's sight, and so the franchise sent Quinn to its farm team in Memphis. Pat and Sandra moved into a complex where several of the Memphis Wings players lived.

The Memphis Wings played out of the Mid-South Coliseum. The team averaged almost four thousand fans a game, a decent crowd in a place where the game was as novel as a professional Aussie Rules football team might be in any North American city today. Teams in the Central League were only allowed to have five guys in the lineup who were above the age of twenty-three. The Wings had a young, talented lineup with players like John MacMillan, Dan Belisle, Gary Bergman, Warren Godfrey, and Ab McDonald (all of whom would make it to the NHL). The team was coached by Vic Stasiuk, who had played for the Chicago Black Hawks, Detroit Red Wings, and Boston Bruins, and still yearned to be on the ice while he wound down his playing career. The Red Wings were constantly shuffling players between Detroit and Memphis.

Quinn was named the team's captain. It was a vote of confidence, especially considering that he'd been an afterthought in the Red Wings organization for years. Quinn's teammates had great respect for him, considering him trustworthy and consistent on the ice. "He wasn't a gazelle," says teammate Gregg Pilling, who reunited with Quinn in Memphis after they were teammates on the Oil Kings, "but he played within himself—found a way to utilize his ability to make the team better." Quinn always thought of ways to find an edge to win the game with what he had, and understood that players could be used like chess pieces. He happened to be a large, immobile one—but he was still a piece to be played, and he found a way to contribute to the greater game plan. He was also, as several teammates would recall, a calming presence off the ice.

Quinn didn't view his responsibility as captain as a sign that he should lay off his other ambitions. He transferred the credits he'd picked up at the University of Tennessee and the University of Tulsa, and enrolled in a couple of courses during the season at Memphis State.

During a road trip that season, Quinn pulled out a huge economics textbook and started into the readings for an upcoming class. Memphis coach Vic Stasiuk walked down the aisle of the bus and saw his captain studying. "What is that?" Stasiuk asked him, sternly. "It's a book," Quinn replied. "Let me see that thing," Stasiuk said, snatching it. If a library filing system were employed to sort the literature found on the buses used by minor pro hockey teams in that era (or any era, really), the only entries would be under section 176 (sex and reproduction) and section 611 (human anatomy), and the only titles listed would be *Playboy* and *Penthouse*.

While admirable to the general public, this tome on economics was offensive to the sensibilities of an old-time puckhound, certainly under the surface argument that it was a distraction from the game, but also as an affront to the unspoken rule that players were employees who worked their shifts on the lines and did as they were told. The system kept the supply of players in the hands of rich owners, and while it had been blindly obeyed in general, it was strictly enforced when rebels stepped out of line. There were few, if any, agents for players to depend on. They took care of any negotiations themselves, and usually left the deliberations happy to have a job at all. Joe Daley, the Memphis Wings' starting goalie who played sixty-eight of seventy-two games, made thirty-five hundred dollars that season, the equivalent of twenty-seven thousand dollars today. Scared that he was making less, or more, than his teammates, Daley never divulged his salary to any other players. "They had you for life. If they didn't like you, they could shit on you from great heights. What are you gonna do about it? Quit? They didn't care," says Daley.

Pat Quinn knew the system was unfair. He believed players, even minor league guys like himself, should have the ability to sell their services for a fair price. He believed they should be businessmen. To him, the argument on the bus was about much more than pregame reading materials: It was a matter of principle. Professional hockey was on the verge of change—expansion, a rival league, agents—a reckoning for decades of player exploitation and bully tactics by management. Even Gordie Howe, the greatest player the game had known, was being hosed by the Detroit Red Wings, who lied as they swore to him that he was the highest-paid player on that team. Trust was an illusion.

Moving his family from city to city on the meager salary of a minor pro journeyman, Quinn could see the hollow scam and felt as passionately about fighting back as the united workers back home in Hamilton's steel mills had. They were no different. The textbook in his lap was Quinn's agency.

"If I ever see that on this bus again you'll be in deep trouble," Stasiuk said, as Quinn recalled years later, reciting the story of his long struggle for education. "What kind of a leader are you?" the coach charged. "*Captain* of the team?" (Later, Quinn said he received a call from Ted Lindsay, who'd helped organize the NHL Players' Association in the fifties, "giving me crap" about taking classes while playing.)

Despite the apparent distraction of higher learning, Quinn finished the season in Memphis with a team-leading 135 penalty minutes. In December 1965, he was fined one hundred dollars and suspended for three games by Jack Adams, then the president of the Central Professional Hockey League, after being cut loose by Detroit in 1963 for striking linesman Fred Gibbons during a game in Tulsa. (The incident earned a brief mention back in Canada in the *Globe and Mail* on December 7.) Quinn was revered as a loyal teammate with a strong sense of family—but he was feared for a reason. He had a furious, explosive temper that often betrayed him. He had no problem settling matters with force. A long list of opponents, and evidently officials, lost arguments with Quinn that way.

The Red Wings left Quinn unprotected in the 1966 interleague draft, in which NHL teams could pick up unprotected players from the minor league systems of other NHL teams. The available players were in the minor pro Western Hockey League (WHL),

American Hockey League (AHL), and Central Professional Hockey League.

The Montreal Canadiens picked up Pat's rights. During training camp that fall, they invited him to play in exhibition games in Halifax and Moncton. During the train ride back to Montreal, Pat was summoned to the last car in the train, which belonged to Sam Pollock, the Habs' general manager. The notoriously restless GM fiddled with his handkerchief and chewed it absentmindedly, like someone might tap their fingers, as he spoke to his new recruit. The Montreal Canadiens had just won their second straight Stanley Cup championship, coached by Toe Blake and led by the great Jean Béliveau, one of Quinn's heroes growing up.

"You know, son, we took you this year but we won the Cup last year," Pollock told Quinn. "There's not much room for you. We like how you play. We want you to go to Houston" — Quinn knew he was getting cut— "and we've got a lot of young kids coming out who are a little bit younger than you," Quinn would recall Pollock saying. "It could be a great setting for us all down there. We want to offer you a contract."

The Habs' defensive core was young and Quinn knew he had little chance of cracking the squad when he made the trip out east. Another season in the minor league meant moving his family for a fourth time in as many years. The nomadic life in hockey had given him one thing, Quinn knew: the chance to pursue the education he'd vowed to complete. Hockey in the minors didn't pay much, but along with the summer work he'd pick up, it paid the bills and helped cover tuition, though it still wasn't quite enough for a growing family. Since he had no agent to negotiate for him, Quinn, just twenty-three, took on the task himself. Pollock offered to sign him to Houston for the same five-thousand-dollar salary he'd earned the year before in Memphis. Quinn remembered the conversation going like this:

"That's not even a raise," Quinn said. "I need to have more than that."

"Well, what do you think is fair?" Pollock asked.

"You took me in the draft so you must have valued me somehow," Quinn said. "Eight thousand dollars."

"I'm not going to nearly double your salary," Pollock said. "You had a good year last year and yes, we took you, but we're not going to do that."

Quinn didn't budge. "Well, I'm not going to sign for the same amount of money," he said. "So what are you going to do?"

"I don't know," Pollock said, "There's not many jobs in the winter in Hamilton, you know."

"Okay," Quinn said and left the car. When he got off the train, he left training camp without a contract, and hitchhiked five hundred miles to Hamilton.

7

One More Shot

The family was sitting around the kitchen table on Glennie Avenue when Pat walked through the back door. Sandra and Valerie, now two, had been staying in one of the rooms the family had previously rented out while Pat was supposed to be at training camp.

"What are you doing here?" his mother asked.

"I left camp," he said.

"What are you going to do?" Jean asked.

Pat told her the truth. "I don't know yet," he said.

He told them that Montreal had offered him a contract to play in Houston, but he didn't think it was a good enough deal. Jean asked her son how much the Habs had offered.

"Five thousand dollars?" Jean said. "Do you know what your father makes?" As a municipal fireman with two decades of experience, Jack Quinn would earn a little less than five thousand dollars that year. But Pat also knew he could earn more than five thousand working a union job down at the steel mill. It wasn't the life he wanted, but might have been the best option left if his gamble with Montreal had backfired.

Luckily, he didn't have to make the choice. A few days later, the phone rang. It was Pollock. He upped the offer to seven thousand dollars.

The Quinns packed their bags and set out for Houston, their fourth home in four years. It was a short stay, however. Quinn dressed for just fifteen games in Houston and found himself nailed to the bench. There were almost a dozen rookies on the Apollos, including Jacques Lemaire and Serge Savard. Because of their numbers, Savard suggested that the rookies try to shave the veterans instead of accepting the usual initiation. It didn't work. Savard was grabbed right away and shaved. But when Quinn arrived, Savard figured no one would be able to initiate a guy as big and strong as he was. He convinced Quinn to go after Bill McCreary, a veteran player who was also the team president. Quinn didn't hesitate. He thought it was a great idea. All the rookies agreed to help. Unfortunately for Quinn, when he went to accost McCreary, all the other players chickened out. "He was off the team the following week," says Savard. "True story." At the rink on Boxing Day, after Quinn had played just fifteen games with the Apollos, the team's trainer informed him that he was being shipped to the Seattle Totems of the Western Hockey League.

Seattle was a long road trip away, with a stop in San Diego to meet up with the Totems there. Pat and Sandra loaded up the Oldsmobile Cutlass with their few belongings: clothes, a television, and a few small items tailored for the instability of life on the road. They headed for San Diego—twenty-two hours southwest. They neared the edge of Texas by New Year's, checking into a motel along the border where they could hear the roar of bullfights across the way in Mexico. When they arrived in San Diego, Sandra stayed in a motel with Val, while Pat joined the Totems on a loop of games through southern California, from Los Angeles and up to Oakland, before returning to San Diego—where the Quinns pulled their lives another twenty hours north along the Pacific coast, heading for Seattle.

With the Totems, Quinn tried to focus on changing his game. He'd become known as a tough guy, and he was tired of it. He was no longer a young prospect, and at twenty-four years old, his odds of actually cracking an NHL squad were diminishing. He needed to prove that he could actually play the game. He was a student of the game, just as he was a student of economics. The league could label him a policeman if that was what would get him noticed—but if he was going to be a cop, he'd be a smart one. He became more judicious about dropping the gloves; his time in the penalty box had fallen significantly when he was the captain in Memphis, and it dropped to nearly half the average of his previous years between Houston and Seattle in 1966–67. The Totems went on to beat the Vancouver Canucks in the Western Hockey League championship.

In the spring of 1967, the NHL doubled in size, adding six new teams—the California Seals, the Los Angeles Kings, the Minnesota North Stars, the Philadelphia Flyers, the Pittsburgh Penguins, and the St. Louis Blues. Vancouver, which many had considered to be a strong candidate for a team, was left out, which sparked outrage across the country. Even

Prime Minister Lester B. Pearson voiced his displeasure. Much of the blame fell to the Montreal Canadiens and Toronto Maple Leafs, who were said to have blocked expansion in western Canada because the organizations didn't want to share CBC television revenues.

This was the first major change in the makeup of the NHL in twenty-five years and it ended the "Original Six" era. It also opened up NHL roster spots for players who otherwise would have toiled in the minors, hoping for a rare chance to move up to the big league. This was actually considered a tragedy by many fans, who believed the league's talent would be diluted, but it was good news for Pat Quinn. In June 1967, he was sold to the St. Louis Blues by the Montreal Canadiens for a paltry sum of cash that no one seems to have taken note of. Pat and Sandra tucked their short west coast experience away, to be remembered as their first of many memories on the Pacific coast.

Quinn spent the summer in Oklahoma, working for the Price family and taking courses toward his economics degree at the University of Tulsa. (Pat also picked up part-time work collecting payments for Shamrock Oil and making use of his imposing frame by working bartending shifts at a local pub when he was able.) When the Blues invited him to the team's inaugural camp that September, Quinn had every intention of being on the roster on opening night. He felt he had a great camp and believed the Blues would offer him a contract. But Lynn Patrick, the Blues' general manager and coach (until Scotty Bowman took over partway through the season), had all-to-familiar news for Quinn. He wanted him to report to the minor league squad in Kansas City. But Quinn said no. He had seen enough of the minors. He walked away from the game. He returned to Tulsa prepared to never play again. At twenty-four years old, a young father with a family to care for, Quinn figured he was done. He would make more working for the oil and gas company in the afternoons while taking classes in the mornings.

The career of Pat Quinn almost ended right there. But the game wasn't quite done with the Big Irishman. Ray Miron offered him another option: If he could get the Blues to loan him back to the Tulsa Oilers, would he consider playing in just the home games? Quinn thought about it. "I could use the extra cash," he told Miron. So Miron went to work, finagling a deal between the Blues and the Toronto Maple Leafs that would see his favorite defenseman return to Tulsa—strictly on loan, and only for the home games.

Having joined a new team every season since junior, Quinn was well versed in the art of first impressions. In Tulsa, he bowled them over.

The Oilers had a regular touch football game on Monday afternoons through fall. Jim Keon, brother of Leafs star Dave Keon, organized the games with goalie Al Smith. It was always a competitive event, with Keon being the captain of one team, and Smith leading the other. When Pat Quinn arrived, Smith quickly announced that he was picking him for his team. "That breakaway speed is really going to help you in touch football," Keon chirped. Quinn didn't say anything. But he squared up with Keon, who was playing quarterback, when the two teams lined up for the snap.

There was a strictly enforced steamboats rule. Quinn would have to count out three before he could rush. Keon pedaled backwards off the snap looking for an open man. He heard

"Three-steamboats" and *whap*, Quinn smacked him across the side of his head and knocked him over.

"What the fuck was that all about?" Keon said.

"I didn't know you were a pussy," Quinn replied.

Keon protested that it was touch football.

"It's football," Quinn shot back with just enough of a smile to let Keon know that to him "touch" was open to interpretation.

And so Pat Quinn turned the Oilers' Monday afternoon touch-football tradition into a game of full-on tackle. "It was fun," Keon recalled. "He had an ability to bring people together."

The Oilers needed a guy like that. Badly. Tulsa was a talented team that was routinely beaten and battered by tougher clubs. Quinn's presence had a dramatic effect, says Keon. "He didn't pick his spots. He sought out the toughest guys on the other teams," Keon says. "He protected everybody." Predictably, Quinn's agreement to play only in home games for Tulsa didn't last long. Hockey players play for each other, and in the end, there was no way Quinn was going to leave his teammates unprotected on the road.

That message was clearly delivered during a game early in the season against the Fort Worth Wings. They had a defenseman named Lou Marcon, who was only five-foot-nine and liked to rush the puck. At the time Marcon wore a beard that grew almost to his eyes, and his nose had been bent a few too many ways and a few too many times. Marcon was burning the Oilers. Mike Pelyk, a nineteen-year-old rookie, known to be an agitator, was paired with Quinn. Midway through the first period, Pelyk turned to Quinn as they caught their breath on the bench. "Paddy, when this guy carries the puck up the ice, why don't you just step up on him. I know for sure he's going to cut up the middle," Pelyk plotted, knowing the Oilers' back-checking forwards would force Marcon toward center ice. "I'm going to bury him." Quinn nodded: "Okay."

It went off as though they'd choreographed it. Marcon started down the boards and Quinn stepped up, forcing him to cut toward center ice. And Pelyk—maybe a buck seventy in his gear—flat out hammered him. Marcon's stick and gloves went flying into the air, like pieces of wood twirling slow-motion from an exploding house. Success. Then fear. Between periods, talk among the Tulsa Oilers shifted from glee over the crushing hit to concerns about Pelyk's safety. Marcon had a mean streak and certainly wouldn't forget the setup that leveled him. "You gotta watch this guy," one of the Oilers said. "He's coming after you." The talk got to Pelyk—"Oh God, he's going to kill me," he thought. "This guy's a beast. *He's going to kill me.*"

Pelyk looked over his shoulder through the second period. Nothing. But in the third, Marcon dumped the puck at center into the Oilers' end. Pelyk went back to pick it up, "scared shitless," as he'd recall, knowing that Marcon would love nothing better than to cross-check him through the end boards. Pelyk tried to cut in close by the net as the puck rolled behind, but he didn't lose him. He forced out his breath, bracing for the inevitable. A moment passed and then, just a loud "Whooo!" from the Tulsa bench. Pelyk turned to see Marcon laid out flat on the ice—Quinn had cut him off with a right hand to the jaw. "He went ass over teakettle," Pelyk remembers. Fort Worth let out a collective "*Oh shit*" and never recovered. "We won the game and life was great," Pelyk says.

It wouldn't be the last time Pelyk found himself indebted to Quinn. During a team party that New Year's Eve at the Civic Center in Tulsa, the festivities continued well into the early hours of 1968. Pelyk, who didn't often drink, imbibed a bit too liberally. He noticed that an American Airlines group was having a party in the same building. Pelyk decided to join them. "I went downstairs and whatever I was doing, I got into trouble," Pelyk says. "And some guy just hammered me. Just coldcocked me." Pelyk was on the ground and on his own, scrambling to get up. Before he could, Pat Quinn arrived, wearing a gold lamé jacket like a muscle-bound Irish-Canadian Elvis. Quinn had followed Pelyk, knowing he was heading for trouble. Quinn tossed a couple of guys away, while two more grabbed him, ripping the jacket right down the seam on the back. "He saved my ass and got me out of there," Pelyk says.

The next day at practice, Pelyk had a foggy memory of what transpired—"I obviously did something stupid; that guy didn't hammer me just for the hell of it"—but knew he owed his defensive partner. Quinn knew it, too. He arrived at practice with his ripped gold jacket in hand, pushed it into Pelyk's chest, and told him he was paying to get it fixed. "He was dead serious," says Pelyk, who was making $404 after taxes every two weeks. But it was only fair considering what the outcome might have been had Quinn not had his back. "It was the cheapest bill I ever paid," he says.

Thankfully, beyond the days of traveling in ancient buses with bunks and no toilets, the Tulsa Oilers flew to games on a DC-3 jet or took an upgraded charter bus to away games. It was one of the few perks of being just a step from the NHL. The fan base in Tulsa had grown steadily, too, with attendance at games averaging close to five thousand. With a roster that boasted guys like Quinn, Pelyk, and occasionally Jim Dorey, the Oilers had earned a reputation as the toughest team in the Central League that season. Hockey as a whole was getting tougher, especially with expansion, and an arms race was underway in every league. In that capacity, Quinn had value. He led the Oilers in penalty minutes that season, with 178 in just fifty-one games—easily outpacing his average of his earlier years in the minors. But the effort he'd put into the other aspects of his game had paid off for Quinn, too. He was skilled at breakout passes and plowed opposing players from the front of the net. He carried a rare intelligence that Ray Miron always admired, on and off the ice.

As a minor league veteran, Quinn wasn't a boisterous presence in the room, but teammates always respected him. It was rare to see him crack a smile until beers were on the table. Then, the fun-loving teddy bear would appear. During inevitable team disagreements, Quinn served as the de facto referee. When linemates Len "Comet" Haley and Ken Campbell tussled at a teammate's stag, Quinn pulled them both outside. There, he watched as they beat on each other in a more appropriate space.

The Tulsa Oilers would win the Central League championship in 1968—a season in which the Stanley Cup–defending Toronto Maple Leafs missed the playoffs for the first time in a decade. The Leafs were battered around all season. They just weren't physical enough to compete in a league that was getting tougher.

In the dust of a dismantled dynasty, a path was made for the lumbering Irish defenseman who'd nearly walked away from the game just a season earlier.

8

Blue and White

The Toronto Maple Leafs were hit hard by expansion. Their roster was aging when they unexpectedly won the Cup in 1967. All of the Original Six had lost twenty players from their systems, as each of the teams had been allowed to protect one goalie and eleven skaters. The Leafs lost regulars Bobby Baun, Terry Sawchuk, Kent Douglas, and Larry Jeffrey, as well as more than a dozen players in their system. Traditionally, the Leafs had a rich farm system, but in 1966 they had sold the farm, hawking the Rochester Americans of the AHL and the Victoria Maple Leafs of the WHL in 1967. All of the players—forty-five in total—were included in the sale, costing the Leafs future talent and bait that could have been sacrificed in the expansion draft, shielding key players. The age of the Leafs' roster had been questioned since the Leafs' Cup win in 1962, but Punch Imlach was set on hanging on to veteran players like George Armstrong, Allan Stanley, and Johnny Bower—and adding more veterans like Red Kelly, Marcel Pronovost, and Terry Sawchuk. Imlach's instincts proved successful.

Toronto won the Cup for three straight years from 1962 to '65, and then again in 1967, with its oldest roster yet (Bower was forty-two; Stanley was forty; Kelly was thirty-nine; Horton and Sawchuk were thirty-seven; and Armstrong and Pronovost were thirty-six).

By that time, old age, the pilfered farm system, and the expansion draft had left a huge hole in the Maple Leafs' franchise. Red Kelly retired after the 1967 win, and Punch Imlach went to work dismantling the championship core. Frank Mahovlich and Pete Stemkowski were both traded to the Detroit Red Wings.

It was within this context that Pat Quinn would finally get his shot at the NHL. In November 1968, Leafs defenseman Marcel Pronovost went down with an injury. Imlach called up Ray Miron, looking for a player to fill the gap. He wanted Quinn. The Leafs had been knocked around by more physical opponents, and Imlach wanted to add some intimidation to his roster to put an end to the idea that the team could be steamrolled.

When Miron told him the news, Quinn was elated—and very nervous. After five resilient years, towing his family around the country, he'd finally skate in the National Hockey League—and for the Toronto Maple Leafs, the team he'd listened to on those broadcasts over the radio when he was a boy sitting with Grandpa Snooze near the potbelly stove back on Glennie Avenue. Snooze, an enormous Leafs fan, had passed away in 1964, taking his final breath in the room next to the stairs where he'd guarded the Quinn kids while Jack and Jean went dancing. He would have been thrilled to know that the grandson with whom he shared such a special bond was now wearing blue and white.

On November 27, 1968, Pat Quinn joined the Leafs on a road trip in Pittsburgh. Sandra stayed home in Tulsa with Valerie, now four—and a new baby girl, Kathleen Allison, whom they would always call Kalli. Pat called Sandra before his first game. The Leafs tied the Penguins 3–3.

The Leafs' defensive core was made up of several aging veterans mixed with an influx of youth. Pronovost and Horton represented the old guard. The new generation included players like nineteen-year-old Rick Ley, twenty-year-old Mike Pelyk, and twenty-one-year-old Jim Dorey. Quinn, at twenty-five, bridged a gap between the generations.

Pat Quinn played his first game at Maple Leaf Gardens on November 30, 1968. He left tickets at the gate for his brothers Barry and Guy, but his parents watched the game at home. Before the game, Quinn explored Maple Leaf Gardens. He'd played there as a junior, but had been to only one Leafs game as a fan beneath its famous domed ceiling, when he was briefly a student at St. Mike's. Now, he'd take to the ice as a player, as he'd dreamed of while learning to skate on the backyard ice rink and in ball hockey games on Glennie, and shinny at Mahoney, and those early morning practices at the Parkdale arena. This was what he'd gone to Edmonton for, and the reason he and Sandra were willing to pack up and move again and again, living like nomads through hockey's minor leagues. Before that first home game against the Minnesota North Stars, Quinn walked through the concourse and found the stairs to the broadcast gondola, where Foster Hewitt had called out the dreams that took shape in his mind as he listened to those Saturday night broadcasts with Grandpa Snooze. He found Hewitt there, in his perch high above the Gardens, and thanked him.

During the pregame skate, as Quinn circled the ice in front of a packed and roaring arena—among stars like George Armstrong, Dave Keon, and Tim Horton—Punch Imlach called him over to the bench and shook him from the dream. "Don't worry, everything is alright with your brother," Imlach said. Quinn had no idea what he was talking about. "I'll tell you about it between periods," Imlach promised.

Earlier in the day, Quinn's brother Guy and a few of his friends had been among the more than thirty-two thousand people attending the Grey Cup at Toronto's Exhibition Stadium. When the Ottawa Rough Riders beat the Calgary Stampeders 24–21 in a thrilling finish that included a seventy-nine-yard touchdown run from Vic Washington, Guy Quinn and his buddies rushed the field and were all arrested. At the police station, Guy—then a large, promising seventeen-year-old football player—tried to inform the officers that he couldn't stay in jail because his brother was about to play his first game at Maple Leaf Gardens. There was a collective "Sure, pal" among the officers, but Guy persisted. Finally an officer agreed to call the Gardens. Imlach sent bail money over to the police station in a cab. Quinn made Guy write a letter to Imlach apologizing and thanking the Leafs coach for bailing him out.

That December, the Leafs put Quinn up in the Westbury Hotel on Yonge Street, just around the corner from the Gardens. Sandra remained in Tulsa, unable to drive up to Toronto while caring for their infant and four-year-old daughters. She relied on Ray and Rowena Miron to help her get around town, to pick up groceries and do the Christmas shopping. As the holiday season neared, Quinn was unsure how permanent his posting with the Leafs would be. During his time in the NHL, Quinn was being paid a salary of around ten thousand dollars. Back in Tulsa, he made quite a bit less. But even with the bump in pay, a flight for his family would have been an unmanageable expense. The Leafs had purchased Quinn a two-way ticket, a constant reminder that his NHL posting was temporary anyway. But, as always, unafraid of requesting what he believed he deserved, he went to Imlach's office at the Gardens and asked if the team would either send him home to visit his family or arrange to have them come be with him in Toronto.

"I've been here all this time," Quinn said. "I'd like to see my family."

"Do you like it here?" Imlach replied.

"Yes, of course I do."

"I can arrange to have you sent back. I don't care," Imlach said. "You can go back there."

"No, no, no," Quinn said. "I like it here. I want to play here."

"Just mind your own business," Imlach said. "We're not sending you back there. We got games to play."

Quinn had heard many stories about Punch Imlach, but through the years he would always maintain that his experiences with the divisive coach were pleasant. Though, of course, he could be blunt. At the time, Quinn would recall, management didn't treat players with much respect because they simply didn't have to. Imlach was a product of a different era. Because of that, his true legacy as a coach would always be debated. He is credited with being the architect of a Leafs dynasty, guiding the team to the Stanley Cup finals in his first season at the helm in 1959, where they lost to the Montreal Canadiens in five games. Under the "Big I"—as he was referred to behind his back—the Leafs won four Stanley Cups through the 1960s, and Imlach swore it could have been five if injuries hadn't wiped out their chances in 1961. Imlach preferred experience to youth, often rolling with proven veterans rather than developing new talent, an approach that was both praised and criticized. What can't be argued is that it resulted in four championship banners. Yet even with his penchant for proven vets, Imlach wasn't afraid to stiff them—a trait that fractured his relationship with some of his key players.

At his core, Imlach was a tactician, an incredible bench coach who could match lines and find ways to win games. But for all his success on the bench, he was a notorious hard-ass. He was an old-school breed, a demanding drill sergeant, a man of few words who dressed in snappy suits and fedoras. His practices were wretched, grueling affairs. He'd run the exact same practice day after day and then bag skate the team on a whim. And he could be vicious. He motivated through intimidation, physically and verbally. His bully tactics drove away young talent like Carl Brewer. He was known to single out players. He ridiculed Frank Mahovlich in the press, often pointing out plays he'd messed up and deliberately mispronouncing his name as "Maholovich." King Clancy, the Leafs' assistant general manager and coach, served as a much-needed balance to Imlach. "We all loved King," says Ron Ellis, one of the young guys on the roster who also had a great deal of respect for Imlach's "strength as a motivator." When Imlach went on a tear, Clancy would come along and calm the situation down, Ellis says. "It was good cop, bad cop."

But Imlach's bad cop routine caused Quinn a great deal of grief through that first shaky month with the Leafs. The team paid for his hotel, but the twenty-five-year-old rookie call-up was on his own for meals. He ate at the hotel restaurant every day, and the cost of living in Toronto mounted exponentially. He had a family to support and rent to pay back home in Tulsa. And a wife and two little girls he hadn't seen in weeks. So Quinn worked up the courage to appeal to Imlach again. This time, he asked for meal money.

"No. There's nothing I have to do," Imlach told him. "You are getting paid."

Resilient, Quinn again asked about his family. He needed to see them. They needed to come to Toronto, or he needed to get back home.

"Well, I'll fix it for you," Imlach said. "You go there but you won't be coming back."

Rejected again, Quinn left the office. But a few days later— perhaps after being visited by the ghosts of Maple Leafs past, present, and future—Imlach softened. He told Quinn that the team would have Sandra and the girls flown to Toronto in time for Christmas.

Quinn scored his first major league goal—a game winner— against Roger Crozier of Detroit in an 8–3 win at home right before the holiday break that year.

Pat spoke over the babble of his baby girl when he answered the phone in his room at the Westbury Hotel that January, where Sandra and their two young children were still staying. What was supposed to be a temporary position had become seven weeks and counting, part of an imposing blue line duo with Tim

Horton, one of the best defensemen in the game. Quinn had impressed Imlach and, fresh off a game against the Philadelpia Flyers, Imlach had just announced that Pat would remain with the Leafs for the rest of the season.

The caller was Dick Beddoes, the *Globe and Mail* sports columnist, who was writing a story about Quinn's long journey to the NHL. He was three weeks away from his twenty-sixth birthday—an unusual age for a rookie. "I was born under the sign of Aquarius," Quinn told Beddoes, kidding, as Sandra settled the girls. "Aquarians are dreamers. We visualize ourselves in positions of power, some glory," Quinn went on, as Beddoes asked him about the instability of his brief tenure with the Leafs and his history of having some "illusions kicked in my professional hockey" through his years in the minors. "The insecure bit, not knowing where you're going to be, keeps [you] off balance," Quinn said, but continued: "Look, don't make it seem like hockey's been all bad for me."

He told Beddoes about the chance that Ray Miron had taken on him, first in Knoxville and then later in Tulsa. And about Leo LeClerc and the Edmonton Oil Kings pulling him out of early retirement in junior, and making him a Memorial Cup champion. Without them, Quinn said, he would never have had the chance to put on that blue-and-white sweater. Just a day earlier, the Leafs had presented Quinn with a souvenir puck mounted on a marble-and-wood base to commemorate his first goal against Detroit, the team who'd sent him down so many winding paths in his junior and minor careers and set up so many roadblocks in his attempts to get an education.

In his column, Beddoes—who had criticized Quinn's rough play during the Memorial Cup—called his journey "the stuff of psychologists, or perhaps poets." "In boyhood we all conceive impossible achievements but in maturity, to stay sane, we adjust to what we are," Beddoes wrote. "But there must be some shred of the child's hope in maturity, or we are doomed to become cynics."

Quinn held no illusion about what he was. He adjusted to achieve the goals he conceived as a boy. Cynicism could have halted him long before he reached the Gardens. It could have rusted him out as a spare part in the minor league. It could have ended his wild pursuit of education. Cynicism would have landed him back in the Hamilton steel mills, grinding out overnight shifts. But he hadn't learned cynicism around the kitchen table back on Glennie Avenue. Jack Quinn's mealtime quizzes, the family-wide hustle for work, the *one-two-boom-boom* delivery of justice—all served to fuel Quinn's tireless thrust into "impossible." It wasn't hope, though. Hope was too weak. It left too much to chance. Stronger than hope, then. More exact. It was resilience and adjustment ... resilience, adjustment ... ever on, fusing his core elements into something unbreakable.

Steel cut through the ice as Quinn tore toward Howie Young during a game in early March 1969. The Black Hawks tough guy had been laying the lumber on the Leafs, which caught the ire of Punch Imlach. Quinn would later recall his coach standing on the bench and leaning down to tell his six-foot-three-inch, 211-pound, twenty-six-year-old rookie: "Somebody's got to stop that stuff out there." Like in any mob hit, indictable words were never used. No one told Quinn to fight. No one had to. But Young found himself in Quinn's embrace, twirling as he tried to avoid his bulky fists. And when they emerged from roughing penalties,

Quinn went to finish the job—this time with a hard, high cross-check. Chicago coach Billy Reay was furious after the game.

"You saw it. It was a deliberate attempt to injure," Reay charged to the press. "That calls for a match penalty. It's in the book."

"I heard a couple of my guys talking on the bench," Imlach (distancing himself from the incident) told reporters. "I won't say who they were, but I heard one of them say, 'There's the son of a gun now. Let's go get him.'"

Quinn wasn't coy in his postgame comments, though: "I got him [with] a pretty good shot," he said bluntly, and that was it. He was sending a message: Pat Quinn doesn't back down.

Quinn's size and strength weren't just of benefit against opponents; they helped in dealings with the Leafs, too. During a train ride home from a game against Montreal, Tim Horton and some of the veterans decided it was time to put the rookies through the team's customary full-body shave initiation. But there were seven rookies on the team and they vowed to stick together. "Take a look around here," Paul Henderson told Horton. "We're vastly outnumbered. If anybody gets shaved, it's not going to be them." There was a big melee—pushing and shoving and wrestling—with Quinn right in the middle, the biggest on the team, protecting his own. "There were bodies flying every which way," says Dave Keon, who was in the mix on the veteran side. Eventually, Horton, Keon, and the rest of the vets retreated, exhausted. They'd lost. No one was shaved. "It didn't go down very well. It was not a success," says Keon. "You could label it a failure."

But avoiding the humiliation of a rookie initiation didn't mean that Quinn was exempt from harsh lessons. Dave Keon wasn't much older than Quinn when he first started playing for the

Leafs—but he was a legitimate star. By the time Quinn made it to the NHL, Keon had won the Calder trophy, two Lady Byng trophies, played in four all-star games, and won a Conn Smythe trophy. The hierarchy was clear. After a bad shift on defense, Quinn returned to the Leafs bench and slammed his stick against the boards. Keon let the rookie have it. "If you do that again, I'm going to give you the stick. You don't show twenty thousand people that you're unhappy with yourself, and you don't show the bench either."

Helping with Quinn's learning curve, Imlach paired him with Leafs legend Tim Horton, whose experience helped compensate for any errors Quinn might make as he adjusted to the NHL. "He could do some things when he played with Timmy, because if he made a mistake, Tim was there to cover it up," says Dave Keon. The duo quickly became one of the most intimidating blue lines in the game.

Quinn idolized Horton, one of the premier defensemen of his era and always one of the strongest players on the ice. The two roomed together on the road, and became good friends. When Pat and Sandra moved into a new place the following year, they didn't have the money for new furniture. Tim and Lori Horton gave the Quinns their dining-room table and chairs to help get them started.

Even though he had earned a spot on the Leafs, Quinn still intended to finish his business degree—planning to take courses through York University in the summer. He received a crash course from Horton, who often worked on the books of his growing coffee-and-donut-shop business in hotel rooms when the Leafs traveled.

Horton had started his business in 1964 with a single shop in Hamilton—less than ten minutes from where Quinn grew up—on Ottawa Street North, at Dunsmure Road. The original Tim Hortons shop is still there today, with a commemorative version of the original signage, which had a drawing of Horton shooting donuts like pucks.

Horton procured Quinn's acting talents in a television commercial when the company opened more stores. The commercial's narrator describes the store's great chocolate dip and orange twist donuts, honey crullers, and Dutchies. "At Tim Hortons there are a lot of great reasons to stop for coffee and donuts," a narrator says, over shots of coffee being poured next to a peach-juice dispenser. "But most of all, you'll meet the happiest people!" the narrator continues, as a row of happy customers sitting on stools at the counter turn, smiling at the camera, donuts in hand. They are a random guy off of the street, CFL defensive tackle Angelo Mosca, and Leafs players Pat Quinn (with a mustache and white blazer), George Armstrong, and Tim Horton.

Quinn would later recall a road trip in Boston that season, where he and Horton were in a room next to Mike Pelyk and Pierre Pilote, the future Hall-of-Famer who was playing a final season with the Leafs after more than a decade with the Chicago Black Hawks. It was an old hotel, with a thin connecting door between the rooms. After the team had been out enjoying a few beers, Horton and Quinn overheard Pelyk asking Pilote about his salary, and Pilote replying, "Fifty thousand dollars." As soon as he heard that, Horton jumped out of bed, pulled his pants on but didn't bother with a shirt, and took off down the hall to Punch Imlach's room, where he pounded on the door so hard it almost seemed he would knock it right off the frame. Imlach had told Horton that he was the top-paid player on the Leafs. But as one of the best defensemen in the game, he made about forty-five thousand dollars—the equivalent of a little more than three hundred thousand dollars today. Players were blind to comparative salaries at the time, and even in the NHL, players weren't aware of what their teammates were bringing in.

Pat Quinn was at home with the Leafs. He was serious and businesslike at the rink, but a warm, jovial personality when the team went out for post-practice beers or took lunch at George's Spaghetti House on Dundas Street. He was a storyteller, among the best on the team, especially after a few drinks. He often had a pipe dangling from his lips, cupped in his hand. He was more of a pipe smoker back then, but cigars would become a Quinn trademark. When Quinn and Mike Pelyk had first been roommates back in Tulsa, he would puff cigars while relaxing, lying back on his motel bed reading a book.

During practices, Quinn kept his head down, studying like he would for an upcoming final. Marcel Pronovost took him on as a special project, working one-on-one with him. During Imlach's grinding practices, the veteran defenseman would take the giant rookie aside and offer advice. Noticing the extra work Pronovost put into helping Quinn, the Toronto press suggested that the thirty-eight-year-old might be instructing himself out of a job. Pronovost didn't disagree, but he also saw the mentorship as a duty he was happy to fulfill, one that reached back through generations of the game. "I've got a lot out of this game. I recall Bob Goldham and Leo Reise going out of their way to help when I broke in with Detroit in the 1950–51 season. I took Lee Fogolin's job and later Lee was sent to New York," Pronovost told Red Burnett of the *Toronto Daily Star*. "That's the way it is in this game. The veteran should help the kid."

Quinn was eager to learn and grateful for the help. He knew he'd have to adjust to survive in the NHL. His size alone wasn't enough. Pronovost was a professor with experience, having spent fifteen seasons with Gordie Howe and the Detroit Red Wings, a system that Quinn hadn't been able to crack early in his career. Having joined the Leafs in 1965, the snow was softly falling on Pronovost's Hall-of-Fame career. He picked up his fifth Stanley Cup as a member of the aged Toronto squad in 1967.

"There are so many little things that become very important when you're playing defense in the National Hockey League. Marcel watches my every move, files away the errors and goes over them with me during workouts and after every game," Quinn said. "He also tells me what I can expect from various players. He'll spend hours with you as long as you're receptive, willing to listen and learn. I think he'll make an excellent coach someday. I can't tell you how much I appreciate what he's done for me—and God knows I need all the help." The following season, Pronovost joined Ray Miron's team in Tulsa.

9

"We Want Quinn!"

The Boston Bruins were a high-scoring threat in 1969—boasting the best offense in the league with stars like Ken Hodge, Wayne Cashman, Derek Sanderson, and, of course, Bobby Orr. Phil Esposito led the league in scoring by a wide margin, followed by Bobby Hull and Gordie Howe. But along with scoring, Boston was known for brawling. If you fought one Bruin, you fought them all. The bruising force had also developed a fierce hate for the less talented but also physical Toronto Maple Leafs. Unlike in the years to come, as the league's size expanded, the smaller league led to more frequent games where guys got to know their opponents more intimately. That also produced the perfect environment for nurturing personal grudges. A season earlier, Leafs center Brian Conacher had been injured in a melee with the Bruins—an incident that pushed the Leafs to get bigger and tougher, creating a need for guys like Pat Quinn.

On March 16, the fourth-place Leafs took on the Bruins at home. During the game, Orr clinched the record for most points in a season by a defenseman with 120. (Orr bested that with 139 points two years later, a record that still stands today.) But the Leafs overcame a 3–1 deficit after the first period to win 7–4—scoring five goals in the third period.

Quinn was volcanic in that game. First, he tangled with linesman Brent Casselman, who tried to hold him back from Derek Sanderson and Don Awrey. Casselman grabbed Quinn, trying to pull him away from the group. "Don't touch me!" Quinn shouted at Casselman, shaking himself free.

Later, Orr tried to jam a puck loose from Leafs goalie Bruce Gamble, whacking him on the glove with his stick. Quinn charged at Orr and cross-checked him into the crossbar. Orr crumbled to the ice and Quinn stood over him. Orr kicked up at Quinn's stomach and Quinn returned with a swift kick to Orr's ass. And then it went off—Orr rising to meet Quinn, and Quinn happy to oblige. They ended in a pile, with Orr on top of Quinn's back like a kid taking a ride from an older sibling. As the linesmen pulled them apart, fans at Maple Leaf Gardens booed Quinn. The papers gave the informal decision to Orr.

Toronto was in Boston the next night. Quinn was left off the lineup because of a groin pull and was sitting near the Bruins' bench. The Boston crowd chanted for him, craving revenge on the cross-check he had laid on their star defenseman the night before. "We want Quinn! We want Quinn!" they shouted as hats, shoes, balls, and garbage were thrown onto the ice as the game collapsed into a series of brawls in an 11–3 landslide win for the Bruins.

The next day, St. Patrick's Day, Quinn offered little remorse for the cross-check on Orr. Speaking to reporters, he wore a kelly-green bowler tipped slightly forward and had a shamrock pinned to his forest-green tie, with a matching cardigan and blazer. He smacked a long, curving shillelagh into the palm of his hand. "All they are is a bunch of backstabbers," he said of the Bruins, a cigar balanced in his lips. "You can't turn your back on them or they'll give it to you, and good. I was eating my heart out not to be out there. I've never wanted to play in a game as much as that one," Quinn went on, proudly sporting his St. Patrick's Day attire, noting that he'd been booed in every rink he'd ever played in.

"There isn't anybody on the Bruins who scares me. Listen, I don't profess to be a fistfighter. But I don't intend to take any guff from the Bruins. I'm going to play their style of game. We've got a lot of small forwards, and if they're going to be hammered by the Bruins, I'm going to do the same in my end of the rink."

Quinn defended his cross-check on Orr, who he said was jamming his stick into Leafs goalie Bruce Gamble, trying to wedge the puck free. "I didn't attempt to deliberately injure him," Quinn said. "But if I didn't do my job, clearing people away in front of the net, the fans would soon be on my back."

He said the kicks were half-hearted—"If I wanted to hurt him I could have. But that's not my style, kicking a guy...." Orr had actually kicked *him* in the scuffle, Quinn said, and maintained he had a bruise on his belly to prove it. "I know he's a star and a great player and I'll never be one-third the player he is, but when he's messing around in front of our goal, I'm going to hit him.... I've read in the paper where I lost the decision. Well, that's the first decision I've lost when I didn't get hit."

Questioned about his assault on linesman Brent Casselman, Quinn simply replied that he had a phobia about officials who grab him. Casselman grabbed his punching arm when he went to fight Derek Sanderson and Don Awrey. "I got mad," Quinn said. "I've taken punishment before when someone was holding my arm. In fact the first time I played Boston this year somebody grabbed me from behind, which is a typical Boston trick."

Quinn told the press that he was convinced the Leafs would make the playoffs and he hoped they'd be up against the Bruins. "I'm not going to say anything that will perhaps come back to haunt me," he said, "but I'd like to get another shot at them." He got his chance. The Leafs sat in fourth place and held on through the final seven games of the season, setting up a first-round bout with the second-place Bruins.

The day before the first game of the series, Quinn underscored his intention to play it physical with the Bruins. "You're not suggesting we play docile or try to beat them with finesse or speed are you?" he asked the *Globe and Mail*'s Louis Cauz. "We've got the muscle to beat them, so why not use it?"

True to Quinn's word, the first game of the series is remembered for its violence, with little talk of the ten goals the Bruins scored in slaughtering the Leafs at the Boston Garden on April 2, 1969. Tim Horton and Boston playboy Derek Sanderson slugged it out in the first period. Horton had to get stitches in his forehead to repair a gash from a high stick.

With two minutes remaining in the second period, Quinn stepped into the play that would define his playing career.

Bobby Orr carried the puck along the boards in the Bruins' zone, as he always did, building his speed before cutting through the middle of the ice, as a slow-footed defenseman reached back uselessly. It was a roadrunner versus coyote gag. Orr was too swift, too brilliant with the puck. He moved where he wanted, controlling the game at will. But Quinn had been watching, studying. There was no way he could stay with the rushing Number 4, but he could identify a weak spot. As Orr gained momentum through the hashmarks, he often dropped his head for a moment. Quinn did the quick calculation. If a slow-moving tank of a career minor-leaguer crosses the blue line just as the most talented player the game has known accelerates from the goal line, the opposing forces—if timed with precision—would collide with devastating effect.

Orr cut out from behind the Bruins' goal, pinned close to the boards by Leafs forward Brit Selby, trying to cut off his path before Number 4 could accelerate out of Boston's end. Quinn had backed up to the blue line, but saw that Orr was looking down at the puck, which he'd lost briefly between his skates. He didn't see Quinn, who took four strides and launched into Orr with his shoulder, which happened to line up with the all star's head.

Orr fell backward as his skates kept moving forward and the back-right side of his skull smacked on the ice. Quinn was airborne. He twisted in the air, following the force of his left shoulder, and was almost parallel with the edge of the glass before he crashed down onto his side.

Orr was unconscious, lying on his back. Right-winger Ken Hodge rushed over, dropped to his knees, and gently put his gloves under Orr's head.

The Boston Garden, filled with 14,659 fans, was as quiet as a Catholic church, Leafs defenseman Jim Dorey recalled. The referee, John Ashley, told Quinn he was giving him a five-minute major for elbowing. Quinn objected as Ashley pulled him to the box. Someone in the stands threw a shoe that landed on the ice near Quinn.

"It was a monstrous hit," says Derek Sanderson, Orr's teammate. "It was a bouncing puck. Bobby never has his head down, ever. His head just dipped to pick up a loose puck … I don't doubt that Paddy felt a little shitty afterwards, hitting a superstar that hard. Wayne Gretzky *never* got hit *that* hard."

Orr lay flat on his back, with trainers and team doctors working on him. Eventually they brought out a stretcher. As Orr was carried off the ice, the Garden heated into a raging fury. A police officer stood in the box to keep fans from harassing players. Fans started to throw garbage and coins onto the ice, hollering obscenities at Quinn. He sat facing the ice. Someone splashed a soft drink on him. Then a fan climbed up the glass behind him and punched him in the back of the head. He ducked to get out of the way, and then turned to the crowd. Several tried to climb into the box. Quinn stood up on the bench and took a few swipes over the glass at the fans with his stick. The officer grabbed him. Quinn took another swing with his stick and struck glass. It shattered, sending fans tumbling into the box. One of the shards cut the officer's face. More fans tried to climb into the box to get at Quinn. He jumped onto the ice and a storm of garbage, change, and even a coin changer fell from the fierce thunder that enveloped the arena. For five minutes, it was chaos. Mike Pelyk and Jim Dorey came to Quinn's defense, jabbing their sticks at fans who were trying to get at the ice through the penalty box. They were joined by Tim Horton and Paul Henderson.

Jean Quinn sat in her kitchen on Glennie Avenue, watching Pat play, with her chair pulled right up to the tube like always.

It was difficult to watch the game with Jean, because you'd have to sit off to the side to angle your view around her. She often yelled at the television, ripping the bumbling referees who kept blowing calls against her son. That night Jean was already riled, given all the animosity built up between the Leafs and Bruins during the team's last meeting of the season. (Jack Quinn was out on call for the firehall, and wasn't watching the game.) Guy Quinn, then eighteen, told his mother he had to watch the game on the television in the basement workshop because it was too distracting to watch it with her. As soon as he flipped on the tube, near the painted net on the wall where Pat used to fire pucks, he saw his brother flatten Orr like a transport truck.

Guy immediately had a vision of his mother diving through the television screen. He charged up the stairs. Jean was already in a fury. They watched the scene at the Boston Garden unfold. Jean screamed at the referee. She screamed at the fans. "She was beside herself," Guy says. "It was quite a scene. I mean, *if she had been there....*"

As the Leafs walked down the tunnel at the end of the second period, fans leaned over the railings and took swings at Quinn, trying to whip him with their coats. A few spat at him. Another called him an animal. In the locker room, the Leafs could hear the crowd chanting: "We want Quinn! We want Quinn!"

Orr was taken to Massachusetts General Hospital to be examined by a neurologist. But before the ambulance took him away, he told coach Harry Sinden that he wanted to play the third period.

Toronto was down by a lot, 6–0. They knew the third period wouldn't be about the score. The game was over, but much more was at stake. King Clancy came into the room, practically jumping up and down, defenseman Jim Dorey recalled. "Somebody give me your equipment," Clancy said, furious. "I'm going out there with you." He was serious, but the outburst cut the tension in the room, earning a few quiet chuckles.

In the third period, Forbes Kennedy challenged almost the entire Bruins team to fight and the game broke into a succession of brawls. Five minutes in, young Jim Dorey fought Eddie Shack, clearing the track with a one-punch decision. For several minutes some actual hockey was played, but with less than five minutes to go, the action erupted into a war fueled by Kennedy. Bruins goalie Gerry Cheevers slashed Kennedy across the ankles, to which Kennedy responded with a cross-check to the goalie's face. Cheevers ripped off his mask, dropped his gloves, and went after Kennedy in a rage. The Bruins' "Terrible Ted" Green jumped in to help his goalie and a brawl broke out. Kennedy took a gash across the bridge of his nose from Green's stick. Bruins backup goalie Eddie Johnston and Bruce Gamble, who had been pulled for Johnny Bower, both left the bench to join the fight. During the dustup, fans reached over the glass throwing punches at the Leafs. When he found a spare moment, Kennedy went after Cheevers again—but linesman George Ashley, who was officiating his first NHL playoff game, stood in Kennedy's way, trying to keep him from getting by. Kennedy punched the linesman in the face, knocking him backward to the ice. After assaulting the linesman, Kennedy turned to Bruins bruiser John McKenzie, who obliged him at center ice. Both left the dance with bloody faces, though McKenzie had the edge over the exhausted Leaf.

As the players piled into the penalty box, six police officers surrounded them to keep the Bruins fans away. Quinn remained mostly free from the fracas, but picked up the final penalty of the night, sent to the box for hooking with just a few minutes left to go.

The game took more than three hours to play. Toronto ended up with seventy-nine penalty minutes, Boston with fifty-six. The scorer used three game sheets to fill in all the penalties. Phil Esposito scored four goals and added two assists, tying a playoff record—but it was an afterthought in most newspaper stories about the game.

Punch Imlach ordered the Leafs' locker room closed to the press after the game, and refused to speak with reporters as he left the arena.

Bruins president Weston Adams Jr. told reporters that he didn't want Toronto to dress Quinn in the second game. "They'll kill him," Adams said. "If they were smart they'd never play Quinn again in Boston. I was afraid something like this might happen. Harry Sinden and Milt Schmidt both warned our players to ignore him and forget what happened in Toronto."

A lieutenant with the Boston police at the Garden said that they had called in backup after the incident with Quinn in the penalty box. "They should get him out of the building now," said the officer, who requested anonymity. "The fans here don't like anybody to touch Orr. He's their Frank Merriwell and Jack Armstrong rolled into one. To me, though, it looked like a clean check." Police officers escorted Quinn past a pack of still-raving Bruins supporters as the Leafs boarded their bus.

The *Boston Globe* said the Quinn hit appeared to be a "premeditated action" and charged: "Since they were outplayed in such essentials as shooting, passing, and skating, the Leafs resorted to the last refuge of the humiliated. They gave a pretty good impersonation of a vengeful gang dedicated to any consolation to be derived by provoking violence."

NHL president Clarence Campbell flew in from Montreal the next day to review footage at the Boston Garden, but Quinn didn't receive any supplementary disciplinary action for the hit, which was deemed to be fair and legal. King Clancy and Forbes Kennedy attended the meeting along with three officials from the game—referee John Ashley, and linesmen George Ashley and Matt Pavelich. Campbell viewed the footage in silence, until he saw the clip of Kennedy slugging George Ashley. "Oh my God," Campbell said, as the linesman hit the ice.

Kennedy sat there in cowboy boots, nonchalantly puffing a cigar as King Clancy attempted to argue against a suspension for the assault. Campbell listened to his arguments and left to make his decision. Ultimately, Kennedy was given a seven-game suspension and fined two thousand dollars. It was the last game he'd play in the NHL, opting for retirement the following season.

Before the second game of the series, Punch Imlach distributed copies of *The Power of Positive Thinking* to his players. During the warm-up, seventeen thousand chanted "Kill Quinn!" and his effigy was hung in several places around the Garden. Orr returned for game two, his face still bruised and battered from Quinn's wrecking-ball hit. It was another laugher for the Bruins. Boston embarrassed the Leafs 7–0. Orr sat out the third period to rest. After the game, he was asked if he planned to retaliate for the hit. "I had my head down," he said, a point that Bruins coach Harry Sinden had admitted as well. Orr had left himself exposed. When a reporter pushed further, asking if the incident was closed, Orr grinned. "Who knows?" he said quietly. (Orr would later write in his book that an anonymous fan would offer to "take care" of Quinn—an offer he declined.)

In the Leafs' locker room, Punch Imlach slumped in the corner, looking exhausted and dejected, trying to explain why his team had been so easily dismantled. He couldn't find the answer. He seemed to know he wouldn't find one. His days in Toronto were numbered. The decision was already made.

The Leafs rolled away from the Boston Garden, beaten, but not discouraged from continuing the team tradition of sending a rookie to pick up team beers for the bus. Quinn was a natural choice. The Leafs' bus pulled up beside an Irish pub just down the street from the Boston Garden that was packed with Bruins fans. Quinn had a feeling the situation was about to get ugly, but pushed through the door and made his way through the crowd toward the bar. Then he heard the first call from behind him: "Hey, it's Quinn! It's Quinn!" He froze, knowing he had pushed his luck too far. The door was too far back, and the fans packed too deep around him. He braced for a fist or a broken bottle, but neither came. Instead, a hand clapped on his back. And another. "Nice hit, Paddy boy. Nice hit." The would-be mob all seemed to agree. The bartender gave him the beers on the house. He walked out with a case in hand, grateful that a man's Irish-Catholic roots were enough to keep the man who knocked out Bobby Orr safe in a Boston bar.

Utterly outmatched, the Leafs would drop the next two games at home at Maple Leaf Gardens. Boston outscored Toronto

24–5 in the series. Quinn and Orr, still suffering headaches from the blow, shook hands over center ice when the series was done.

Punch Imlach was fired as Leafs GM and coach by Leafs president Stafford Smythe immediately after the final game of Boston's sweep of Toronto. "That's it, the end of the road," Smythe told the press at Maple Leaf Gardens. "The end of the Imlach era." A reporter asked if, after eleven years and four Stanley Cups, Imlach might stay on in some capacity—perhaps as general manager. "No, he's fired," Smythe answered. "I am buying up the last year of his contract and we parted friends." Smythe announced that Jim Gregory would be the team's new general manager. Only thirty-four, Gregory had served as a Leafs scout through the season and previously coached the Vancouver Canucks, the Leafs' affiliate in the Western Hockey League. Gregory had learned from the venerable Father David Bauer and was a trainer with the St. Michael's Majors, an experience Quinn missed out on while attending the school.

Before the Leafs players were told of the firing, Imlach walked around and shook each player's hand, not mentioning what had just occurred. In a public declaration of allegiance and discontent that would be rare in an NHL locker room today, several players voiced their dismay over the firing. Johnny Bower, then forty-five, announced that he too was leaving when he heard the news from reporters. "That's it for me," he said. "I'm leaving with him. He's the reason I stayed around. I thought I could help him in this rebuilding season. Personally, I thought he did a great job with the green defensemen. We might have gone further if a few guys had shown a little more desire."

Tim Horton, who played his first game with the Leafs in 1949 and had apparently settled his salary feud with Imlach, echoed Bower. "If Imlach is through, I go with him. There's nothing to keep me here now."

Leafs captain George Armstrong said, "I'm too emotionally upset by our four-straight games loss, plus the firing of Punch, to say anything about my future. It's a terrible shock."

"That's burning the corpse while it's still warm," said another player.

In truth, though, Imlach had really been done in December. After not making the playoffs the year before, and with the team clearly in a rebuilding mode, Smythe had tried to move Imlach solely to the general manager's office and replace him on the bench with John McLellan, then the head coach in Tulsa. Imlach had told Smythe to either leave him alone or fire him. Later in the season, forward Mike Walton left the team, saying he'd no longer play for Imlach. Walton, a client of rising NHL agent Alan Eagleson, who helped found the NHL Players' Association, said Imlach had constantly been negative about his on-ice performance and his haircut. Over his tenure, Imlach had also clashed with Carl Brewer, who walked away from the Leafs, and had well-known run-ins with Bobby Baun, Brian Conacher, and Eddie Shack. Frank Mahovlich, who had crumpled under the ridicule of Imlach, scored forty-nine goals after he was traded to Detroit.

He may have been a legend, but Punch Imlach was far from infallible. Still, he'll always be the guy who brought Pat Quinn to the NHL.

10

Figures and Shillelaghs

He tied up his skates and pulled his Toronto Maple Leafs sweater over his head and shoulder pads. Then Pat Quinn stepped onto the ice to take figure skating lessons.

In the lead-up to the Leafs' training camp in 1969, the perpetually bumbling Quinn took a series of lessons with renowned skating coach Bruce Hyland. Hyland and his team worked with some of the best figure skaters in the world and had recently branched out into a new method of training that could be applied to hockey players. It was known as "power skating." Hyland wore figure skates when he taught, which often threw rugged NHL clients off. He tried to apply the fundamental balance of figure skating to the rough, fast-paced flow of hockey. And he'd had success. Hyland had already worked with Peter Mahovlich when he was in the juniors, and the Canadiens star went on to win four Stanley Cups. Quinn saw it as another opportunity to improve—especially as he continued to haggle with the Leafs for his contract for the upcoming season. Leafs general manager Jim Gregory suggested that Quinn do the training. "I guess he thought if it would succeed with me it would succeed with anybody," Quinn quipped to a reporter.

Through the month of September, six days a week, Quinn laced up at the Tam O'Shanter rink in Toronto to practice the fundamentals of skating alongside Judy Williams—the junior Canadian figure skating champion—and other national-level figure skaters like Bob Emerson, John MacWilliams, Anna Forder, and Richard Stephens. Quinn, on the ice in his full gear with everything but a stick, was trounced by Williams, who beat him in a race around the ice in which he skated forward ... and she skated backward.

Quinn was a stiff, almost straight-legged skater, observed John Wilde, one of Hyland's top instructors, who worked one-on-one with him. The only thing holding back Quinn's speed, Wilde said, was that he'd never been properly instructed. All of the hours spent skate ... skate ... skating at Mahoney and the Parkdale arena had ingrained his terrible form. Quinn didn't know how to create speed. In nine sessions, he said he felt everything changing.

"The chest and shoulders are the heaviest parts of your body. To keep balance you must have them over your front gliding foot, at all times," Pat explained, recounting what he had learned to Bob Pennington. "You lean into a corner from the waist down just as you lean into a hill from the waist down in skiing ... [and] keep that inside shoulder up as you turn." The trainers had Quinn doing quick stops and starts, over and over. "I'm doing things now that I wouldn't have dared to try before. Y'know I've always stopped on my front foot. Today I'm using both feet.

I'm still making a lot of mistakes but I realize why I'm making them and how to correct them. It's tough to shake off the bad habits of nearly twenty years. Sometimes I think I'm doing fine and then John Wilde puts pressure on me as a rival would, and I go back to my old and familiar style. To be effective, technique must almost be instinctive," Quinn said. "There's a hell of a long way to go before training camp opens next week, but I'm trying. At worst, I'll report fitter than I have ever been."

When the Leafs' training camp opened in 1969, there were nine defensemen fighting for an everyday job with the team, and Quinn had to fight as hard as any of them. At the time, Quinn hadn't agreed on any contract with the Leafs and was still in negotiations with Jim Gregory, arguing that he deserved not only to stick with Toronto—but to be paid more for his services. Quinn was in the lineup against the New York Rangers for an exhibition game in Kitchener on Sunday, September 21, during training camp. He was still in salary negotiations but knew he needed the ice time. "One game is worth several scrimmages," he said. "I'm the kind of person who has to work hard at my job."

During the Leafs' training camp scrimmages, the six-foot-three-inch giant squared off against the talented five-foot-eight-inch defenseman Rick Ley. It was common for small skirmishes to come to blows during practice and intra-squad games. It was, after all, impossible to be teammates if you didn't make the team. Camp was about survival. There was plenty of time for beers and pleasantries at the bar after they got off the ice. "We both understood," says Ley. "We were trying to feed our families." The wounds were strictly superficial.

Quinn and Ley were different kinds of players. Ley was five years younger, and had been a top prospect in the Leafs' system. Quinn was a rounding error that found a way to stick around. Both kept their spots on the Leafs' roster for the 1969–70 season, and they'd remain connected—as best friends—through the next four decades.

That season, Pat and Sandra rented a townhouse in Mississauga, just around the corner from Rick and his wife, Ellen. Murray and Helen Oliver also lived nearby. The teammates often drove to practices and home games together in Ley's green Plymouth Sports Fury or Quinn's bright-blue Lincoln. Quinn usually directed the conversation with a cigar dangling from his lips. Between puffs, he'd lecture his teammates on players' rights and contract negotiations.

Quinn was well versed in the business of the game. He knew the details of several other teammates' contracts, which were for the most part closely guarded secrets. He was aware of what most of the other players were making. The information was important, because it was power—not over his teammates, but over a corporate structure that had always worked in favor of owners and ensured that the players were compliant and willing to work for much less than they deserved.

At the time, Quinn was still completing his studies at York University and was just a few courses away from finally obtaining his business degree—nearly a decade after he'd started. During those rides to the Gardens and back home to Mississauga, Quinn puffed his pipe professorially, lecturing Ley on the many ways they might keep and save the little money they did manage to get out of the Leafs. There were lessons in military history, too, with

Quinn being an aficionado in all matters of war—especially when Canadian troops were involved. He often told stories of Romans and Greeks and ancient battles that still offered lessons today. "I could ask him what something was in Latin and he'd know," Ley says.

While Quinn lectured Ley on war and finances, Sandra made her own impression on Rick's wife, Ellen. The two would catch a ride to Maple Leaf Gardens with Helen Oliver, who was the only driver among the three. They sat beside each other during the games. Ellen watched with passing interest while Sandra, who she remembers always looked perfectly put together with matching outfits, took notes, keeping track of Quinn's plus–minus record. It was astounding, Ellen thought, how much Sandra knew about the game. She wasn't just a passive observer. Sandra knew hockey—she studied it, like Quinn did. "She cared about every facet of it," Ellen says. The constant moves, packing up the car to drive from town to town with no stability—all of it had been part of the Quinns' unified pursuit. Anything Pat had achieved had been earned with Sandra propping him up, never quitting on his dreams. Ellen and Sandra would often joke about their different perspectives on the game their husbands played. If Rick Ley was sent down for conditioning, he'd be going on his own. "Ellen never went to the minors," Sandra teased.

Quinn served the purpose Jim Gregory signed him for. "We were always concerned about our team getting pushed around," says Gregory. "When you have players on your team like Paul Henderson and David Keon, you have to make sure you have people who make sure they don't get manhandled." But Quinn's contributions to the Leafs were appreciated off the ice as much as, if not more than, on it. In a year and a half, the Big Irishman had become a locker-room favorite—more relaxed with NHL experience. "He always had a big smile on his face and a cigar, laughing and joking," says Mike Pelyk. "He didn't always play regularly, but you knew when he was there, you could count on him. There are guys like that, that are like the glue." Star players can put up the numbers, but every hockey team needs character guys who support the squad in less tangible ways. As a player, that was Quinn's role. It was one he'd circle back to years later as he utilized the kind of hard-nosed, spirited players in whom he saw a younger version of himself.

During post-practice, the game meal was at George's Spaghetti House on Dundas Street or a smattering of bars in the area that welcomed the Leafs. Quinn often regaled his teammates with his tales of life in the minors and back-in-the-day accounts of growing up in Hamilton's east end. Hours would pass, glasses filled and emptied and filled on repeat, with the laughter as constant as hazy clouds of cigar smoke above them.

On the road, court was held in hotel lobbies—"lobbying up," they called it—as they sat around in plush chairs and swapped stories. Plane rides were for games of bridge or reading, where Quinn always had a book in his massive hand, even if he fell asleep with it in his lap having only gotten through a page or two.

The memory of Bobby Orr being crushed by Pat Quinn was still fresh in the minds of Bruins fans in 1969. The Leafs and Bruins faced off four times before the New Year, tensions rising in each up to the fifth meeting of the season between the rivals, on February 1, 1970. A wild, sellout crowd of 14,831 packed into the Boston Garden for a game that was televised in both the United States and Canada.

In the second period John McKenzie took a shot at Quinn, who lashed back at the Bruins' enforcer. Phil Esposito threw a few punches at Quinn before Orr came rushing in and jumped on him. The benches cleared and the ice turned into a free-for-all brawl. In the mix, Quinn was pulled to the ice from behind and buried beneath a pile of Bruins as the Boston crowd chanted, "Kill Quinn! Kill Quinn!"

The Leafs lost the game 7–6. Referee Bill Friday issued eighty-four minutes in penalties: a relatively even forty-three for Toronto and forty-one for Boston.

A couple of days later, sitting in his stall at Maple Leaf Gardens after an off-day practice, Quinn scanned the news reports of his fight with Orr. The Boston papers scored a clear win for Number 4. One of the articles showed all-star defenseman Fred Stanfield tugging at Quinn's sweater from behind— the safest way to approach the angry Irishman. "Restraining Quinn," the caption read.

"Oh, he was restraining me, was he?" Quinn grinned. "He hit me one good shot on the head when I was down," he continued, turning to the matter of Orr. "But I hit him a good one when we were standing up and split his lip. It's not a decent fight if you don't take at least one shot. I wound up on the bottom, so it's cut-and-dried I guess. I lost, or at least that's what they say.

"He's well coordinated, has good balance on his skates, and is very strong," Quinn allowed of Orr's merits as a physical player. "He's a pretty good fighter. I guess if he wanted to be a boxer or a high-wire walker, for that matter, he could do it."

There is a certain respect that comes with rivalry, particularly in hockey. Orr was the best player Quinn would ever skate against, a one-of-a-kind talent, arguably the greatest that has ever played. They sat on opposite ends of the NHL spectrum. Quinn was just hanging on to his place in the NHL, fitting into a role that was the product of the increasing physicality of the game. In that position, though, Quinn learned to see the game unfold around him. He learned to process it in ways that Orr never would. If Orr was Picasso, Quinn was the scholar who found beauty and meaning in his strokes. Of course, that served little use to a player with limited skills.

To survive in the league, Quinn had to play the villain. There was no other way for him to fit in. He was often a healthy scratch for the Leafs through the 1969–70 season, and the best currency he had was those jeers from the bleachers—"Kill Quinn! Kill Quinn!"—a tribute to the man for doing his job. And even those Bruins fans had a strange affection for the man they tried to despise. His warm reception in that Boston bar the night of the hit the previous spring proved as much. And even after they called for his head in the Boston Garden, Quinn was one of the Leafs they surrounded for autographs after the game. Many fans adored Quinn and the role he played even though hockey purists, even then, labeled the position a stain on the game. Quinn would have much preferred to be known for the electrifying end-to-end rushes that his apparent nemesis was famous for, but his only meal ticket was to spark chaos. "At least if they're hooting at me, I'm being noticed," he said. "And maybe it will help me keep a job." And it would. But never with stability.

Under coach John McLellan, the Leafs finished sixth in the East Division that season with just twenty-nine wins, and didn't qualify for the playoffs. They were eighth of twelve teams in goals for; ninth in goals against.

Quinn dressed in just fifty-nine games, and was sent down to the minors in Tulsa for a time. He finished with five assists, no goals, and eighty-eight penalty minutes. Despite his charisma with teammates—and friendship with Gregory himself—Quinn just didn't factor into the Leafs' plans enough to protect him in the 1970 expansion draft. Two new franchises—the Buffalo Sabres and Vancouver Canucks—would make the NHL a fourteen-team league.

Vancouver had been passed over during the first round of expansions for the start of the 1967–68 season, as the NHL granted six new franchises to American cities, sparking outrage across Canada. After all, the west coast had a rich history in the game. When the Stanley Cup was still a challenge prize, the Vancouver Millionaires claimed the trophy in 1915 from the Ottawa Senators, beating the defenders in three straight games in front of crowds of seven thousand at the Denman Street arena. It was the first time the Cup was awarded to a team west of Winnipeg.

The Canucks started as an amateur team in the Pacific Coast Hockey League (PCHL), which formed in 1945. The team played out of the drafty, arctic-cold Pacific National Exhibition forum. The PCHL professionalized three years later and merged with the Western Canada Senior Hockey League in 1952 to form the minor pro Western Hockey League. For a logo, the team used a rendition of Johnny Canuck, the Canadian superhero, skating with a wide, powerful stride.

Fred Hume, Vancouver's mayor for eight years through the 1950s, bought the Canucks of the Western League in 1962 from the Pacific National Exhibition. At the time, the club's assets amounted to two players, a set of sweaters, sticks, and a few rolls of tape. Hume funded the team out of his own pocket, putting more than two hundred thousand dollars of his own money into the Canucks.

Toronto Maple Leafs president Stafford Smythe was actually credited with planting the seed for bringing NHL hockey to Vancouver, when he inquired into the possibility of creating a western franchise in the early 1960s. Smythe said he'd build a three-million-dollar rink if the city provided the land. But Vancouver turned down the offer. The NHL announced plans to expand in 1965, rekindling hope that the NHL might come west.

Hume sold the Canucks to a group of Vancouver businessmen just before the NHL expansion in 1967. The Canucks moved to the brand new Pacific Coliseum, despite still being members of the seldom-attended minor pro Western League. Three years later, during the next wave of NHL expansion, Vancouver was finally granted an NHL team along with Buffalo. (The price tag for entry had jumped from two million dollars in 1966 to six million dollars in 1970.)

Bud Poile, the Canucks' general manager, attended the NHL annual meeting on June 10, 1970, at the Queen Elizabeth Hotel in Montreal, prepared to pick the core group of leftover players that would make up the inaugural Vancouver Canucks roster. Each of the league's twelve teams had submitted its list of protected players, leaving a group of leftovers that would fill out the rosters for the Buffalo Sabres and Vancouver Canucks. The

Sabres won a coin toss and picked first, taking Tom Webster from the Bruins' system. The Canucks took defenseman Gary Doak, also from Boston, with their first choice. Next they selected veteran centerman Orland Kurtenbach from the New York Rangers, who had played for the Canucks in the late 1950s and won two Western League championships with the club. Kurtenbach would be the first captain of the new NHL team. Poile took forward Ray Cullen from Minnesota with Vancouver's next pick. In the fourth round, the Vancouver Canucks selected Pat Quinn.

Once again, the young Quinn family packed their bags and went west.

11

"It's Been a Great Life"

OH, THAT CLANCY! OH, THAT CLANCY!
Whenever they got his Irish up,
Clancy lowered the boom …
Boom … Boom … Boom …
Boom … Boom … Boom …

Pat Quinn's well-tuned baritone carried through the Vancouver Canucks' locker room as he sprayed on his deodorant. He'd picked up the right can after spraying hairspray under his arm the first time, wincing as he discovered the error. Several of his teammates laughed along as Quinn—whom they'd nicknamed Clancy—regaled them with the ditty by entertainer Dennis Day while they dressed after practice at the Pacific Coliseum.

O'Leary was a fighting man,
They all knew he was tough.
He strutted 'round the neighborhood

A-shootin' off his guff.

He picked a fight with Clancy,

Then and there he sealed his doom!

Before you could shout, "O'LEARY, LOOK OUT!"

Clancy lowered the BOOM!

After practice that day, on November 27, 1971, Quinn was in a rush to take his seven-year-old daughter, Valerie, to her first Brownies meeting, but he stopped to chat with reporter Tom Watt of *The Province*. Watt was writing a feature about the twenty-eight-year-old Canucks defenseman who was having a difficult start in the team's second season.

Quinn had viewed his first season in Vancouver as a chance for a new beginning in the NHL, after it had become apparent that he didn't fit into the Leafs' plans. The rag-tag Canucks were a great fit for him. It was a team of spare parts, a thrown-together bunch that would be lauded for being rich with "character," which some might interpret as a kind way of saying they lacked raw talent. But despite the varying reaches of their careers, the inaugural Canucks roster did share a common experience: They were a team that knew something about instability and disappointment. They knew what uncertainty felt like, constantly having to prove that they belonged in the NHL.

The Big Irishman had immediately established himself as one of the social leaders on the team. During training camp the players went out to dinner and Quinn took charge of plans to meet up at the beer hall afterward, where pints were twenty-five cents each. Vancouver general manager Bud Poile's son, David Poile, was attending the camp. He'd just finished at Northeastern

University, where he'd played hockey, and was looking to follow his father into the business side of the game. Poile was drawn to Quinn from the moment they met. "He was larger than life to a young guy like me," says Poile. "You could just feel his presence. I've never met somebody that you just wanted to be around as much as him. There was a combination of comfort and knowing that you're going to have fun." At the beer hall, the younger guys on the team (and David Poile) were unable to keep up with the more seasoned drinkers, but when they tried to tap out, Quinn said, "Oh no, you're not going anywhere." The next morning, the veterans skated circles around the hungover youths, including Poile, who'd laced up for the practice. They couldn't do anything. "So there was a method in his kindness—or madness—to be inclusive, if you will," says Poile. "He was indoctrinating us into pro hockey."

Vancouver was all-in on the new NHL franchise. The Pacific Coliseum was packed with just over fifteen thousand people for the Canucks' opening game on October 9, 1970, which was broadcast coast-to-coast on *Hockey Night in Canada*. A seventy-three-member pipe band played. The players stood at center ice with the Stanley Cup, on which were etched the names of the former Vancouver Millionaires, who won it once in 1915. Eighty-seven-year-old Cyclone Taylor, the last surviving Millionaire, was on hand as well, and the crowd went nuts for him. But things fell flat from there. The Los Angeles Kings scored halfway through the second period, followed by two more goals for a 3–1 win. Barry Wilkins scored the Canucks' first-ever goal in the third period, while Quinn picked up two minors and a misconduct.

Playing out of the East Division, the Vancouver Canucks faced a punishing travel schedule, as the team's closest divisional opponents were Detroit and Toronto. The Canucks would travel by bus to Seattle and wait in the terminal to catch a commercial flight to begin a two-week road trip along the east coast, playing as many as seven games. "Beer doesn't even taste good after ten days," said Orland Kurtenbach, the team's captain. "It's just awful." It was common for the Canucks to play games on Wednesday, Thursday, and Saturday, and often to finish in New York or Boston on Sunday—before getting up (often hungover or not having slept at all) at 4:30 A.M. to catch a flight to Toronto, to sit in the terminal and wait for a flight back to Seattle, fly for five hours (losing three), to get on a bus to Vancouver, where the team would practice in a fog that afternoon to get ready for a regularly scheduled home game on Tuesday night, which they'd often lose.

During one of the Canucks' practices at the Pacific Coliseum, Quinn and Kurtenbach (who was a trained boxer) got a little too rough with each other while scrabbling for the puck along the boards in a drill. Both were too competitive to let up. As Quinn hammered Kurtenbach into the boards, Kurtenbach threw up an elbow for protection. Then two of the toughest players in the league threw down their gloves and fought. Eventually, coach Hal Laycoe and a few of his players jumped in to pry them apart.

After cooling down, neither held a grudge. But it wasn't the end of their competitive rivalry. During a trip through California, the Canucks went out as a group for dinner. Walking home, the conversation turned to past athletic accomplishments. Quinn noted that he had been an excellent football player through high school. "Well, you must have played the line," Kurtenbach said. "A big guy like you, you're not too fast."

"Pardon me?" Quinn replied. "I'll beat *your* ass."

There was a light post about 220 yards away, and they wagered one hundred dollars on who could get there first. Kurtenbach thought it would be an easy win, as Quinn was carrying about 220 pounds then, compared to his 195. But when he reached the post, Kurtenbach recalls, Quinn was basically waiting for him. "Who's running the line now?" Quinn said.

The Canucks relied on that kind of confident competitive streak in their first year in the NHL. They refused to be pushed around. Teams could outplay them, but it was hard to intimidate them. They refused to back away from battles, in the corner or after the whistle. Even the Big Bad Bruins had a hard time pushing them around. Quinn was at the forefront of most of it, defending teammates and knocking opponents off their game. "I'll do anything to win," Quinn told *The Province*'s Tom Watt. "As long as it isn't morally wrong."

Vancouver finished sixth in the East Division, twenty-six points out of the playoffs.

Despite the lack of team success, Quinn felt he'd had one of his best seasons. Hal Laycoe matched him with twenty-four-year-old Gary Doak as the team's top defensive pairing, and the two were a formidable shutdown combination. Quinn played in seventy-six games and finished plus-two on a team that had 296 goals scored against it, third worst in the league. He scored two goals and finished with thirteen points, while leading the team with 149 penalty minutes.

In his second season with the Canucks, everything changed. Doak was injured in training camp, missing seven weeks of the season, and as soon as he was healthy, the Canucks traded him to the Rangers. "Pat Quinn must be the unhappiest player in the NHL today," the Canucks' coach said after the trade. "He had his greatest season last year with Doak." Quinn and Laycoe spoke shortly afterward and Pat was left with the understanding that his coach felt Quinn's success the previous year had been because of the partnership. Without Doak, Laycoe didn't have confidence in Quinn's ability. He was pushed aside.

"Believe me, it was ego shattering to hear that," Quinn told Watt after he'd finished serenading the dressing room that day. He'd already been a healthy scratch several times in the young season and was anxious to play with more regularity. "A big guy has to play a lot. I'm not the type who can just do spot duty," he said. "They can't say to me, 'Go over to the boards and hit someone.' Hitting is a lot like scoring. Sometimes you can play a whole game without getting a guy lined up and other times you get four in a row."

The Quinns lived in a rented townhouse just off the Mountain Highway in North Vancouver, about ten minutes from the Coliseum. They lived in the same complex as the Canucks' first goalies, Dunc Wilson and Charlie Hodge, and veteran journeyman Murray Hall. Quinn took his daughter Valerie to catechism classes at nearby St. Stephen's parish. The family couldn't afford very much on Quinn's salary, but they quickly came to feel a strong connection to the city. They'd adored the west coast since that brief stint with Seattle; it was so different from the many, many places they'd lived before. The family had returned to Hamilton in the summers, as Quinn chipped away at the final credits of his economics degree at York University. He was only two courses away from the diploma now, and admitted that the marathon pursuit of an education had worn on everyone, growing tired of summers dominated by classes. Now, it seemed, they were on the brink of completing the journey they'd embarked on nearly a decade earlier just as part of the end goal— playing in the NHL—was slipping away.

Despite the discouragement that came with being pushed off the Canucks' top defensive pairing, let alone being scratched from the regular roster, Quinn had done his best to keep his spirits up in the locker room. He'd relax from the stress with a pipe and a book. He enjoyed popular novels but was particularly drawn to histories—though he admitted that he'd given up on *The Rise and Fall of the Third Reich* because he "just couldn't hack it." He'd recently picked up the complete works of Winston Churchill and was looking forward to starting them. When he couldn't escape to old war stories, he found strength and support in Sandra and their two little girls at home. His wife was an "avid Pat Quinn fan," he assured Watt, with a laugh. "She keeps saying I'm better than this guy or that guy. I guess all wives are like that. I'm low at the moment, but if all this ended tomorrow, I'd know I had a lot of great years doing something I loved. You know, some guys work all their lives at jobs they hate." That he could just as easily be working an overnight shift pulling molten steel in a Hamilton mill was never lost on Quinn.

Even though his playing time had dwindled in Vancouver, he remained a fan favorite because he always took the time to chat with fans. "My philosophy is that it's no skin off my teeth to stop and talk to them," Quinn told Watt as they sat in the Canucks' locker room. "Taking the time to talk to people is something I learned from Tim Horton when I played with the Leafs. If a great athlete like Horton can spend the time to do that, then so can this guy."

At the time, the days when fans would stop to chat must have also seemed somewhat numbered. Even as he kept up his high in the locker room, bellowing out "Clancy Lowered the Boom" for his mates, there was a sense of an ending in his conversation with the reporter, before he rushed out to make it to Brownies on time: "I just hope when I'm finished playing I can find a career I'll enjoy as much as hockey," Quinn said. "It's been a great life."

Vancouver won twenty games, lost fifty, and tied eight in its second season—the worst record in the league. (The Canucks' forty-eight points put them one point below the LA Kings for the inglorious distinction.) They were second worst in league scoring, with just 203 goals for; they were also second worst in goals against, with 297.

Quinn didn't know what lay ahead, but he thought it unlikely that he would return to the Canucks. The team didn't intend to protect him in the upcoming NHL expansion draft, in which the new franchises—Atlanta and Long Island—would select the core of their team. Pat was twenty-nine now, past a player's usual peak, but with just four years in the league. But the upstart World Hockey Association (WHA) was about to launch its inaugural season, creating a whole new market for players like Quinn to find work. The Alberta Oilers, one of the WHA's twelve founding franchises, flew Quinn in hoping to sign him.

The Quinns traveled back to Hamilton that spring, moving in with Jack and Jean and Pat's teenage brother Phillip. The girls spent their days playing in the backyard with their cousins and walking to the corner store to get ice cream bars. Jean regaled them with memories of how she used to cover her eldest son's paper route. Pat went back to work making sales calls for a trucking company while finishing the final course of his economics degree at York University.

The emerald-green house on Glennie Avenue needed a new roof, but before they could lay the shingles, the Quinns had to remove the large old metal television antenna. Guy Quinn was home from his football scholarship at Youngstown State, but was recovering from knee surgery, and Pat's future in hockey depended on his physical health, so Jean wouldn't let either of them up on the roof. The job fell to Barry, who was working at a Hamilton steel company at the time. He climbed up to the top of the roof and tied himself off, just like Jack had shown his boys to do. It was drizzling out, and he didn't want to risk slipping. Pat took the rope's end on one side of the house and Guy took the other, holding their brother in place. Barry knocked the pin out of the base of the antenna, expecting it to unhinge, but the antenna didn't move. He cut the wires attaching the antenna to the roof and gave the antenna another shove, hoping to knock it forward—but it fell left, and went tumbling toward the hydro wires that ran close to the house and along the street beside it. As Pat and Guy shifted and pulled on the ropes to keep him upright, Barry grabbed the end of the antenna just as it struck the top wire—KABOOM. Fiery sparks exploded from the wires that danced in the air and crackled down the roof next to Barry, who had fallen backward. A huge arc of white smoke shot into the sky. The lights went off in the house with the bang, and Jean came running out the back door to see what had happened to her sons. "Where's Barry? Where's Barry?" she asked, frantically.

"Mom, go back in the house," Pat said, trying to calm her, guiding her back inside. Unable to get by her eldest son, Jean ran through the house and charged back out the front door, just as Barry leapt off the roof, trying to get away from the live wires thrashing around. He crashed down next to her.

Several blocks away at the Woodward Fire Station, where Jack Quinn was sitting with his crew, the lights were also out. In fact, the power throughout a large chunk of east-end Hamilton was down, and would stay down for several hours. "That's my boys," Jack said. Moments later a call came in and a firetruck was dispatched to 252 Glennie Avenue.

The damage, beyond shattered egos, was minimal. Barry finished the roof on his own.

On a June afternoon that year, the Quinn family were sitting in the living room at Jack and Jean's when the phone rang in the kitchen. It was for Pat.

"Hello," he said, taking the receiver in the kitchen. Pat listened, confused. "Okay, okay—who?"

"It's the Boomer," the man on the other end of the phone repeated. He had a thick French-Canadian accent.

"Who?"

"The Boomer!" the man insisted.

"Okay. Who?"

"Pat, it's Boom-Boom Geoffrion. I picked you for my team!"

The south was a new frontier for hockey, a risky market that needed to draw fans who had no relationship with the sport. It was an enormous task, and the ownership group in Atlanta asked a young, relatively unknown hockey executive named Cliff Fletcher to be the general manager of their Atlanta Flames. Fletcher got his start in the Montreal Canadiens' organization, managing the Junior Habs, before becoming a scout with the new St. Louis Blues when they started in 1967. He was quickly promoted to Blues assistant general manager under Scotty Bowman, until both were fired in 1970 after falling out with the team's owner, Sid Salomon Jr.

Fletcher asked Habs legend Bernard Geoffrion to be his coach, and before they had even selected their players, Fletcher and Geoffrion took to promoting the Atlanta Flames in Georgia. Boom-Boom starred in a Miller Lite commercial. He was stout, in his early forties, with a flat nose and parted hair overgrown with sideburns, and he wore a tuxedo as he skated onto the ice carrying a bouquet of flowers. "To all you people in the south," he said, with his thick French-Canadian accent, "I offer you these beautiful roses. Now come and see our game. You are going to see something unbelievable—action, fights, whatever you want. It's better than football or basketball. Come to the hockey game." Strange as the appeal was, it seemed to work. The lure of this new ice sport that offered action and fighting and "whatever you want" helped ticket sales take off. People in Atlanta were ready for hockey, even if they weren't quite certain exactly what it was.

As had been the case two years earlier, there was little to choose from in the expansion draft on June 6, 1972. For their six-million-dollar expansion fee, the Atlanta Flames and New York Islanders were allowed to select twenty-one players, but collectively no more than three from any one of the other fourteen teams. The existing franchises were allowed to protect fifteen of their best players and two goalies from being selected. The rest was slim pickings.

The Vancouver Canucks left Quinn unprotected, and Atlanta took him with the thirty-fourth pick. Along with the well-established physical presence of the thirty-year-old Quinn, the Flames picked up defensemen Ron Harris, Randy Manery, and Bill Plager. They added veteran defenseman Noel Price after the draft, for cash. Cliff Fletcher did best with his picks in goal, stealing Phil Myre from the Canadiens and Dan Bouchard from the Bruins. Up front the Flames took a long shot on centerman Bobby Leiter, who had a steel plate in his arm and hadn't scored more than fourteen goals a season. After the draft, they also picked up centermen Rey Comeau, who had played four games with the Canadiens the season before, and Larry Romanchych, who played ten games and had two assists for the Black Hawks. "If you tallied up the career NHL goals for all the players we drafted, it was less than seventy," says Fletcher. "That's the talent they made available to us."

Quinn and Fletcher met in a room at the Bristol Place hotel near the Toronto international airport to negotiate a contract that would bring Quinn to Atlanta. Quinn told Fletcher the WHA was an option for him and that he was strongly considering the Oilers' offer. The thirty-six-year-old first-time general manager was hearing that a lot, actually. The upstart WHA was eager to steal talent from the NHL and salaries were on the rise because of the new competition for talent. Fletcher had never met Quinn before, but had heard about his stubbornness, and knew his reputation for being a staunch negotiator. When Quinn arrived at the meeting, Fletcher was immediately impressed. Quinn had a presence to him, Fletcher recalled. He was statuesque. "When he walked into a room, everyone knew he was there," he says. Fletcher was also impressed by Quinn's determination, as demonstrated by the degree he had just completed after a decade of studying his way through the minors and into the NHL. Fletcher wanted Quinn for his size and strength, but also for his resilience. Fletcher knew that if Quinn made a commitment, he wouldn't waver. They agreed on a one-year contract for fifty thousand dollars.

"We overpaid him, I'm sure," says Fletcher.

12

Rejects and Has-Beens

It took five different universities and ten years, but in the fall of 1972 Quinn finally graduated from York University with a bachelor of arts. "I suppose you could call me a plugger," he said. "It took me a few years—in fact, more than a few—to become an NHL regular and to earn that degree. Well, I made it to both of them." Pat Quinn, BA, didn't attend the commencement ceremony, however. He was busy starting a new life in Georgia.

Pat and Sandra had been welcomed to Atlanta by a familiar face. David Poile had been hired as Fletcher's assistant with the Flames, and his first major job was to pick up the players upon their arrival. So David and his wife, Elizabeth, met the Quinns at the airport and took them out to dinner at the Midnight Sun restaurant in Atlanta. It was the beginning of a lifelong bond between the Quinn and Poile families.

The Quinns unpacked their boxes at their new condo in a complex called Windy Hill in Marietta, Georgia, a suburb about thirty minutes outside of Atlanta where most of the Flames' players lived. Pat and Sandra didn't have the time or money to return to Vancouver, so they had everything in their place packed up and sent south, making Valerie and Kalli Quinn the only kids in the area with snow pants and toboggans.

In their close proximity, the team developed a tight-knit bond. They had all traveled similar winding paths, exhausting paths, to get to Atlanta. The group lived in a new place, through the same experiences. Several players had young families, and the wives helped each other with the kids when the team was on the road.

During a preseason exhibition game in the Flames' first season, Quinn set a bold tone when he faced off against his former teammates on the Leafs at a game played in Ottawa. Mike Pelyk was up on forward killing a penalty and managed to move out of Toronto's end with the puck, sliding past Quinn by breaking to the outside and cutting back in toward the Flames' net. Beaten, Quinn turned and gave Pelyk a vicious two-hander across his shin. Pelyk fell to the ice, sliding hard through Flames goalie Phil Myre. As Pelyk slowly got to his feet, Quinn hustled over to apologize to his friend. "Mike, I had to do it."

The Flames opened up the season on the road in Long Island against the Islanders, winning 3–2. They went to Chicago for their third game, where a hockey reporter wrote that the Flames were "the worst assemblage of rejects and has-beens ever in the history of hockey" and that they were unworthy of playing at Chicago Stadium. They lost to the Black Hawks 4–1 and went on to finish their first road trip with one win and three losses.

The players were treated like heroes, however, when they arrived in Atlanta for their first home game at the Omni on

October 14, 1972, against the Buffalo Sabres. The Flames sold more than seven thousand season tickets and were expected to average about thirteen thousand fans a game. But on opening night the rink was absolutely packed, with more than fifteen thousand people in the stands. Fans dressed up like they were going to a cocktail party; women wore dresses and men, ties.

"Listen fellas. I've got to tell you this," Geoffrion said before the game. "I'm not the greatest coach in the world. But if you look around this room you'll see that I don't have the greatest players either." He got some laughs, and continued, "If you go out there and prove to these people that you want to play this game they will appreciate you."

The Sabres were coached by Punch Imlach, who started Quinn's good friend and mentor, Tim Horton, on the blue line. When the puck was dropped, Gilbert Perreault won the draw back to Horton, who skated nonchalantly to center ice and flipped a shot in on net. Flames goalie Phil Myre corralled it easily against his chest. The Omni went nuts, and the thousands of dapperly dressed fans gave Myre a standing ovation. The Flames and Sabres tied 1–1. But even in a low-scoring affair, the Atlanta fans were hooked on hockey. Through the first few months, people would come down to the gate to stand on the ice, just to see what it felt like. The Omni was consistently filled to more than eighty-percent capacity, and there were regular sellouts. Having shed their formal wear for more arena-appropriate attire, the crowds were beer-fueled and vocal. They cheered at everything, especially the big booming hits laid out by Pat Quinn, and they continued to applaud every routine save made by goalies Phil Myre and Dan Bouchard. "They were being educated to a new sport," says Myre. "It wasn't like today with all the exposure the NHL gets. It was a great experience." (As a marker of the time and place, the Flames had a fan who would come to every game in a gray Confederate uniform and would wave the Confederate flag every time Atlanta scored a goal.)

The Flames rode goaltending and defense that first season, and were in contention for the playoffs, battling for third place until the first week of February—when they went on a skid that sent them to seventh place, eleven points behind the fourth place St. Louis Blues.

Despite the collapse, the season was considered a success. The Flames had Atlanta's attention, even if the fans still weren't quite sure what was happening on the ice. Boom-Boom Geoffrion had become a celebrity, as the city grew more enamored with the charismatic, quirky, and at times temperamental French Canadian. Geoffrion proved to be the perfect choice to take a bunch of marginal players and inspire them to collectively become something more. He did it with humor and he did it with sincerity. When the team played the mighty Boston Bruins that first season, Boom-Boom colorfully told his players, in broken English, "I wouldn't change any of you guy for one of those guy!" He paused, then added, "Well, maybe one or two."

Quinn would later say Geoffrion wasn't necessarily the best teacher of skills but he was the best coach he'd ever played for at preparing his players for a game. "Boomer convinced us that the only way we could accomplish anything was through hard work. We had no trouble believing him," Quinn said in an interview while he played for the Flames. "When Boomer played himself, he wasn't gifted with great natural ability but he became a superstar through sheer hard work and determination. In fact, I doubt if any player who achieved superstar status had less natural ability. Boomer used to run on his skates but he ran pretty darned hard.... So when that guy tells you that you can accomplish anything you want if you want it badly enough and work hard enough, you believe him."

Quinn—who grew his hair out, letting it flow over his ears and down the back of his neck—played along with his tough-guy role as the Atlanta fans that packed the Omni cheered every time he hammered an opponent to the ice. "They have names for Pat Quinn around the National Hockey League," sports writer Jim Huber wrote in a profile of Quinn. "Most of them can't be repeated in a family publication. He's not the league's most beloved player. Mean Pat Quinn the enforcer."

"I LOVE physical contact. I always have. I like nothing more than to give out a good beating," Quinn told Huber, who described his face, cartoonishly, as being "worthy of a sleazy gymnasium above a tobacco shop in the wrong section of town," but added that off the ice Quinn was "the picture of cool, splendidly dressed with an ever present pipe in his mouth."

"They call me mean but I'm not, really," Quinn said. "I prefer to think of myself as tough. I don't play dirty. But a man has to look after his family and his job. And since I have never been a very good skater, I've had to compensate in other ways." Quinn then pointed to the scar tissue above both his eyes and shared a story about the grudge he'd carried for the Chicago Black Hawks' Stan Mikita since he was fifteen years old and playing junior. Mikita, Quinn said, hacked him with his stick when he dropped his gloves to fight. "Someday, I'll get him back for that too."

Quinn finished his first season in Atlanta with two goals and eighteen assists. Continuing with his long tradition, he led the team in penalty minutes. No one was going to mistake him for Bobby Orr, but at thirty years old, Pat Quinn was playing the best hockey of his life. Through the off-season he worked hard to slim down ten pounds to 205, hoping to increase his mobility on the ice.

After the Flames' first season, in the summer of 1973, Pat volunteered at a charity event at Emory University. To help raise money he put his face in a cut-out piece of plywood and fans bought pies that they chucked at him. During the event a large man—six-foot-seven, 270 pounds—walked up to Pat and stuffed the pie right in his face. The man was Mike Tilleman, a defensive tackle with the Atlanta Falcons, who had just been traded from the Houston Oilers. Mutual friends from Houston had told Tilleman and his wife to connect with the Quinns in Atlanta. So Mike decided to make a lasting first impression on the Flames' enforcer. "Afterwards I heard about what he had done to Bobby Orr," Tilleman says. "I got scared."

That summer Pat got a job doing sales for an Atlanta brewery and the Quinn family moved to a two-story home in the north end of suburban Marietta. Pat converted the garage into a playroom for the girls. It was the first time in their many moves that Valerie and Kalli didn't have to share a room. In the evenings when he was home, Pat, the bruising tough guy, would tuck his girls into their beds and sing them "Teddy Bears' Picnic."

The Quinns were only ten minutes away from the Tillemans, who had kids close in age to Valerie and Kalli. Quinn was a year

older than Tilleman, and both found themselves in the twi-
light of their careers as professional athletes at the same time.
The Quinns' backyard became the de facto spot for social gatherings, as they hosted regular barbecues for the Flames and
other friends. "If they had forty home games, [there were] probably forty parties," says Tilleman, who almost always attended.
The Tillemans and Quinns also gathered each New Year's Eve,
when their kids would bang pots and pans on the front porch as
the clock struck midnight. Every summer, the Tillemans hosted
a "Happy Birthday, America" party, where the families would
bob for apples and have pie-eating contests.

Pat often tried to educate his NFL friend on fine wines
and grappa—always while puffing on a Cuban cigar—and their
conversations frequently turned to business opportunities outside
the game. With his fresh degree, Pat was eager to embark on
something entrepreneurial. "The thing we had in common was
neither one of us started out making any money," Tilleman says.
"There was no money in the games." Mike was interested in
starting a series of car dealerships back home in Montana. Pat
was intrigued by an opportunity in Atlanta to open gas bars with
stores attached.

Through the next four seasons, Atlanta became the most consistent place the Quinns had lived since the beginning of their
hockey journey. Valerie and Kalli went to school there through
the formative period of their childhood, and both started to
swim competitively.

On the ice, a slimmed down Quinn continued to improve.
He had a career high, five goals and twenty-seven assists in the

1973–74 season, as the Flames finished fourth in the West Division and made the playoffs for the first time (where they lost to the Flyers in four straight). For a team just two years from conception, reaching the playoffs was considered tantamount to the Philadelphia Flyers winning the Stanley Cup in their seventh season. The Atlanta Flames were one of the biggest success stories of the NHL. While the team was led by the stellar playing of Dan Bouchard and Phil Myre in goal—they'd also found themselves a star player in twenty-year-old rookie Tom Lysiak, who led the team with nineteen goals and sixty-four points.

The following season, in 1974, the Flames were moved to the new Lester Patrick Division. It was a tough division, physically, with the New York Islanders, New York Rangers, and Philadelphia Flyers. The Flames finished fourth in the division and didn't make the playoffs.

Team captain Keith McCreary retired at the end of the season. Quinn was named his replacement—a decision that Fletcher called a "no-brainer." "He was a total leader. He commanded respect," Fletcher said. "It was the easiest decision we ever made."

The trajectory of Quinn's career was incredible, when you think of it. He went from being an afterthought defenseman, drifting through the minors, to being named captain of an NHL team. Given the opportunity, Quinn proved his value. And it had nothing to do with his talent on the ice. Here was a player who found a way to survive against the odds. He was smart and calculated. He was determined. And, in his own way, Quinn became an asset.

On November 30, 1975, the Flames played against Oakland Athletics owner Charlie Finley's California Golden Seals.

Quinn, now playing with a "C" on his chest, picked up a penalty and was stuck in the box. When the penalty expired, the play was breaking out of the Flames' end. Defenseman Noel Price fired a pass and hit Quinn at center ice. The Golden Seals had a young defenseman, Rick Hampton, and Quinn lumbered in on him, one-on-one. Quinn dropped his shoulder and checked Hampton aside "all the way to the second row of the seats" and went in alone on Gilles Meloche. Quinn pulled off a forehand–backhand deke, and put it in the top shelf. "I pissed my pants," says Cliff Fletcher, who watched the game from the manager's box with assistant general manager David Poile. "I've never seen a goal like that in all my life. If he tried that a million more times he wouldn't have got it." Quinn tried to play it cool—"with his big Irish smile," Fletcher says—going back to the bench like it was a routine play. The Flames won 4–1. In six decades of NHL hockey, Fletcher swears it's the greatest goal he's ever seen. "Looking at the types of skills that I had, that goal was way out of line," Quinn later recalled. "That was not the sort of goal one might expect from a Quinn."

Through the years in Atlanta, Fletcher, the young general manager, and Quinn, the aging player, became close friends. "The Irishman was a fun-loving, gregarious guy," Fletcher says. "When he was with his friends, there was no one more fun to be around, smoking a big stogie and singing Irish songs." For his part, Quinn admired the way Fletcher ran the Flames. "To me, it was how he treated people. He was a player's manager.... He made himself available," Quinn said in an interview in 2010. "He didn't interfere, but at the same time you got to know who he was. He wanted to have people respect the players. He wanted them to be treated properly."

As captain of the Flames, Quinn viewed his role as the one to communicate to the coaches what the players in the locker room were feeling and thinking. He was their representative. "Most players hide stuff from their coaches or try to; they don't want anybody to see the pimples," Quinn said later. "Sometimes as a player, you have to have the insight for your team to be able to pass on information to the coaching staff that they should have to help make the team better, not to get somebody into trouble or anything of that nature, just to actually help the player. I think that's the captain's responsibility too. At the end of the day, to be able to help everybody be good, that's that link that captains have."

Quinn was already the team rep for the NHL Players' Association, attending the annual meetings run by Alan Eagleson as they worked to continue a trend to increase player pensions and salaries. At the meetings he developed a close friendship with the Philadelphia Flyers' star, Bobby Clarke. Clarke admired Quinn's intellect. He carried strong opinions and wasn't afraid to share them, but he never just spouted them out. Quinn would sit quietly in the meetings, taking the information in and carefully considering it. When he did speak, the entire room paid attention. "You always knew when he said something, you'd better listen," Clarke says. Clarke played for one of the game's great innovators, Fred Shero, and something about Quinn back then made Clarke think that while their styles were different, he'd make a similarly effective coach.

At the time, Quinn had never considered a career behind the bench. But he was thinking about a future in law. He'd become friends with Dick Babush, an Atlanta accountant and attorney who did some work for the Flames. Quinn was intrigued by the intellectual challenge of law and considered it a possible career when his playing days were through. He looked into studying at Emory University in Atlanta.

But on the ice, Quinn found himself more in demand than he had ever been. The Phoenix Roadrunners, an expansion team with the rival WHA, tried to lure Quinn away from Atlanta. As a result, Fletcher locked him down with a long-term deal with the Flames. "I figured I've been with enough expansion teams for one career," Quinn said.

He'd become a smarter player by then. By his own admission, Quinn said he'd thrown himself out of position by lunging too eagerly and aggressively to check players in the past. He'd learned to be patient, waiting for the right time to strike with less frequent but more effective body contact. Quinn was sometimes compared to Allan Stanley, the stay-at-home defenseman who was a key part of the Leafs team that won four Stanley Cups through the 1960s. He worked the same way, the *Toronto Star*'s Frank Orr noted. He rushed only when the danger of being trapped was at a minimum, he'd stand up at the line as back-checkers came to help, and he cleared out the front of the net like a bulldozer. He was the cornerstone of the Flames' defensive core, which also featured thirty-nine-year-old Noel Price, Randy Manery, and Bob Murray, as well as a young pair in Dwight Bialowas and Jean Lemieux. Despite finishing last in the Patrick Division in 1975, the Flames were fifth best in goals against out of the NHL's eighteen teams, with 233. On the other hand, they were fourth worst in goals for, with 243.

Boom-Boom Geoffrion resigned from the Flames near the end of the 1975 season. The stress of coaching had been taking a toll on his health—he'd smoked two packs of cigarettes a day and lost fifteen pounds during training camp that he'd had trouble putting back on. He was having a hard time getting some of the younger guys to listen to him and felt he might have lost his touch. Mostly, though, he'd had a disagreement with Fletcher about whom to play in goal and didn't want anyone interfering with his coaching decisions. Fletcher replaced him with minor league coach Fred Creighton. The French Canadian was still one of the Flames' most popular personalities, though, and his departure was a blow to the trajectory of the fan base. After he left, Atlanta's attendance started to dwindle and soon the team struggled to get ten thousand people into the building. The team didn't make the playoffs that year or the year after. Fletcher ended up bringing Geoffrion back as vice-president of season ticket sales and promotion and a color commentator on the telecasts.

Quinn's massive frame teetered on the tiny skateboard, picking up speed as he hurtled down the hill toward the street at the end of his driveway. He'd been out in the front yard watching his daughters play with their new red and green skateboards on a summer day in 1976. He tried to show them that he could ride, too.

It was his biggest mistake.

Just before the end of the lane, Pat leapt off the board like an action hero driving a car toward a cliff. But instead of making a graceful dismount, Quinn landed on the side of his ankle, which snapped under the momentum of his body. The girls ran down to him as he lay on the ground, writhing in pain and cursing. An ambulance was called to take him away.

For any hockey player, a broken ankle is a severe setback. For the thirty-three-year-old slow-footed defenseman, the broken ankle was a fatal blow to his playing career.

Quinn tried to push through the 1976–77 season but was hampered by his injury the whole time. He played in only fifty-nine games and, at the end of the season, Fletcher told his friend that the Flames planned to go with a younger core on the blue line. Pat Quinn would never play for another professional hockey team again.

But his real legacy in the sport was about to begin.

Quinn still had a year to go on his contract. Fletcher called Ray Miron, Pat's old friend from Tulsa, who was now the general manager of the Colorado Rockies. He asked Miron if he'd like to have his old friend join his organization as a consultant or assistant coach. "Cliff, I'd love to have him," Miron said. Fletcher offered to have the Flames pay half of his salary through the duration of Quinn's contract, if the Rockies would take the other half. To Miron, it seemed like the perfect deal. He went to the Rockies' president, Munson Campbell—with whom he didn't often see eye-to-eye—and said he wanted to hire Quinn. Campbell said they couldn't afford his salary. Miron argued that Quinn would be a huge asset as an assistant coach, and for half the price. Munson refused to budge and, to Miron's everlasting disappointment, the Rockies passed.

"I always thought that players like Pat—who were marginal players, who played for a lot of teams, who played in the minor leagues for a ton of coaches—they absorbed a wealth of hockey knowledge that most people don't have," says Cliff Fletcher, remembering the incredible success his dear friend Pat Quinn would have on the other side of his life in the NHL. "When you're a healthy scratch, when you're playing and then sent down," he said, "when you're called up, on different teams, different coaches—if anyone would be prepared to deal with players coming up, it would be someone who experienced what Pat did."

In Philadelphia, under legendary head coach Fred Shero, the Flyers had become one of the first NHL teams to name an assistant coach. First, Shero hired Mike Nykoluk to join the Flyers as an assistant, then hired Flyers defenseman Barry Ashbee to run the team's defense after he suffered a career-ending eye injury during a playoff game against the New York Rangers in 1974. With Ashbee on the bench next to Shero, the Flyers won their second straight Stanley Cup in 1975. Tragically, Ashbee passed away from leukemia in 1977, when he was only thirty-seven years old.

Remembering Quinn's work with the NHL Players' Association, Bob Clarke recommended him as the team's new assistant. Keith Allen, the Flyers' general manager, called Quinn to see if he was interested in the assistant coaching job. Quinn said no. He wasn't ready to let go, and still harbored visions of making a comeback as a player in the NHL or WHA.

But as the summer went on, it became clear to him that he was in no condition to play, that he'd be lumped into the pile of old, broken players. He'd been thinking about his exit since those early days in Knoxville when he promised himself that he'd be prepared for something new when the game spat him out on the other side. That time had come.

There was no ceremony, no heart tugging wave to the fans, no sweet goodbye. In the busy sports section of the *Toronto Star* on

August 6, 1977, the notice was a single sentence, a tiny bullet point:

ATLANTA—Atlanta Flames defenseman Pat Quinn, a 14-year-veteran, will retire from active play with the National Hockey League club, a spokesman for the Flames said yesterday.

Officially retired, Quinn considered enrolling in law school at Emory University, but missed the application cutoff and would have had to wait another year. Then Keith Allen called again. The coaching job was still on the table. "Why don't you come and try it?" Allen asked.

13

Coach Quinn

The apprenticeship of John Brian Patrick Quinn began at 6:00 P.M. on Tuesday, August 9, 1977, when the Flyers officially announced that he was joining the organization. "We checked him out thoroughly. He's intelligent, well respected and very enthusiastic. Once he gets his feet wet he'll be an excellent addition to our organization," the Flyers' release read.

Quinn would serve as an assistant coach to head coach Fred Shero, replacing the late Barry Ashbee, working with the team's defense. Terry Crisp was also named an assistant coach, looking after the offense.

During the Flyers' rookie camp that year, about fifty young players were invited to try to earn a spot at the main training camp. During a luncheon with the Flyers' brass, one of the bosses told the bunch of eager players that they were all going to make the big camp—creating a sense of hope built on false promises. During practice the next day, Quinn—now a clean-shaven thirty-four-year-old with a bowl haircut, parted neatly across his forehead—gathered all of the prospects and, at considerable risk to his long-term employment, contradicted what the executive had told them. "A lot of you are going home," he said. It was a deflating message, but an honest one. One of the players in the pack was a rookie named Brian Burke, who had just finished at Providence College. "That was my first impression of Pat Quinn," says Burke. "Making sure we all knew what was going on, telling the truth even if it caused him some aggravation."

Truth-telling was a trait that had been engrained in Quinn growing up in Hamilton, where a man's character was all that mattered, a sentiment Quinn had lived out in fourteen years of ups and downs in professional hockey. Even if the truth was unpleasant, it had to be said. This was the foundation upon which Quinn built his coaching philosophy; much of the rest, he'd learn from Fred Shero.

Shero had been one of the NHL's most successful coaches through the 1970s. He was famous for using systems that integrated his offensive and defensive strategies. For Shero, it was about simple sets of rules he'd drill into his players, some about fighting. "Never go offside on a three-on-one or a two-on-one," "No forward must ever turn his back to the puck at any time; know where the puck is at all times," "Never pass diagonally in our zone unless one hundred percent certain." Shero would often quiz his players on his rules, which started off as ten and grew to sixteen by the 1975–76 season.

The former pro hockey player wasn't an excitable, charismatic personality like Boom-Boom. Shero had picked up the nickname "Freddy the Fog" during his playing career because he was reputedly the only player during a 1948 game in Minnesota who could see the puck through a heavy mist. Over the years, though, the moniker came to more fittingly represent his enigmatic personality. People would often catch the Winnipeg native deep in thought, unable to be distracted. He was quiet and didn't engage with his players much beyond repeatedly drilling his systems into them, though at times he'd make them do drills that didn't make any sense. When players like Bob Clarke would question his methods, Shero would reply: "Yeah, I know that. I was just waiting for someone to challenge me on it."

Shero did, however, often write philosophical and inspirational messages on the chalkboard of the Flyers' locker room. He famously wrote, "Win today and walk together forever," before game six of the 1974 Stanley Cup final. After carving his name on the Cup that year—along with receiving the Jack Adams Award for being coach of the year—Shero coached the Broad Street Bullies to another championship in 1975. The Flyers returned to a third straight final in 1976, but lost to the Montreal Canadiens.

Quinn looked for opportunities to catch Shero in his office when no one else was around. Shero would always keep his door shut and Quinn would listen to hear if he was there. Then he'd knock and ask the coach if he had some time to chat. Shero's office at the old Spectrum was tiny, and could barely fit both men. Quinn considered it a rare privilege to have these one-on-one conversations with the man he viewed as the most innovative and revolutionary coach of the era. "It was like a private audience with the Pope," he said.

Shero's analytical approach gave him a strategic advantage over other coaches and it gave Quinn another perspective. "He was a different sort of man," Quinn said. If a biopic were made about Shero today, the comedian Drew Carey would emulate his look perfectly, a dead ringer right down to the black, heavy-framed glasses.

Shero had little to do with bringing Quinn to the Flyers. That was Keith Allen's call, coming from captain Bob Clarke's strong endorsement. But the two men had a lot in common. They had both experienced the game from many different angles, and at all levels. Shero played only three seasons with the New York Rangers in the late 1940s before spending another decade in the minors. Shero turned to coaching with the Moose Jaw Canucks of the Saskatchewan Junior Hockey League in the late fifties and worked his way through the minor pro leagues until being named the Flyers' coach in 1971.

It's hard to imagine NHL teams operating today without myriad coaches, performance consultants, and analytics specialists that make regular games seem as involved as a trip to the International Space Station. But it all started with Shero. He was always looking ahead, trying to gain whatever advantage he could over teams by thinking differently about the game.

During their one-on-one chats, Shero would lean back in his chair and look up toward the ceiling as he'd philosophize about the game. It looked like he was imagining a rink in the sky, Quinn said. Shero would put himself up in that rink and just talk and talk. It didn't have to be a particularly good question, Quinn recalled. Quinn could just sit down and say something, any-thing—and Shero would go on for hours, talking hockey.

During one of their first meetings, Shero imparted to Quinn one of his most influential nuggets of advice: "I know who you are a little bit and you may know lots about the game but probably what you know is how you had to play the game," Shero said, as Quinn would recall. "If you ever want to coach and be a good coach, you're going to have to learn how to help others know how to play the game and that's your biggest job right now. Not just your knowledge; take your knowledge and try to fit it so that you can help others learn how to play."

"Okay," Quinn said. "How do I do that?" It was something he'd have to learn. Quinn spent hours watching footage of old games, scrutinizing the intricacies of what the Flyers did right and wrong on the ice. More and more coaches were using tape at the time, but none as thoroughly as Shero. He'd watch tape of other teams, but mostly he focused on his own. Shero came up with systems for every scenario on any part of the ice. Everything was organized. Everything had a plan. It was all preparation. He concentrated on his team's execution in much the same way as the legendary UCLA basketball coach John Wooden did, Quinn said. And so Quinn studied the way Shero operated on the bench, in the locker room, and in practice. He started to take notes—something he'd do throughout his career, scribbling down every idea or observation he made. Quinn took his own master's degree in the mind of Fred Shero's systems, watching how those X's and O's translated to the action in the games and how his drills during practice worked to implement a larger plan.

Quinn often drew up his own drills and would ask Shero if they could try them at practice, a request that was usually rejected. (Shero's practices were always the same—intense and repetitive. He wanted precise execution.) "Not during my practice," Shero would say. "You can keep the guys out afterwards to do that." And so Quinn did. He spent hours on the ice with

Paul Holmgren and Kevin McCarthy, two of the new, younger players on the team.

Shero was steps ahead of all of the game's innovative thinkers, Quinn would later say. And he made him realize how much Quinn enjoyed the art of coaching and inspired him to want to do more—to be a head coach.

Quinn also had great respect for Keith Allen who, like Shero, wanted his organization to create a tactical edge through practical intelligence. And owner Ed Snider, a savvy businessman who'd brought the Flyers to Philadelphia during expansion, shined up the Spectrum and was heavily involved in putting the team together. Pat thought he was smart and dynamic and "probably a bit ruthless, too." The Flyers developed a standard written-evaluation process for their scouts to report on prospects. Traditionally assessments had been verbal—"He had a good game," or "He had a bad game"—just a description of what the scout saw. The Flyers created an evaluation system that could rank and analyze the players they were looking to bring into the organization, which, despite its success, was still in its infancy. Allen increased the scouting department to five full-time scouts and pumped three hundred fifty thousand dollars into the annual scouting budget. Allen also hired Gil Brandt, chief scout of the Dallas Cowboys. Brandt was one of the NFL's most creative minds, who went against conventional thinking about the game. He used computer progams to quantify and measure skills—and had a lasting impact on how talent was evaluated in the NFL. Allen had Brandt develop a computer system to assess talent for the Flyers. A computer stationed in Santa Clara, California, soon held data on more than two thousand pro and amateur players, rating them on a scale of one to ten.

At the time, Quinn was thinking about becoming a head coach. But as he learned more about the industry, specifically within the Flyers' organization, Quinn was confused by the decisions being made by management without the input of the coaches. If he were a head coach, Quinn decided, he would certainly want to be on the inside of what the organization's thinking was. How is the team choosing players? How is the coach expected to use them? He wanted access to the information the managers had. Maybe it would be useful, maybe not—but the point, Quinn believed, was to have the information, regardless. He felt the Flyers' attempts to keep Shero out of the management side of the team inevitably led to Shero's departure from the Flyers for the dual coach and general manager's job with the New York Rangers following the 1977–78 season.

After the Flyers finished that season second in the Patrick Division and lost to the Boston Bruins in the Stanley Cup semifinals, Shero sent a letter of resignation to the Flyers. The departure was controversial. Shero still had a year left on his contract but believed it would be void after he signed a two hundred fifty thousand dollar contract with the Rangers. The Flyers refused to accept his resignation and a few weeks later the Rangers had to give up their first-round draft pick and cash to avoid tampering charges. Philadelphia drafted centerman Ken Linesman.

Shero's departure was an enormous opportunity for Quinn. He thought there was a good chance that he might get the head coach's job in Philadelphia. But the Maine Mariners, the Flyers' farm team in Portland, had just won the American Hockey League championship, led by Bob McCammon, who was named AHL coach of the year. McCammon already had five years' experience as a head coach and Quinn had just that single season as an assistant to his name. Keith Allen offered Quinn the head coaching job in Maine. Angry that he wasn't offered the Flyers job, Pat nearly accepted an offer from Mike Tilleman to join him in Montana and start a car dealership. But Sandra and the girls weren't convinced. So grudgingly, Quinn accepted the position in Maine.

The Quinns rented a doctor's summer home on the coast in Portland, Maine—a visual upgrade from the place they'd been renting in New Jersey. The girls didn't mind another move. "We kind of packed up and moved every summer," says Kalli. Maine was just another stop on the journey they'd been on throughout their young lives. And this one had an ocean view.

The Mariners were a team of young prospects who were well versed in the legends of Pat Quinn. They immediately took to the man who had knocked out Bobby Orr. Quinn had them from the moment he walked into the locker room. He brought swagger, a new style of coaching—and, of course, cigars. There were no rules about smoking inside buildings or on buses in those days, so Quinn almost always had a cigar in his mouth. He'd light one up on the rink or in the locker room. Pretty soon a third of the team was carrying cigars on the bus. Everyone wanted to be like Quinn. They'd always wait for him to light his, and then several of the players would light up.

The Mariners' road trips took them to places like Halifax, Nova Scotia, which was nine hours away; Rochester, New York, seven hours away; and Springfield, Massachusetts, three hours away. The card players sat in the back of the bus, while the readers sat closer to the front. Quinn always settled himself in the second seat from the front because it had a light above it. He'd spend his time on the bus reading books or drawing up plans for an upcoming game, always while smoking or chewing on a cigar. One of the books Quinn carried around during his time with the Mariners was a book written by Fred Shero, *Shero: The Man Behind the System*.

Mike Emrick was a young broadcaster doing play-by-play and public relations for the Mariners when Quinn arrived in Maine. He sat in the seat in front of Quinn through those long road trips. Emrick and his wife, Joyce, sometimes went over to the Quinns' for dinner, and the conversation was almost always about hockey, he remembers. One evening, Quinn told them about a hilarious new movie called *Slap Shot* that had just come out, considering it very similar to the life he'd lived in the minors.

The Mariners developed a heated rivalry with the New Brunswick Hawks (an affiliate of Chicago and Toronto). The Hawks' roster included future NHL coaches Bruce Boudreau, Ron Wilson, Joel Quenneville, and Darryl Sutter. They were coached by Eddie Johnston, the former Bruins goalie who had been on the bench when Quinn knocked out Bobby Orr. Fights erupted in several games between the Hawks and Mariners that season. Maine had a team that was built for brawling. During a game in Moncton, a few fights escalated into a bench-clearing brawl (which wasn't uncommon for the era). The Moncton arena sat seven thousand passionate fans and the team benches were right next to each other, with only a small pane of glass between them. Quinn saw one of his players being taken on by two Hawks in the far corner, while all of his other players were tied up. He stepped up on the edge of the boards, over the Hawks' bench, trying to get to his player. Johnston stood in his way and put up his hands to stop him, but Quinn pushed him aside and Johnston fell back off the bench. He may have been wearing a suit, but in his mind, Quinn still hadn't hung up his skates. He jumped onto the ice and went slide-running toward the fight when a Hawk grabbed hold of his sport jacket from behind, tearing it from the bottom up to the collar—putting into practice the lesson that if you're going to grab Pat Quinn, it's best that he not see you. The officials had to pull Quinn back to the bench, with his coat dangling off of him.

While Quinn was paying tailors' bills and gaining experience as a head coach in Maine, the Flyers floundered through the first fifty games of the 1978–79 season. Philadelphia sat last in a difficult Patrick Division and was winless in eight games in January 1979, when Keith Allen fired Bob McCammon and assistant coach Terry Crisp, and called Quinn up—on his birthday—to take over as head coach. Quinn packed his belongings from his office in Maine into two cardboard boxes and carried them out to his car. The apprenticeship was over.

In Philadelphia, Quinn outlined his coaching philosophy, giving credit to the mentors who had taught him along the way: "Bernie Geoffrion was the best I played for as far as handling players," he told reporters. "He was personable and loved his players. [Punch] Imlach was one of the master psychologists. The game has changed since, but Punch dealt with people the way he felt they should be dealt with. Make some fearful, praise others, or [use] intimidation. His philosophy was to win a hockey game by having everybody ready. He used to work on me by telling me how bad I was.... The one coach who had the most influence on me, at least in the tactical sense, was Fred Shero. But I never did get my finger on how he motivated players. He was deceptive to the extent that I didn't even know what he was doing here—and here I was working for him."

Shero had taken parting shots about increased management interference with how he coached. Quinn made it clear who was in charge as soon as he took over and laid out a blueprint for winning.

"We've got to establish a leader and eliminate all the innuendo, double-talk, and confusion on the ice," Quinn said in one of his first interviews as the Flyers' new coach. "These things aren't done without having someone in control of the situation. The first thing we have to do is rebuild the confidence on this team. We need to build confidence between the coach and players. The players need to build it in each other. But that kind of confidence can only come through success, knowing where you're going, having goals, and accomplishing them."

The Flyers clicked under Quinn and made a late-season surge in the standings—with eighteen wins, eight losses, and just four ties—to finish second in the Patrick Division. (Philadelphia pulled it off without star goalie Bernie Parent, who suffered a career-ending injury on February 17 when he was struck in the eye by a stick.) The Flyers narrowly beat the Vancouver Canucks in the first round of the playoffs, but lost to Shero's New York Rangers in the quarterfinals.

"We returned to the basics, for one," defenseman Behn Wilson said after the season, about the Flyers' resurgence under Quinn. "And right off from the start he gave the players new confidence in themselves. If a player made a mistake, Pat didn't yell or berate the individual. Instead, he offered … constructive criticism because he remembered when he was a player. It serves little purpose to lose a player's confidence through harsh criticism."

There were rumblings in the off-season time that Don Cherry would be hired to take over the Flyers, but Quinn had no intention of stepping aside. "I'm not an interim coach and the Flyers don't want that arrangement," he said. He went to work negotiating a lengthy contract with the Flyers, with the help of his friend and attorney from Atlanta, Dick Babush. With job security in hand, Quinn then asked his friend and the Flyers' longtime leader Bob Clarke to become his assistant coach, while still playing.

Clarke wasn't sure about the move. "I don't think it's a good idea," he told Quinn. "I don't want to do it." But Quinn was persistent. He felt that Clarke's stature with the club would be a valuable resource in the coaches' office. It was an unconventional—perhaps risky—move, which showed that, like Shero, Quinn wasn't afraid to be unconventional. Clarke relented and agreed to join the coaching staff.

At thirty-six, Quinn had begun demonstrating that he had the ability to succeed as a coach at the NHL level. But a third of a regular season and a single playoff series win would mean very little if he couldn't continue the success in his first full campaign as head coach.

And it started terribly.

After opening the season at home with a win over the formidable New York Islanders, Quinn's Flyers traveled to Atlanta to play his former team. It was a blowout. The Flames dismantled the Flyers 9–2 on October 13, 1979, in humiliating fashion.

"Holy smokes," thought Quinn, deflated by the loss. They had just spent a month in training camp, and this is what they had to show for all the preparation and work. The embarrassing result didn't bode well for the rookie head coach.

Quinn climbed into the plane to fly back to Philadelphia feeling a devastating uncertainty about the upcoming season. The Flyers were playing the Darryl Sittler–led Toronto Maple Leafs the next evening at home. There was little time to find and fix whatever it was that had gone so wrong.

Whatever plan Quinn devised in the sky that night worked, however. The Flyers wouldn't lose again for three months.

14

The Streak

The secret was Hugh Hefner. All through the Philadelphia Flyers' unmatchable thirty-five-game undefeated streak in the 1979–80 season, Quinn regularly consulted the *Playboy* tycoon. Hef, his head slightly cocked and a pipe dangling from a rascal's grin, had his arms around two bunnies—one, a brunette in a pink one-piece, cut low at the chest and high at the thighs; the other, a blonde in a green bikini. The trio were posed in front of the famous grotto, their cartoon likeness perched at the end of Quinn's pinball machine, next to an ever-growing score as the Flyers' coach hammered on the buttons, thwacking the ball into a maze of Hefner's finest bunnies, posed with arched backs to show off the curious angles of their lingerie. The machine—branded for Bally's Las Vegas casino—rumbled and angled and dinged and flashed with Quinn working his way to the exact score he needed, the same every time, a number now long forgotten but nevertheless essential. Pat Quinn would joke throughout his life that he wasn't a superstitious man. "I just do it in case," he'd often say.

The "Playball" pinball machine was meant to be a Christmas gift for his adolescent daughters, and it was hidden in a storage room at the Quinn home on Springhouse Lane. But Quinn started using it well before the girls knew it existed, sneaking a play before leaving for the rink as the Flyers kept winning and winning through the first half of the season in 1979.

The streak was improbable, if not seemingly impossible. It will most certainly never happen again, as long as ties remain extinct in the NHL. Philadelphia slipped past the Toronto Maple Leafs 4–3 at the Spectrum on October 14, 1979, and then faced the Flames—who had crushed them just a week before—and beat them 6–2.

At first, they paid no attention. But then the wins continued to mount and a few close calls ended in a tie, and soon a couple of weeks had turned into a month. The Flyers remained undefeated. Quinn's superstitions would change randomly over time, his desire to win shifting to a new lucky outlet every time he needed it. The Playboy pinball machine was the charm that helped put him in the record books.

Or part of it, at least. Another secret to the Flyers' remarkable success that year was the hours Quinn spent studying his team. He analyzed the strengths and weaknesses of each player, each part, while locked in his office on the main floor of his house where his York University diploma hung proudly on the wall and his bookshelves groaned under the weight of his growing collection of biographies, histories, and management texts.

Quinn saw the Flyers as a problem to be solved, a set of chess pieces to be deployed. Philadelphia was a franchise in flux, moving out of the Broad Street Bullies era—a time when the

Flyers had bashed their way to consecutive Stanley Cups while utilizing Fred Shero's sixteen-rule system.

By now the roster was a mix of established NHL players and guys making the jump up from the minors. Philadelphia still boasted established stars like Bobby Clarke, Bill Barber, and Rick MacLeish. Mel Bridgman took over Clarke's position as captain. But the roster also included a host of relatively unknown players. Keith Allen added pieces from the Mariners, including defensemen Norm Barnes, Frank Bathe, and Mike Busniuk, who were known as the "three Bs." They had all played for the Maine Mariners under Quinn, and they ended up being key players for the Flyers. In the absence of Bernie Parent, Philadelphia picked up goalie Phil Myre, Quinn's old teammate from Atlanta who had been playing with the St. Louis Blues. Myre split games with rookie goaltender Pete Peeters, who had also played for Quinn in Maine.

The Flyers' strategy had to change, Quinn thought. Fred Shero had told his team that if they wanted to skate, they should join the Ice Capades. At the time, every team in the NHL used a north–south, up–down strategy. The Flyers weren't known for mobility, but Quinn wanted to change that. "A static team can't win anymore," he said. Quinn had his forward crisscross with the puck as the Flyers attacked, with the winger crossing into center ice and the center crossing over to the wing, confusing the defense. Aside from the powerhouse Montreal Canadiens, the style was not familiar in the NHL. But this was the way teams had seen the Soviets play the game—and in many ways it was a throwback to the way hockey had been played on frozen Canadian ponds for generations. The strategy allowed the Flyers' offensive players the freedom to attack without the restraints of the predictable north–south strategy they were used to. Quinn diversified his attack as well, changing it up at times so his players attacked more slowly to throw opponents off with two speeds on offense. "Most of us that had played for Shero had played the same way for seven, eight years. We needed a change," says Bob Clarke. "This was something different. This was something new. It changed the game of hockey."

As the winning streak stretched on, Quinn didn't relent on his grueling practices. He'd give his players a day off, but the next time they were on the ice it was a grind. They skated constantly.

Quinn made sure the team was prepared physically and mentally. In practice the team ran through every possible game situation, whether they were winning, losing, pulling the goalie, tied and trying to win, or tied and trying to prevent a loss. In practice, Quinn's drills focused on skating, puck handling, and perpetual motion. And like a general leading his troops, Quinn ran through the strengths and weaknesses of upcoming opponents. It was all about strategic preparation for battle.

Puck possession and handling was key. The longer his team had the puck, the better. The less the opponent was in the Flyers' end, the better. Quinn wanted his players to move the puck quickly, and with precision. Puck support was essential. Every Flyer on the ice had a part in each unfolding play. Quinn was years ahead of his time. Few coaches in the NHL were thinking in these terms. Within two decades, everyone would be.

At the same time, Quinn sought to keep the atmosphere light. Every Monday—which they called "Funday"—the Flyers split into four teams to play each other in soccer, touch football, volleyball, or softball, or to skate in races on the ice. They also did weight training. "Athletes take themselves too seriously," Quinn said, when asked about the unorthodox training. "It gives everyone a chance to laugh at themselves."

Quinn looked to revitalize players who he felt had been underused or used ineffectively. Reggie Leach, a Conn Smythe Trophy winner, had scored sixty-one goals in the 1975 season but hadn't managed the same tally in the next two seasons combined. It looked like Leach would be sent to the minors, but Quinn brought his career back to life. Shero had taken ice time away from Leach, benching him at key moments in games—a tactic that enraged instead of inspired. Quinn took a different approach, ramping up Leach's responsibility as a penalty killer. "I thought I saw a determination, a desire to prove that he was a good player because he went through so much crap here in the last year," Quinn said of Leach at the time. Leach led the Flyers with fifty goals that season.

Quinn also cut back on Bobby Clarke's shifts, knowing the previous years had punished his body. He dropped Bill Barber to defense on the power plays, and told him to rush the puck, instead of playing it safe—"I don't have you back there for that," Quinn told him. "I want you to go, get involved with the attack. Make things happen."

When several of his players told him he was spending too much time explaining drills and game plans during practice, causing the team to freeze their asses off in the chilly Spectrum, Quinn said, "You know what, you've got a good point," and immediately cut the lectures short.

In between periods, Quinn would take a seat outside the locker room and Barber would come sit down beside him and they'd chat.

He was great at listening to the advice of his players. Together, they'd talk about what they needed to adjust to win the game.

The Flyers also knew that Quinn would defend them, regardless—to management, the press, whomever. "He was a player's coach," says Leach. He was also honest. If he needed more out of a player's performance, he told them. He didn't dance around the issue. Quinn was firm in his opinions, and he could be blunt. "If he gave you heck as a team, your team deserved it," says Bob Clarke. If a player asked him a question, about hockey or anything else, he'd stop to consider his answer thoughtfully. "If he asked you how you're doing, it wasn't just a question pulled out of the sky," says Clarke. "He wanted to know how you were doing, and he was listening for your answer."

Paul Holmgren had been an underused right-winger under Fred Shero and Bob McCammon, but Quinn saw potential in him. He bumped the six-foot-three Holmgren up from the checking line and used his size as a strength on the offensive attack. On and off the ice, Quinn became a source of confidence that the young forward previously lacked. His philosophy was to let players play the way they knew how—and then to use their strengths as tools to win. Quinn didn't try to change his players, on or off the ice. Instead, he tried to implement a system that considered the pieces he had to work with.

"Everyone stayed within their means—there was no disagreement of roles, of what was expected from you as a player," says Bill Barber. "He let everybody be themselves.... And yet, everyone played for one another when the puck was dropped on the ice."

The press's interest was piqued when it became apparent that the surging Flyers weren't a fluke. The thirty-six-year-old sophomore coach who preferred three-piece suits, expensive cigars, and cream ale started to garner more ink. One Canadian newspaper dubbed his team "the Broad Street Smoothies." But the Flyers weren't pushovers. In fact, they led the league in penalty minutes that season. They were involved in a brawl against the Los Angeles Kings on December 6 for which they were fined three thousand dollars, but the Flyers won that game 9–4. They were six games from breaking the Montreal Canadiens' NHL record of twenty-eight games without a loss, which they'd sewn up in 1977–78, before the dynasty went on to win their third consecutive Stanley Cup.

At home, Quinn continued his pregame meetings with Hef and the bunnies, making sure every cosmic angle was covered. His biggest fans—Sandra, Valerie, and Kalli—did their best to carry on as though nothing special was happening. Speaking of the streak would surely ruin it. For eleven-year-old Kalli, there wasn't much remarkable to comment on anyway, as she was convinced that her dad could do anything. "Oh yeah, he just keeps winning," she thought. And there was nothing strange about that.

The Flyers tied the Black Hawks, and then beat the Nordiques and Sabres. On December 16, they tied the New York Rangers 1–1 in Madison Square Garden—and the Flyers were one game away from tying the unbeaten streak. By now the streak was known as The Streak, and the national press took notice. *The New York Times*, the *Boston Globe*, *Sports Illustrated*—all praised Quinn and his remarkable reinvention of Philadelphia. "The Flyers are back on top again, picking up wins like broken teeth … but incredibly without breaking many," wrote *Newsweek*.

The Pittsburgh Penguins were all that stood in the way of the
Flyers tying the Canadiens' streak. They traveled to Philadelphia
to play at the Spectrum on December 20. The Flyers dominated
the game, throwing shot after shot at Greg Millen, but the
goalie stood on his head. Nothing worked. Philadelphia trailed
the Penguins 1–0 late in the third. They could feel the streak
they never spoke about slipping away. "It was really scary," says
Phil Myre, who was on the bench that night. "It looked like we'd
gone this long, this hard, and we wouldn't even be able to tie
the record."

That's when Hefner and the pinball gods shifted the course
of sports history in favor of the Mighty Quinn.

With less than five minutes to go, Pittsburgh's Bob Stewart
picked up a hooking penalty. The crowd grew wild. Quinn and
the Flyers knew the powerplay was their only chance to keep the
streak going. Off a faceoff in the Penguins' end, the puck shot
into the corner. Dennis Ververgaert battled through a crush of
bodies to emerge with the puck. He passed it to defenseman
Behn Wilson who had snuck in from the right point and slipped
behind the Pittsburgh defense. The pass hit him in the skates
and trickled toward an open net, as Millen reached for it. Wilson
tapped it in just in time. The red light went on. The Spectrum
went bonkers. More than seventeen thousand fans stayed on their
feet while the tense final minutes ticked off the clock as the
Flyers held on for the 1–1 draw. Philadelphia had tied the record.

The Flyers traveled to Boston two nights later to play the
Bruins at the Garden, a rink they hadn't won a game on in five
years. The Bruins (featuring an eighteen-year-old Ray Bourque)
were a powerhouse team. And they were tough. They'd finish

with the second-most penalty minutes of the season, behind Philadelphia.

Jack Quinn was watching from the stands. He had been flown to Boston on a private plane with Flyers president Bob Butera to see his son coach in the potential history-making game.

Before the game the Flyers were prepared for a battle. Every town they played in was louder and angrier as the streak grew. Opposing teams treated every matchup against the Flyers like a playoff game. Everything was on the line because no one wanted to see the Flyers get the record. Boston's fans were notoriously rough. Of course, no one knew that more than Quinn. And he acted like it was just another game. His team needed the win like any other day.

Around the locker room, though, the tension was silencing.

On the ice, everything fell Philadelphia's way. As expected, it was a war—but on the scoreboard, Boston was never in it. When the clock ticked down to zero in the Flyers' historic 5–2 win over the Bruins, Phil Myre leapt into the air in his crease as the team piled onto the ice, finally free to celebrate the impossible. Quinn found his goalie near the net and gave him an enormous hug. No one could ignore it now: The Flyers had made history. Even the fans in the Boston Garden stood to applaud.

"We looked like a M.A.S.H. unit coming out of the Garden in Boston," says Bill Barber. Even Quinn allowed himself a little satisfaction in securing the record. But the real prize was yet to be won. The Streak, as the Flyers now allowed themselves to call it, continued for six more games, carrying it into the New Year.

On January 6, they beat the Sabres in Buffalo to make thirty-five games without a loss. The next evening they were in

Bloomington, Minnesota—playing in front of nearly sixteen thousand at the Met Center, the loudest arena Phil Myre had ever been in. The North Stars were on a streak of their own that night, having won eleven games in a row, and were on the cusp of setting their own club record. The Flyers' Bill Barber scored early in the game, but the North Stars came back, scoring three by the end of the first period. A Paul Holmgren goal was disallowed in the second period because an official spotted an extra player on the ice. The North Stars capitalized on the errors with two more goals. Even as the game slipped away, incredulous Flyers talked like they could pull themselves back into it. Fights broke out as the North Stars attacked and attacked and the Minnesota fans grew wilder with every goal, shouting, "Go home, Flyers! Go home, Flyers!" Minnesota coach Glen Sonmor, the one-eyed Hamilton high school basketball coach turned pro hockey coach whose advice Pat had sought two decades earlier, had to be restrained because of his protests with an official over Philadelphia's conduct. The Flyers finally lost, in a 7–1 drubbing. North Stars general manager Lou Nanne gave his players trophies in jest for stopping The Streak.

In the Flyers' locker room after the loss—just the second of the season—there was a sense of disappointment, but also a strange relief. They were part of history now. It was nice to have the conquest behind them.

The party was fun while it lasted, but now it was time for the hangover. The Flyers had won a lot of close games against bad teams; any number of them could have swung the other way. Their accomplishments would mean little, Quinn thought, if his Flyers didn't finish the season with the prize he was really searching for. "The Streak was silver," Quinn said. "The Stanley Cup is gold."

Though his eyes were fixed firmly on the Cup, Quinn did allow a little room for celebration. And there was no better time than St. Patrick's Day. On the afternoon of March 17, 1980, Quinn—dressed in his green knickers, knee-high socks, and a paddy cap—embarked on a marathon day of libations and Irish cheer. He went to a pub with a few close friends, including Flyers president Bob Butera and Bob Curran, who was the attorney general in Philadelphia. As is customary on St. Patrick's Day, they drank several pints of beer as Quinn regaled them with old hockey stories and sang a few Irish songs. It was a lively affair, which stretched into hours and eventually evolved from pint glasses to drinking straight from pitchers. "He could drink more beer than any man I've ever met," says Curran, affectionately. As usual, the beers kept coming from patrons who stopped to chat with Quinn. But unbeknownst to him, a Flyers fan club had arranged to present him with a trip to Ireland as a present. Butera was sworn to secrecy—and faced the implausible task of getting Quinn to the club's meeting in New Jersey that evening. "We were having so much fun at the bar I don't think he even wanted to go," says Butera. But he managed to pull Quinn away from the Irish pub and they arrived at the Flyers fan club meeting. Butera wasn't sure if Quinn would be able to make it up to the podium but his friend had a remarkable talent for remaining composed and coherent regardless of the quantity of alcohol consumed. He accepted the gift with gracious eloquence, with nary a slurred word to be heard. "How he ever handled that situation is beyond me," Butera says.

The Flyers struggled through the final stretch that season, winning just seven of their last twenty games. But regardless of the slide, the team still finished first in the Patrick Division— twenty-five points ahead of the second-place New York Islanders. Under Quinn's weaving attacks, the team was second in league scoring with 327 goals.

But for all the attention given to Quinn's new Soviet-style offense, the Flyers never actually abandoned the grit they were famous for. Philadelphia led the league in penalties that season, finding themselves shorthanded 381 times.

Quinn complained that officials and writers still thought of the Flyers as the Broad Street Bullies, which led to more penalties being called against them. "We are still categorized as the team of 1974 and '75," he told reporters. "People back then just didn't understand honest hard-working hockey players, guys who were willing to drop the gloves if things got heavy and not carve people up with sticks ... I still believe you can play aggressively within the confines of the rules." For all Quinn had gained from exposure to Russian hockey, he opined that hockey's long-standing code of ethics was now being ignored. "The code held up until we started playing the Europeans," he said. "They would do things that we would never do—spearing, kicking the skates out from under you—and when we tried to get back at them in the good old American or Canadian way— drop the gloves, lay it all out on the table—the press jumped all over us.

"If we ever take the emotion out of the game," Quinn continued, "we'll be just like the goddamn Russians."

In the first round of the 1980 playoffs, Philadelphia met the Edmonton Oilers and a nineteen-year-old Wayne Gretzky—who had finished with 137 regular season points, winning his first Hart Memorial Trophy as the league's most valuable player. The Oilers were coached by Quinn's former Oil Kings teammate Glen Sather, who took the helm during the team's inaugural season in the NHL after moving over from the WHA. The Flyers swept the dynasty-in-waiting in three straight games in the best-of-five preliminary round.

Next, Philadelphia faced the New York Rangers, the team that had knocked them out the previous year, coached and managed by Quinn's mentor, Fred Shero. This time the Flyers had their revenge, knocking out their former bench boss four games to one.

After that quarterfinal win, Quinn sat down with *Hockey Night in Canada* broadcaster Brian McFarlane on a bench in front of a backdrop of Rangers and Flyers jerseys. McFarlane, in a powder-blue suit and holding a long silver microphone, asked Quinn, "Paddy, you've come over another big obstacle on your way to the Stanley Cup. You said earlier this year after The Streak, the streak wouldn't mean very much if you didn't cap it all by winning the Cup. How do you feel about this victory over the Rangers?"

Quinn looked down and smiled and then rubbed his cheek before answering. "Well, very pleased. We had trouble with them last year and it became more of a psychological barrier for us than if we'd have played someone else at this stage."

With one mentor, Fred Shero, beaten, Quinn turned his sights to another, Glen Sonmor. The Minnesota North Stars had already played spoilers to the Flyers' ambitions, having ended the unbeaten streak. They looked to do it again in the semifinals. In front of fans at the Philadelphia Spectrum, the North Stars beat the Flyers in a close 6–5 opening game. The Flyers responded, blanking Minnesota 7–0 in the next game and then sweeping the next three.

With just two losses in thirteen playoff games, the Flyers had momentum running into the Stanley Cup final against the New York Islanders, the team they had beaten in the first game of the season. The Islanders were put together by general manager Bill Torrey and coached by Al Arbour, who were both destined for the Hall of Fame. (Arbour would finish his career as the coach with the second-most wins in NHL history, with 782, behind Scotty Bowman who had 1244.) Torrey had pieced together an Islanders team that would become the first dynasty of the 1980s.

New York was led by Bryan Trottier, who won the Hart Trophy as the league's best player in 1979, having led the league with 134 points. The Islanders also boasted one of the game's most prolific scorers in Mike Bossy, who had scored a league best sixty-nine goals in 1979—and would go on to become only the second player to reach Maurice Richard's mark of fifty goals in fifty games. Meanwhile, Denis Potvin was a three-time Norris Trophy winner as the NHL's best defenseman. Along with those stars, the Islanders also had a top talent in the pipes, in the fiery Billy Smith—who was well known for hacking at opponents who drifted too close to his crease. Following his lead, the Islanders sat just behind the Flyers as a league leader in penalty minutes. The series promised to be explosive from the start.

In his first full season as an NHL coach, Quinn had led his team on a record-breaking undefeated streak and taken them to the Stanley Cup final. He knew he owed Hugh Hefner a great deal of gratitude for that. And as the Playball-branded pinball machine flashed and pinged before him, he hoped the rally would roll on—just four more wins to the game's biggest prize. He'd never come close to the Stanley Cup as a player with a struggling Leafs franchise and two expansion underdogs in Vancouver and Atlanta. Just a few years removed from nearly walking away from the game altogether, almost moving to Montana to open up a car dealership, Quinn had a chance to put his name on it.

Philadelphia had home advantage in the first game of the Stanley Cup Final, which was tied at three at the end of regulation. Two minutes into overtime, referee Andy Van Hellemond called the Flyers' Jim Watson for holding John Tonelli—a marginal infraction, usually not called in overtime. Quinn would later call it a "rather chintzy" penalty—something that he'd never seen whistled down in a sudden-death extra frame before. In fact, when Mike Bossy scored on the man advantage, it was the first time a powerplay goal had ever been scored in overtime in the history of the Stanley Cup Final.

Afterwards, Quinn said his team had allowed too much chatter about the Islanders to affect the way they played. "Our players listened too much to all the stories about how the Islanders were a tough team and how they could hit with us," he said. "We respected them too much. All we heard was that this would be a physical series, and we stood around waiting for it to happen … We didn't win the battles in front of the nets. We didn't get a second shot [from a rebound] all night. When Mike Bossy scored for New York, he had three shots."

Off Quinn's charge that they'd played too soft, the Flyers stormed over the Islanders in the second game of the series. Before a bloodthirsty crowd at the Spectrum, the Flyers suffocated the Islanders on defense and bashed their way to an 8–3 win. A second-period stick-swinging battle between Bill Barber and Gord Lane highlighted a violent affair that included eighty-four penalty minutes.

After the game, it was Al Arbour's turn to vent. "All the Flyers do is wield their sticks," the Islanders coach fumed. "If they want to make it a back-stabbing series, okay … We'll prove we can back-stab with the best of them. They have a lot of spear carriers out there. Next time, we'll have some too."

Arbour then departed with a string of expletives. Billy Smith, who was pulled after two periods and got into a tussle with Paul Holmgren in the hall, echoed his coach's rage. "Maybe the referees were intimidated in this building, but running after a guy after he passes the puck, like the Flyers do, is ridiculous," he said. "If they keep doing that our guys are going to have to retaliate. They are going to have to put their sticks up … otherwise I'm afraid someone will get hurt."

Sandra drove sixteen-year-old Valerie and twelve-year-old Kalli down from Philadelphia to Long Island to watch the games. It was an exciting time for the family. But it was also disappointing. Quinn was honored with the Jack Adams trophy as the NHL's coach of the year at a luncheon in New York before the third game of the series. But the celebration was spoiled that evening when the Islanders pounded the Flyers 6–2. To make matters worse, Paul Holmgren injured his left knee, and Jim Watson injured his shoulder. Both looked to be out for the rest of the series.

Despite being battered and shorthanded, the Flyers fired thirty-six shots at Billy Smith in game five—but only manged to score two goals in a 5–2 loss.

Trailing three games to one, the Flyers' record-breaking season was on the brink of ending in disappointment when the series returned to Philadelphia for the fifth game. The Flyers lineup was battered and exhausted. But Quinn's men refused to fold. Paul Holmgren returned with a patched-together knee in a rubber brace. Jim Watson suited up with a cracked collarbone. Bob Dailey played with a wounded shoulder that would need surgery in the off-season.

Once again, the Spectrum thundered with the Flyers faithful as Holmgren opened the game with a crushing hit on John Tonelli. But the game remained tight until the third period when the Flyers opened up on a 3–2 lead, scoring three more goals to put the game out of reach. Down 6–3, Billy Smith capped off another violent battle by snapping his stick across the ribs of Flyers' mustachioed captain, Mel Bridgman, during a skirmish at the end of the game.

They returned to New York for game six. If Philadelphia could win one more game away, they'd carry the momentum into a game seven final standoff back at home. Knowing the Islanders had a history of falling apart in the playoffs, Quinn turned to psychological warfare. "They have a bugaboo in their past that I'm sure they'll give lots of thought to," Quinn jabbed ahead of the game, noting that the Islanders were tightening up. Despite having the third-best record in the league in 1978, the Islanders lost to the Maple Leafs in the quarterfinals. In '79, the Islanders had the best record in the league, but lost to their crosstown rivals, the New York Rangers, in the semifinals. "It will give them something to think about," Quinn said.

Game six opened rough, continuing the bloody series with a lengthy scrap between the Flyers' Bob Kelly and Islanders' Bob Nystrom in the first period as the Nassau Coliseum went wild.

Quinn, the Jack Adams Award winner, paced the Flyers' bench wearing a light-tan suit and chewing hard on a stick of gum. The Flyers opened the scoring on a power play goal from Reggie Leach, who beat Billy Smith. A short time later, Denis Potvin tapped a rebound out of the air near his shoulder, past Pete Peeters. The Flyers went after referee Bob Myers for a high stick call, but the goal was allowed.

Then came the goal that would haunt Pat Quinn for decades and cement his lifelong contempt for the men in stripes. The Islanders' Butch Goring carried the puck up past center and passed it ahead to Clark Gillies, streaking down the wing. Gillies crossed the Flyers' blue line with Reggie Leach on him. Linesman Leon Stickle, about three feet behind the blue line, swung out his arms to call Gillies onside, just as Gillies dropped the puck back to Goring. The puck crossed the blue line by about half a foot before it reached Goring, who quickly broke into the Flyers' zone.

Stickle missed the call.

Goring cut to the top of the circle and passed the puck across the ice through three Flyers to a streaking Duane Sutter, who snapped it over the sprawling Pete Peeters.

Phil Myre, who was on the bench right next to the play, said it was about two feet out. "Leon Stickle is the only guy who didn't see it," he says. Linesman Ray Scapinello, who was sitting in the stands on standby, knew immediately that it was a missed call. "It was out by a minimum of a foot," he says. "You can't defend it." Quinn would allow himself some creative licence in his retellings: "It wasn't a foot offside, it was ten feet. I have the film," Quinn later said.

Before the first period was over, Brian Propp had scored off a pass from Holmgren to tie it at two. A single section of Flyers fans cheered.

The Islanders scored twice in the second period to take a 4–2 lead heading into the third. Once again, Quinn's Flyers looked like they were almost out of miracles. Two goals down with just a period to play—Philadelphia looked beat. But two minutes into the third, towering defenseman Bob Dailey scored on a blast from the point, and the Flyers faithful couldn't help but believe. Among a mob of Philadelphia fans at Nassau Coliseum, Keith Allen and Ed Snider tossed around high fives.

"Quinn looks so cool at the bench," said Jim Robson, who was calling the game, as the camera zoomed in on the Big Irishman chomping on his gum as he considered a line combination. "If he is, he's the only cool person in the building."

A few minute later, Moose Dupont fired a one-timer off the boards into traffic in front of Billy Smith. The puck nicked the edge of John Paddock's skate and deflected into the net.

The Flyers had done it—4–4, with fourteen minutes to go. In the stands, Ed Snider turned and embraced a fan behind him.

"They've been doing it all year and here they are again, knocking at the door," said Gary Dornhoefer, Quinn's junior-hockey nemesis who was doing the color commentary for *Hockey Night in Canada*.

The tension only increased the hate between both teams. While other teams might have shied away from the rough stuff with the season teetering in every play, the Flyers and the Islanders refused to back down. Paul Holmgren and Clark Gillies fought with twelve minutes remaining, both picking up seven minutes in the box. Through the final ten minutes of regulation, all the fans—Islanders and Flyers—were on their feet clapping wildly. Meanwhile, the end-to-end rush raged on. Peeters and Smith sprawled to make several spectacular stops on what could have been game-winning goals. When the horn went on the third period, Quinn couldn't help but think that the game would have been over had Stickle not blown that call in the first period. Now his team's incredible run to the Cup faced sudden-death overtime.

For a time it had seemed improbable that Quinn would ever get the chance to skate on an NHL team. Now he was the best coach in the league, owner of the longest unbeaten streak in the game, and a single goal away from a winner-takes-all showdown for the Stanley Cup. Quinn's rise from hockey obscurity to the ranks of the sport's most respected names was already a remarkable success story. It was just missing one thing: his name on the Cup. Being this close, just a year into his coaching career, it seemed inevitable that "Pat Quinn" would one day be scratched onto hockey's holy mug.

But that day would have to wait. Seven minutes into the extra period, the Colosseum still deafening, the Islanders' John Tonelli broke into the Flyers' end as Bob Nystrom cut toward the net past the Flyers' defense. Quinn believed the two were offside as they crossed, though video of the play is inconclusive. Nystrom corralled the puck and slipped it in under Pete Peeters's two-pad stack, winning the Stanley Cup—the first of four straight. The Flyers' dream season was over.

The Nassau Coliseum erupted as the Islanders mobbed each other on the ice. "Outcome Never in Doubt!" flashed on the scoreboard screen in white lights, followed by a pixelated graphic of the Stanley Cup. The Flyers, dejected, consoled Peeters and quickly left the ice.

The Flyers were supposed to charter home immediately after the game that night—anticipating a seventh game in Philadelphia. Instead, they took their time, undressing slowly as the agony of just how close they'd been settled in. The regret—the what if—would never leave them. Quinn, who'd gain a reputation for his quibbling with referees, and for claiming biases and conspiracies against his teams, would always carry the loss.

Quinn walked into the Flyers' locker room, emotionally and physically spent, like the players. His eyes were red and wet with tears.

15

Finding an Edge

"It's a pretty interesting world when you get fired. You drop right off the face of the earth. For three days, everybody's calling you, then you're gone. He wasn't going to feel sorry for himself. I know he was pissed. He went back to school. He got his life going again."   —*Bob Clarke on Quinn going to law school*

After the success of The Streak and the disappointment of losing in the Stanley Cup finals, Quinn sought out new ways to win. He believed that the slightest advantage could be the difference that would win a Stanley Cup.

First, Quinn looked to give his team a physical advantage. Paul Holmgren had been working with a young trainer and karate black belt named Pat Croce, who had helped his core strength and fitness tremendously. Seeing the results Holmgren gained from his time with Croce, Quinn asked him to join the Flyers as a full-time conditioning coach in 1980. Croce says it was the first hiring of its kind. Players used to come to training camp with a case of sticks under one arm and a case of beer under the other, he says. Suddenly, the Flyers were thrust into a regimen of weightlifting and dry-land training. At first, it didn't go over well with old-school players like Bob Dailey, Rick MacLeish, or Reggie Leach. The Flyers suddenly had to think about nutrition. And Croce implemented anaerobic testing throughout the season. They ran as a team through the streets of Philadelphia before practices. "It was something new to us," says Leach. "You have to lift weights, you have to run now, you have to do that stuff. Here we are, I'm thirty years old, Billy Barber's thirty years old, and us guys are going, 'Holy shit, do we have to do this stuff?'"

Quinn would stand in the weight room after practice, chomping on an unlit cigar, while the Flyers grumbled through the workouts. He was so curious about new ideas in training that he sent Croce to Sweden to study the techniques used by the Swedish national team. "The credit is Pat Quinn's," says Croce, who says Quinn gave him his start in what would become a lucrative physical-fitness-training empire. "He was a pioneer."

But Quinn didn't just look for physical advantages. Next, he turned to the mind.

When he was working under Fred Shero, Quinn had met with Canadian psychologist Wayne Halliwell, who was focusing his research on the psychology of sport. Halliwell was coaching Dawson College's hockey team and finishing a master's degree in psychology at McGill University. Shero had first encountered Halliwell at a coaching conference in Russia, and when the Flyers traveled to Montreal, Shero and Quinn would meet with

Halliwell to discuss philosophies about ways to get their players a psychological edge over opponents.

Recalling what he had learned from Halliwell, in 1981 Quinn had the Flyers hire Julie Anthony—a thirty-four-year-old former professional tennis player who had competed at Wimbledon, Roland-Garros (the French Open), and the US Open—to work full-time with the team. Anthony had studied at UCLA and completed her PhD in clinical psychology while competing on the professional tour. Sports psychology was in its infancy and no professional sports team was known to have hired a full-time psychologist on staff. It was a groundbreaking experiment.

"I grew up hearing that hockey was fifty percent physical and fifty percent mental," Quinn said at the time. "So if fifty percent is mental, why not devote more time to the development of the brain? I figure I would get someone whose business is brains. There are so many things that I don't have answers for. When you have a player who isn't achieving, he isn't putting the puck in, he isn't picking up the man, and no matter what you try, it doesn't work, sometimes you can start to second-guess yourself. You wonder if you're overcoaching. I finally decided to get someone who would be available to me and to the players who was more qualified to help solve mental problems."

Coming from the polished world of professional tennis, Anthony walked into the Flyers' locker room and found an unmitigated disaster. The players smoked between periods and drank beer and soft drinks after games. One day during team pictures after a practice, Bobby Clarke asked if she would do him a favor and go get his teeth for him; he kept them in his locker, inside his tennis shoe. As such, the Flyers had to get used to having a female around. "It was kind of cute because they kind of had to clean up their act a little bit and when they swore in front of me they'd get embarrassed. They were very sweet." But it took a while for the players to decide if they could trust her, or if she would take the information to management. "Psychology seemed very suspicious to them," says Anthony.

She attempted to build a bond with the players. She gave talks on nutrition and physical fitness—and even had the spit- and sweat-drenched carpets removed from the Flyers' locker room to create a more hygienic environment. She lectured on meditation, relaxation, and mental preparation.

The second year, in 1982, Anthony dug deeper. She set up meetings to consult with the players on nutrition—something they were more comfortable with—but then geared the discussions toward psychology. Anthony worked with active volcano Ken Linseman on exercising patience when he was provoked on the ice. "The whole concept of mentally preparing for a game was new to most of the players," she said. "They would just show up, get dressed, and play." In the one-on-one sessions, Anthony helped the Flyers with everything from handling the pressure of performing at a professional level (something she knew more about than any of them) to the stress of accidentally getting a girlfriend pregnant.

The rules Anthony suggested—no smoking between periods, no drinking beer after games—were a tough sell to some of the veterans on the team. But Quinn and Bobby Clarke, the star and assistant coach, were adamant. Nobody messed with Quinn to begin with. Put Bobby Clarke next to him? Dissenters didn't have much of a chance. "They wanted to change things," Anthony said. "They wanted the information."

Quinn also asked Anthony to work with his daughter Valerie, who was excelling as a competitive swimmer and would soon earn a scholarship to Penn State. She'd meet with Val—a tall teen with freckles—and helped her prepare mentally for her swim meets. As a father of two talented athletes, Quinn tried to remain simply a supportive fan and leave his coach's cap at the rink. He'd slip into their swim meets attempting to go unnoticed, but always turning heads as the hard-to-miss, dapper coach of the Flyers. And while he did his best to limit the coaching to those on the pool deck at the 5:00 A.M. practices Valerie and Kalli attended, he couldn't help but bring his natural whistle to their swim meets. Kalli would hear the loud, piercing sound right as she got ready to dive into the water. It was a warm whistle, familiar and reassuring. It was a Quinn talent, that whistle, passed down from Jack to his sons—and Pat made good use of it, the way his father had. It reached his daughter, letting her know that her father was there and that he was proud.

His pride didn't cause him to shrink from disciplining the girls when he felt it was needed, though. When Kalli was twelve, she ran afoul of one of her coaches at the Westchester Aquatic Club. He pushed her hard and was constantly critical. One day, he pushed her too far while she did shoulder presses in the weight room. He'd walked away, but turned back just as she mouthed, "Fuck off." The coach kicked her off the team. The girls were rarely called into their father's office, unless there was trouble, but Kalli was called in now. He never yelled, but he told her in no uncertain terms that she was to go back and apologize, which she did. (Years later, Kalli would discover that her parents had been laughing about the offence before she came home.)

For all the joy Quinn had found playing the game and the success he'd had in his early years of coaching, his family remained the most important, happiest part of his life. *Family and then hockey, always in that order.* It was a mantra Quinn would also repeat to his players. After long stretches on the road, family dinners at home were a cherished time for all four Quinns. On family vacations when the girls were small, Pat would bring them out golfing and let them drive the cart around the course with him. He'd work the pedals as they steered across the open fairways, taking whatever paths their young hearts desired. The group would often travel to Hilton Head Island in South Carolina to spend time by the ocean as well. One summer—his overactive imagination recalling a scene from one of the Jaws movies—Pat thought he saw a fin and charged into the ocean to retrieve his girls, both clutched tight in his massive arms as he carried them to shore.

Yes, family—that was the one essential thing. Nothing else could sustain him through inevitable dark times in the precarious world of professional sports. Sandra stood by him through the many long years bouncing around the minor leagues in the 1960s from team to team, never certain when or if Quinn would get his chance to live his dream. She was there to raise their daughters when he was on those long bus rides through middle America, and when he'd wake up early on those summer days to pick up employment in the off-season—and late into the evening when he pushed through textbooks and wrote papers, working, working, working toward a degree that always seemed far away. Even when he finally reached the NHL, his family was there when he was left dangling on those unprotected lists, deemed unessential and dispensable.

These were the Quinns—by way of Hamilton, Edmonton, Knoxville, Tulsa, Memphis, Houston, Seattle, St. Louis, Toronto, Vancouver, Atlanta, and Philadelphia and all the roads traveled in between. And so they would be, still, when it came time to change again.

Suffering a plague of injuries, the Philadelphia Flyers finished second in the Patrick Division in 1981, behind the surging New York Islanders. On St. Patrick's Day 1981, the thirty-eight-year-old Quinn was rewarded with a brand-new five-year contract, which would make him the Flyers' head coach through to the end of the 1987 season.

"One of the secrets of our success has been our stability," Flyers majority owner Ed Snider said in a press release announcing the deal. "We've probably made fewer personnel changes than any team in hockey over the past fifteen years. When you have stability you have direction. That's what we want throughout our organization."

The Flyers went on to beat the Quebec Nordiques in the first round of the playoffs. They fell behind three games to one early in the quarterfinals against the Calgary Flames, which were sold and relocated from Atlanta in 1980. But facing elimination, the Flyers stormed back in game five. Brian Propp scored three goals in Philadelphia's 9–4 romp over Quinn's former team, which was still run by his good friend Cliff Fletcher. In game six at the old Stampede—where the Flames had not lost since February— goalie Rick St. Croix stopped thirty-four shots, leading the Flyers to a narrow 3–2 win. Philadelphia hammered Calgary throughout the game, and the rough play prompted the home

crowd of seven thousand to shower the ice with cans and pro-
grams. The Flyers didn't mind. They had forced a seventh game
and were heading back to the raucous Spectrum with a chance
to finish off the incredible comeback.

But Calgary wasn't about to lie down. In game seven, the
Flames scored two power-play goals in the first—taking advantage
of the Flyers' eight penalties in the period. Playing catch-up, the
Flyers continued to draw penalties, leading to another power-play
goal for the Flames in the second. Calgary went on to eliminate
Philadelphia with a 4–1 win in front of a stunned and deflated
crowd at the Spectrum. "We thought they might have folded here,"
Quinn said after the loss. "We underestimated them."

The following season, Philadelphia started off smoothly with
just one loss in their first ten games. But the Flyers hit turbulence
after that, bouncing through runs of wins and losses. Quinn
managed to get his team back on track by late January, as the
Flyers sat second behind the Islanders in the Patrick Division.
That month, the Flyers traded for Darryl Sittler, the beloved all-
time leading scorer of the Maple Leafs who had been embattled
in a public feud with Toronto owner Harold Ballard. The Flyers
looked poised for another strong run in the playoffs.

"Pat Quinn's future here looked more secure than Ronald
Reagan's," one paper wrote. "Nobody would have dreamed it was the
beginning of the end." But over the next twenty-eight games, the
Flyers only won six. The team's defense and goaltending collapsed.

Despite the long-term contract they'd just given him, Ed
Snider was questioning whether Quinn should be the team's head
coach. According to the team's president, Bob Butera, Snider
wanted to fire Quinn but general manager Keith Allen wanted to

ride out the slump. Allen resisted Snider for weeks as they delib-
erated over what needed to be done. (Butera was part of the conversations, but operated on the business side of the franchise and
did not involve himself in running the hockey operations.)

By the middle of March, Allen couldn't hold Snider off any
longer. On March 17—St. Patrick's Day—exactly a year after
Quinn had signed his new five-year deal, the Flyers lost to the
New York Rangers 5–2. There were only eight games remaining
in the regular season.

Snider, Allen, and Butera watched the game together, and
afterward, Allen finally relented. "Okay, I'll talk to Pat tomorrow
and terminate him," he said. It was a big, risky move, especially
given that Quinn still had four years on his contract that would
have to be honored. The three executives agreed to meet the following day at 8:00 A.M. in Snider's office to confirm the decision.
Butera and Allen arrived and waited for Snider, who eventually
walked in saying, "Boys, I've changed my mind. I slept on it. You
do whatever you want." He left the room and closed the door. Allen
and Butera, left alone, just looked at each other and then started
laughing. But after three weeks of arguing about it, Allen knew
Quinn had lost the owner's confidence.

He fired Quinn on the morning of March 19. Bobby Clarke
was relieved of his assistant coaching duties too, along with Bob
Boucher. Bob McCammon—the man Quinn replaced in 1979—
was called back up from the Maine Mariners to replace him.

The decision did not go over well with the team. Paul Holmgren
found out that Quinn had been canned when he came to the arena
for practice that morning and heard the other Flyers talking about
it. Holmgren was devastated, and the news brought him to tears.

Quinn had turned around Holmgren's career on the ice and had been an important support to him personally. "I think we were all sort of shocked," Holmgren says. "Maybe we were underachieving a little bit but nobody thought we were in jeopardy of the playoffs." Holmgren managed to speak to Quinn a few days later, and was still very emotional. "Things happen," Quinn told him. "It's the nature of the business. Don't worry about me. I'll be fine."

Holmgren wasn't the only player upset by the decision. "I just don't think they had really thought about it that much," says Reggie Leach, who was essentially released from the team at the same time, when he was told to sit out the remainder of the year. "Maybe because he was more of a players' coach, he was more for his players than for anybody else. You know, I loved the man. I loved him. Because he backed me up."

Bob Clarke, who would later go on to serve two decades as the Flyers' general manager and remains an executive with the organization, still considers Quinn's canning to have been an enormous blunder by the team. "The club didn't bounce back for quite a while from that. It was a poorly made decision," Clarke says. "He got screwed there, and Mr. Snider knows it and admits it…. [He] has said a number of times that it's the worst mistake he made in hockey."

The shake-up didn't help the Flyers against the Rangers in the first round of the 1982 playoffs. They opened the series with a 4–1 win, but were swept in the next three in the best of five first-round games.

After he was fired, Pat went home and told his daughters before they could hear about it from the press. He never wanted them to learn about changes in their lives that way. Kalli cried when she heard the news, wondering what her father was going to do.

But Pat already had a plan, not to mention four more years of salary from his contract. He'd become good friends with Bob Curran, the former US Attorney in Philadelphia, and while he was coaching the Flyers would often stop by Curran's law office before they'd head out to lunch, where Quinn would ask questions about the craft. Quinn's interest in law was initially sparked by his friend in Atlanta, Dick Babush, who helped him negotiate his coaching contracts with the Flyers, including the most recent deal that would pay him while he went back to school. Quinn had never considered hockey to be a lifelong job and wanted to find a challenging profession that might sustain him after his time in the game was done. And even if he stayed in hockey, there were practical applications for a law degree. He could see himself as a players' agent, perhaps. Or, like Ray Miron, Cliff Fletcher, and Keith Allen, he could become a general manager or even a team president. Curran had introduced Quinn to Esther Clark, the dean at Widener University School of Law in Delaware. Clark was a high-profile lawyer in Philadelphia who had risen from being the only female student in her law class at Rutgers University to being a public defender making forty dollars a day in the 1960s to becoming the first woman to be the head of the Delaware County Bar Association. Clark was also a big hockey fan, and Quinn would give her tickets to the Flyers games.

Quinn turned down an assistant coaching offer from his old friend Glen Sather with the Edmonton Oilers and another one from the Vancouver Canucks to coach under Roger Neilson. He was told the Oilers job could lead to a head coaching position, if he proved himself—but Quinn figured he'd done all the proving necessary. The Canucks didn't promise anything beyond the assistant's role, but he said he had great respect for Neilson and general manager Harry Neale. Pat thought that a return to Vancouver would have been a comfortable move, but he wasn't looking for something comfortable. Quinn wanted to be a head coach who had control over the management of his team.

That—or maybe he'd become a lawyer.

Quinn wrote his law school entrance exams that summer, and when no other offers from NHL teams arrived, Esther Clark helped secure his enrollment. And so, in the fall of 1982, Pat Quinn—the nearly forty-year-old fired Flyers coach—became a first-year law student. For the next two years, while the NHL moved on without him, Quinn attended three hours of classes a day and studied for another six to seven. He drank coffee and smoked cigars in the student union lounge. The Big Irishman lined up against his much younger, lilliputian classmates in intramural football—imparting the same bruising lessons he'd once given Jim Keon. Quinn also returned to rowing, a sport that he competed in as a teenager with the Leander Rowing Club in Hamilton. While attending law school, Quinn joined the storied Vesper Boat Club on the Schuylkill River. He sculled in eight- and four-man races at several masters regattas, and was in a crew with Olympic rower John Kelly Jr.—the son of three-time gold medalist Jack Kelly and brother of movie star Grace Kelly. Sandra and the girls would cheer them on from the bank of the Schuylkill.

But Quinn was also an everyman. He was steadfast in his commitment to the Clucks, a slow-pitch softball team made up of local businessmen in the Newton Square area. Their logo was a rubber chicken with a noose around its neck, and the entire team wore number 5. The Quinns' neighbor, J.B. Smink, wore a Big Bird costume to games, serving as the Cluck's mascot.

But rubber chickens aside, law school was a difficult adjustment for Quinn. A few months in, he found himself overwhelmed by the workload thrown at him. It was hard to keep up and he worried that his previous piecemeal degree, completed over nearly a decade, part-time and during the summers, had not taught him the discipline he required to get through the program. Quinn had spent years poring over biographies and history books. He loved learning about great leaders—trying to understand how they'd accomplished what they did. But in law school, the reading was dense and overly technical. It was confusing. And it was a grind. "I'm getting better at it; each day I feel more prepared," he said at the time. "But I still have a ways to go."

Quinn wondered if he'd made the right choice, but he came to view the experience as similar to playing hockey in the minors. "It's an apprenticeship that has to be served," he said. Over time, the learning became easier.

But he missed the game. He knew he'd be lying if he said otherwise. At his house in Newtown Square, Pennsylvania, Quinn would flip on channel 29 and watch the Flyers carry on without him. Bob Curran would often get tickets to the games and ask Quinn to come along, but for a long time he declined.

The change in his lifestyle was drastic. Away from the rink where he was always the boss, he entered the world of lecture halls and case studies, and was at the mercy of his professors, beholden to course assignments, and in competition with other students.

But it did have benefits. He was home more, for starters. As his girls continued to excel as competitive swimmers, he was able to spend more time taking them to practice and to put his whistling to work at their swim meets. He was able to drive Val and Kalli to school and pick them up on his way home.

The lifestyle change helped distract his mind from ruminating on what might have been if he'd had the chance to fulfill his contract with the Flyers. But it also fueled his ambition to return, in even greater capacities than when he'd left. If the right offer from an NHL team came, he'd consider it. But it would have to be one that met his terms and guaranteed him the opportunity to move higher—and to have control. "All the years in hockey I really loved," Quinn said at the time. "I always said I would be a lucky man if when I had to leave the game I could find something that would come close to bringing me that satisfaction. Maybe a combination will."

During one lecture, a young lawyer who was making a name for himself as a players' agent was a special guest in one of Quinn's classes. After a single season with the Maine Mariners in 1978, Brian Burke had gone to Harvard Law School and embarked on a career representing hockey players. Quinn and Burke had become friends after they met at the Flyers' training camp during Quinn's first year as an assistant coach. When Quinn had taken over as the Flyers' coach, Burke would go for lunch with him whenever he was staying in Philadelphia. Now, Quinn was sitting in class listening to Burke explain how he'd forged a career combining his experience in hockey with his expertise in law. Quinn admired Burke's intelligence. He was combative and proud and hardworking. He was truculent, with cutthroat confidence. Burke was the kind of character Quinn knew he could work with—someone he could depend on, who already had great experience in contract negotiations. He was built for the front office.

When the semester was over, Quinn worked at the Butera, Beausang, Cohen & Brennan law firm, in King of Prussia, Pennsylvania. Bob Butera's younger brother John was a partner there, and Quinn shadowed him to get real-life law experience. He was an articling student, in a way, if you can imagine an articling student who wears three-piece suits, puffs expensive cigars, and holds court over beers in the clubhouse at the Spring Ford Country Club after a round of golf with the firm's senior members. "He had an audience, that's for sure," says John Butera. "I don't think Pat liked anything more than sitting around, having a couple beers, and telling stories." On one of those occasions, Quinn was asked about whether he'd fought Dave "The Hammer" Schultz, the well-known enforcer from the Flyers' Broad Street Bullies era. Quinn puffed out his chest and replied, proudly: "Dave Schultz would never fight me."

Quinn would lean over his desk in the office the firm gave him, reading and sorting documents. He'd speak to clients on the phone, trying to develop answers to interrogatories or prepping them for depositions. "He just hated every minute of it," says Butera. "He did not like the practice of law. At least as we did it in suburban Philadelphia." Quinn often shadowed Butera at the Montgomery County Courthouse. The Flyers were a huge deal in Philadelphia at the time, and the appearance of big Pat Quinn at depositions and motion court hearings usually created a stir. He was gracious with every fan who asked him for an autograph or wanted to talk hockey. He had a facility for it, Butera says. He was unassuming, despite his enormous presence and the reactions that followed him.

Through the summer, although Quinn never admitted it, it became clear to Butera that Quinn didn't have a passion for law. Quinn was earnest about becoming a lawyer, however. "He tried his damnedest to do what he was supposed to do, but I don't think he liked thirty seconds of it," says Butera. "It was just his personality. If he was given a task that challenged him, he was going to face it—and make it…. Pat was smart. And he was damn sure he was going to get that degree."

16

The Right Direction

It took some convincing to get Pat Quinn back to the NHL. When Rogie Vachon took over as the Los Angeles Kings' general manager in 1984, he called Quinn up right away. The two had been teammates briefly on the Houston Apollos (before Quinn was shipped to Seattle), and Vachon respected the discipline he brought to the bench. He wanted Quinn to take over rebuilding the LA franchise.

But Quinn wasn't quite ready to take the call. He was in the middle of his second-year law finals, and needed to study. Vachon had to be persistent.

The Quinns had settled into life in Philadelphia, having lived in Pennsylvania for eight mostly solid years (minus that partial season in Maine and, of course, the firing). Valerie was about to attend Penn State on a swimming scholarship. Kalli was in the middle of high school. Another move across the country, leaving stability after living so many years on the road, just didn't seem appealing to Pat and Sandra.

There was also the matter of Pat's law degree. His paid exile from the Flyers had served as a scholarship of sorts for him, as he could study while receiving a secure paycheck. Very few students could claim that kind of comfort. Now, just a year away from graduating, could he really walk away from it?

The Kings were an abysmal failure. Los Angeles had twenty-three wins, forty-four losses, and thirteen ties in 1983–84, and missed the playoffs for the second straight year. They had won only fifty-one games over the previous two seasons.

They were weak in goal and average on defense—but still had decent pieces to work with up front. Along with Marcel Dionne, the Kings still had all-star winger Dave Taylor, a thirty-goal scorer in Jim Fox, and one the league's premier offensive talents in Bernie Nicholls. With a crop of young prospects ready to join the league, and with a few trades, Los Angeles could actually have a shot at a winning season. That is, if they had the right man on the bench. Vachon continued to place calls to Quinn, hoping to convince him. Even Dr. Jerry Buss, who owned the fabulously successful LA Lakers as well as the Kings, phoned Quinn's representatives to try to enlist his help.

But it wasn't just the comforts of life in suburban Philadelphia that made Quinn hesitate. His ambitions had evolved. He didn't want to be just a coach. He knew how management traditionally treated coaches. If a team was in a dive, the coach was almost always the first to go. Quinn knew that firsthand now. The experience of being fired in Philadelphia had hardened his perspective on how a team ought to be run. "While the challenge of coaching is very rewarding," Quinn told Bill Fleischmann in *The Hockey News*, "you wonder, even when you think you do a pretty good job, whether someone will wake up someday and say, 'This guy's no good for our team anymore—let's boot him out' …

"The coach is the one job that is defenseless when other parts of the management team aren't working together. It's almost an attitude that pervades the game, that everybody knows that's the job that's gonna catch fire…. I've heard Freddie Shero say that the coach gets isolated by the management team. They want him to be management, but they won't treat him like management. That's why he becomes a players' coach. It's a defense mechanism against the backward thinking that goes on."

In short, Quinn wasn't interested in being just a coach. He wanted to be involved in the management of a team—he wanted to be a boss. Quinn flew out to Los Angeles to meet with Vachon. Both men had the same vision for the direction of the team, and it was clear that the old teammates could work well together. Not only that, but Quinn's ego was calling him back. The firing in Philadelphia had bruised him, he admitted. He still had something to prove.

Around the same time, Quinn was also courted by the New Jersey Devils, of which his friend Bob Butera was now president. Pat flew out to New York to talk but he cut the conversation short because he'd already given his word to Los Angeles that he was interested. "Another example of the integrity of the man," Butera says, adding he thinks that, deep down, Quinn would have preferred to stay in the east. "He probably could have made a better deal in New Jersey."

According to Dick Babush, who negotiated the contract in Los Angeles for Quinn, it was understood that Quinn would come in as the coach, and the following season he would become the general manager—and also serve as the coach, if they didn't yet have a replacement.

The contract was signed, although it would turn out that the two parties had very different ideas about what it said. The interpretation would soon thrust Quinn into the most controversial scandal of his NHL career.

On May 30, 1984, the Los Angeles Kings announced that Pat Quinn was heading west to become their new coach. Quinn took his two years at Widener and arranged to complete his law degree through correspondence and summer courses at the University of San Diego. He had no intention of abandoning his pursuit of that degree. "If I hadn't proceeded in that law thing and was selling cars or doing some other job that I didn't like, it would have been an easier decision," Quinn said.

Pat and Sandra went house hunting in the LA area, and hoped to live near the Mission Viejo swim club, where Kalli could continue to swim competitively. "But for what we think we can spend, what they showed us is like moving into an apartment," Quinn said. "I think I've negotiated a fair contract, but it appears our lifestyle will go down from the economic standpoint." The Quinns eventually found the perfect place in Laguna Hills, with a pool of its own. The town sat halfway between Los Angeles and San Diego, which also made it easier for Quinn to get to class in the summers, when he was a full-time student.

Before the season, Quinn and Vachon posed in matching black tuxedos sitting in studio chairs outside the Los Angeles Forum, for the cover of the Kings' 1984–85 media guide. They both balanced large cigars between their index and middle fingers. They looked like brothers, down to the matching mustaches.

Quinn's mustache, carefully trimmed to the edge of his grin, a flat line across, looked like it had been cut out of a Tom Selleck movie poster. His hair, dark but with a few hints of gray now, had length on the side but was cropped neatly to the top of his ears and straight across his forehead. The sky above the red-and-yellow Forum was the perfect blue of a California afternoon.

"A benefit here for me is that I know Rogie very well and we have the same ideas about what needs to be done," Quinn said before the season started. "My first task was to assess the talent we had, determine who can play and what we might be able to accomplish with them, and try to change what had grown here over the past couple of seasons."

During training camp, Quinn looked to set a tough tone for the team. He declared that the balmy California weather and the Kings' rough travel schedule would no longer be an excuse for mediocrity. "The weather shouldn't be an excuse; it should be a bonus," Quinn said. "For a professional, it should be great to go to the rink, work hard for two hours, and then have the good weather in a beautiful city. The teams coming in from the cold parts of the country are the ones who should be zonked out by the warm weather and the sudden exposure to it. Sure the travel is rough but the big drawback of it is that this club missed about thirty practices a season, which is tough in a league where workout time is hard to find for any team."

Previous coaches had placed a ban on tans, to keep their players from being distracted by the beach in LA. Both Bob Berry and Don Perry gave a thirty-five-hundred-dollar fine to any players who showed up at the rink with a sunburn. Quinn got rid of those rules, however. "The sun, the beaches, and all the other benefits

California offers are here and why shouldn't hockey players take advantage of them? All I ask is that they be professional about it, not overdo it and look after themselves, and have their game faces on when they come to the rink to practice or play."

The Kings' players lived scattered around the sprawling LA area, so they couldn't spend much time socializing. An evening get-together could mean two hours of driving (this, evidently, before the Kings players regularly became inhabitants of Manhattan Beach and Hermosa Beach, two of the richest zip codes in the United States). So Quinn tried to get the team together in other ways, splitting the Kings' twenty-two-man roster into four teams with four captains, for a series of competitions in things other than hockey. The first event was a bowling tournament after the team's first of two games in a row in Winnipeg. The Kings lost the first game but won the second game against the Jets, 5–2, after bowling.

In Quinn's first season as coach, the Kings finished fourth in the Smythe Division with eighty-two points—a significant improvement over the dismal previous season. They lost three straight games in the first round of the playoffs to the powerhouse Edmonton Oilers, taking two of the games to overtime.

With the turnaround, Quinn was a strong contender for the Jack Adams Award against Jacques Demers of the St. Louis Blues, Bryan Murray of the Washington Capitals, and Mike Keenan of the Philadelphia Flyers, who were also in the running. Murray won it, however.

That season, Quinn became close friends with Mike Murphy, who had been named his assistant coach. "His presence was always so overpowering," Murphy says. "His physical stature, his deep voice, his articulation, those things almost immediately almost overpowered you—but once you talked to Pat, he was engaging and kind and soft. He was full of questions and open to listening to you." Quinn would ask Murphy for his thoughts on the game, or a practice, and would then actively work his thoughts into the game plan or next practice. "He taught me so much about the art and skill of coaching," says Murphy.

He got to know both of Quinn's parents when they came out to visit in LA. Of Jack, Murphy says, "He was a great ball of laughs, who loved to sing and loved to dance." That love of music had been passed on to his son. Whenever the Kings went to Chicago, Quinn would take Murphy out to a jazz bar and spend the evening listening to the brass bands play. Occasionally, usually after a few drinks, Quinn would sing an Irish tune in his deep baritone.

After games, Quinn and Murphy would discuss a variety of points that needed to be addressed, but before speaking to the team Quinn would distill everything down to two or three key takeaways to be sure the players would get the message. He used his love for history—Canadian, British, Irish, ancient, and military—and would often try to relate battle strategies to hockey. Quinn would describe British battle formations from the seventeenth century, and relate them to explain why the team needed to play the box when they were a man short so no one could penetrate the center. "When he'd speak to the team he'd catch their attention because he'd speak on something that was completely unrelated to hockey, but it would make the point," says Murphy. *"This is why we do it, this is how we do it, and this is the right way to do it."* Players would often laugh at Quinn's analogies, but they'd accomplish what he wanted.

"He wasn't just a great coach," Murphy says. "He was a great educator." Some of the lessons were filled with insight, combining an erudite sense of history and shrewd application to the matter at hand. Others, less so. "Coaching is like having a bird in your hand," Quinn told Phil Myre, his old teammate and player, who joined the Kings as a goaltending consultant after he retired. "If you squeeze him too much it's going to die; if you're too loose it's going to fly away. The only thing for sure is that it's going to shit in your hand."

As always, during the season Quinn would bury his head in biographies and histories, scribbling notes to retain what he was learning. Through the summer, Quinn commuted south to San Diego, finishing off his course load. He received his law degree from Widener that fall, when the school accepted his credits from San Diego. He didn't attend the graduation ceremony, continuing an accidental lifelong trend of never going to any of his commencement celebrations. Hockey had always kept him from the podium.

For all of Quinn's admirable traits, however, he could also be a hard-ass.

His second season with the Kings started off terribly, again. They had just three wins, one tie, and ten losses when the Montreal Canadiens came to Los Angeles on November 9, 1985, and beat the Kings 6–0 in front of thirteen thousand booing fans.

Quinn reamed his team out after the game. "They should spend some hours thinking about their occupation because some of them certainly aren't hockey players," he said. "We had a lot of guys with no will to play. We had no attack. In the second period, we mounted absolutely nothing … When you stink like that you can hardly point to one person.… I should have benched twelve players and played with three."

The Kings fell apart through the 1985–86 season, finishing fifth in the Smythe Division with fifty-four points—the team's worst season in more than a decade. They didn't make the playoffs.

Given his availability that spring, in 1986, Quinn was asked to be the coach of Team Canada at the World Championships in Russia. Murphy went along as an assistant coach. During a game in Sweden before the tournament, Quinn was struck in the face with a puck that knocked him out cold and took a couple of teeth for good measure. He was on the ground, cut wide open and bleeding, as the team's doctor tried to help him. They tried to get him to leave, but Quinn refused. "I'm alright, I'm alright," he said, still clutching the notes in his hand. Finally, the team dentist convinced Quinn that he had to get his mouth taken care of immediately, and so he left reluctantly, after handing his carefully considered notes to Murphy. Quinn walked around during the rest of the tournament with a horrible scar and missing teeth.

Still, the small dental problem wasn't enough to keep Quinn out of the bar, even behind the Iron Curtain. Somehow the Canadians found themselves seated at a table surrounded by a rough crowd. A large and quite drunk Finnish man sitting next to them kept butting his cigarette in the ashtray at their table, which he kept missing. They didn't say anything for a while. But as it continued, Quinn felt it was rude and asked the man to stop.

The man ignored him. The next time the man leaned across their table to ash his cigarette, Quinn kicked the chair out from under him and the man fell flat on his ass. "It was about our first or second night in Moscow, and I'm thinking we're going to jail," says Murphy. The big guy got up off the floor and came toward Quinn. Quinn stood up. That was the end of it. "He took a look at Pat and ducked into the crowd," Murphy says. They sat down and finished their beers.

Canada ended up finishing third in the tournament, but the real disappointment was unfolding back in LA. Quinn had only moved out west with the understanding that he'd be taking over the GM role from Vachon. But it was clear that Vachon had no intention of moving on.

Quinn had made up his mind. He wanted out of LA. And thousands of miles away in an office in Atlanta, the telephone was ringing.

Dick Babush answered his line.

It was Arthur Griffiths in Vancouver.

17

Quinngate

"We made a short list that was Pat Quinn, Pat Quinn, and
Pat Quinn."   —*Arthur Griffiths*

O f all the words used to describe Pat Quinn—*tough, intelligent,
stubborn, sophisticated*—the two most common are *loyal* and
honest. Those true traits sat at the core of Quinn's persona. He was
a man of principle—staunchly so. That is what made the scandal
that plagued Quinn through the late 1980s so baffling.

Frank Griffiths, owner of Vancouver media conglomerate
Western Broadcasting Co., bought the franchise in 1974 for nine
million dollars. With the new ownership, the team began to show
signs of progress, and Griffiths was rewarded with a Divisional
Championship in his first season. Eight years later, after a few
bumps and some smart trades, the team, shaped by GM Jake
Milford and coaches Harry Neale and Roger Neilson, reached the
1982 Stanley Cup Final. They lost in four straight to the New
York Islanders, but judging by the fans you'd have thought they

were the victors. The day after the defeat that took them out of the running, close to a hundred thousand Vancouverites cut work to attend a celebratory parade. The city was enamored with its hockey team. And at the beginning of the next season, many thought the team had found a winning stride. Sadly, frustration followed and in subsequent years the Canucks fell back into mediocrity.

One night, a fan at the game hurled an insult toward Frank Griffiths: "I'm sick and tired of wasting eighteen dollars on this crap!" Griffiths turned and retorted, "Well, I'm sick and tired of wasting fifty thousand dollars a night on this crap." He was desperate to create a team Vancouver could be proud of again. Griffiths and his family members, who were also involved in the business, searched for two years to find the right person to come in and run the Canucks' hockey operations. They knew that Pat, now coach of the LA Kings, was one of the original members of the team in 1970. "We made a short list that was Pat Quinn, Pat Quinn, and Pat Quinn," says Arthur Griffiths, Frank's son.

Unsure of what Quinn's contractual status with the Kings was, they called his representatives two summers in a row in 1984 and 1985. When they reached out again in the summer of 1986, Dick Babush suggested that Arthur Griffiths call back after October 1.

When Griffiths called back that fall, Babush told him that the Kings had not made clear what Quinn's future with the organization would be. His contract with Los Angeles contained a "two-pronged" option—which stated that either Quinn would be rehired as head coach for another season, in 1987–88, or he would become the general manager for a three-year term (which didn't look like it would happen, because Rogie Vachon wasn't going anywhere). Regardless, neither option was given to Quinn by the October 1, 1986, deadline that was stipulated in his contract. Because of that, Quinn's representatives believed he was free to discuss employment with other teams for the upcoming season.

Arthur Griffiths checked with the league to see if Quinn's contract with the Kings had been officially registered with the NHL's head office. It had not. Under league bylaws, if an employee contract is not registered, anyone is free to contact that person. For that reason, the Canucks operated with the belief that they were not committing the offence of tampering.

Griffiths, already in Florida for an NHL board of governors' meeting, met with Babush to discuss terms of a potential contract at the Ritz-Carlton Hotel in Buckhead, just outside of Atlanta. "I remember being nervous because of course I'm meeting with the lawyer of someone who's coaching a team in the NHL and I'm thinking about being discovered," says Arthur Griffiths. "I felt a little bit of 'cloak and dagger.'" He and Babush discussed the possible terms of what it would take to get Quinn to join the Canucks for the 1987 season, and over the next couple of weeks, the fine points were negotiated and a contract was drawn up.

A written summary of the NHL's subsequent investigation and decision into what the media would dub "Quinngate" lays out the facts all sides appeared to agree on.

On December 9, 1986, the Canucks sent Quinn's representative a written offer of employment, which was to be an "agreement in principle" for him to become the president and general manager of the Canucks, starting on June 1, 1987, or earlier if his employment with the Los Angeles Kings was terminated.

Two days later, on December 11, Quinn agreed in principle to the terms of the contract.

Frank and Arthur Griffiths then traveled to southern California to meet with Quinn in person for the first time. Late in the evening on December 15, they met at the Hotel del Coronado, a luxurious Victorian-era beach resort on Coronado Island, just outside San Diego. They sat on the covered hotel patio and Quinn puffed a cigar as they talked. Frank Griffiths was a straightforward, no-bullshit type of man, who was upset with the Canucks' current direction. They discussed ownership philosophy and the state of the franchise, and laid out exactly what Quinn's authority and responsibilities would be.

Quinn asked Frank Griffiths what he hoped to accomplish with his coming to the Canucks, who were facing criticisms for their last place standing in the Smythe Division. "I need someone who's going to come here and run this hockey business," Griffiths told Quinn. "I want you to bring respect back to the franchise."

On December 23, the Kings and Canucks played against each other in Vancouver. The Canucks won 6–4. That evening, Quinn sat with Frank and Arthur Griffiths in a meeting that carried on past midnight. With the sky still dark on Christmas Eve morning, he signed the formal contract to become president and general manager of the team. The agreement outlined specific details of Quinn's duties with the Canucks, starting on June 1, which included that he would have "responsibility for all hockey operations ... selection and control of the coaching staff ... responsibility for the acquisition, termination, promotion and demotion of players, scouting, drafting and predraft investigation."

The agreement also provided for the payment of a hundred thousand dollar signing bonus. "This was my dad's way of ensuring the contract would never be forced to be broken or otherwise," says Arthur Griffiths. They agreed that Quinn should inform the Kings as soon as possible.

Quinn called general manager Rogie Vachon on Christmas Day, and asked to meet him for lunch the next day. When they met on December 26, Quinn told him about his deal with the Canucks and asked Vachon to keep the information to himself, so he could finish the season coaching the Kings. Vachon informed Dr. Buss later that day, however, and both of them were very upset.

Los Angeles had been climbing in the standings that season, and GM Vachon was pleased with how the team was coming together. Quinn coached the Kings to victories over Boston and Philadelphia on December 27 and 30.

In the New Year, the Kings returned to Vancouver to play the Canucks on January 2. After the morning skate that day, Arthur Griffiths gave an envelope to a Canucks trainer and told him to make sure it got to Quinn. "Nobody knew at the time it was a check except me, Pat, and the accountant," says Arthur Griffiths. "I couldn't [deliver the envelope]. I think the more common thing to do today would have been to do a wire transfer." "It was not Pat's idea," says Dick Babush, about the hundred-thousand-dollar signing bonus accepted while Quinn was still coaching the Kings. "That's what the Griffithses wanted to do." Regardless, Quinn accepted the money.

Quinn and the Canucks planned to keep the deal a secret until the end of the season, when the Canucks would announce that Quinn would be the team's new superboss. But between Christmas and New Year's, a source told Canucks broadcaster Tom Larscheid that Quinn had signed a contract with Vancouver. The source remains anonymous. But Arthur Griffiths wasn't surprised that the information got out. "It was highly likely," he says. "Everybody's got loose lips."

On January 7, 1987, the Kings were still on the road and were playing in Edmonton. Larscheid, who'd been sitting on the news for about two weeks, called the hotel where the team was staying and was put through to Quinn's room. "Can you confirm or deny that you are going to be the next GM of the Vancouver Canucks?" Larscheid asked him. There was a long pause. "Can I call you back?" Quinn said. "What's the number?"

After he hung up from Quinn, Larscheid called Rogie Vachon, dialing several times without getting through. Then Vachon's secretary answered. "I have information that Pat Quinn is going to be the next general manager of the Vancouver Canucks," he said. He was put through to Vachon's office right away. Vachon initially told Larscheid he didn't know anything about it. Then he asked if he could call the journalist back. After a while, Larscheid called back several more times and was told that Vachon was in a meeting. With some persistence the journalist eventually got through. "Where did you get this information?" Vachon asked him before telling him again that he'd call him back. He never did. Neither did Quinn.

Larscheid, who'd been working on the story since nine that morning, decided that after twelve hours of stalls he was going to press. "Just the fact that no one would confirm or deny it was good enough for me," says Larscheid. At the time, he thought it would be big news because it meant that the Canucks' current GM, Jack Gordon, was going to be out and Quinn would be in.

What he didn't realize was just how big the fallout would be.

On January 8, NHL commissioner John Ziegler learned about the contract between Quinn and the Canucks. That day, Kings owner and president Dr. Jerry Buss told Ziegler that he hoped to get the Canucks to reverse the deal.

The next day, Quinn confirmed to Ziegler he'd accepted the hundred-thousand-dollar advance, a fact he'd not told the Kings about. Buss and Vachon were furious. Ziegler announced that Quinn was expelled from the league effective immediately, pending an investigation by the league's general counsel, Gilbert Stein. (A decade earlier, ironically, it was Stein who had first recommended that Keith Allen consider Quinn for the assistant coaching job in Philadelphia.)

"I was not the only one upset," says Rogie Vachon, who characterizes his conversations with Quinn at the time as "not very friendly." After Quinn's deal with Vancouver leaked out, Vachon went to the locker room and addressed the team. "Everyone was in shock," he says. "Everyone was disappointed ... most of the players loved to play for him."

Stein completed the investigation on January 20. Ziegler spent another ten days conducting interviews. He would later reflect on how difficult it was to deal with both Frank Griffiths and Pat Quinn in the case because of the immense amount of respect he had for both of them. Ziegler had been a guest on Griffiths's yacht several times and considered him to be a man of honor. "But they did wrong," Ziegler would say. "They did very wrong." On January 30, he released his decision. While acknowledging that all parties involved *believed* that they were operating within their legal rights and were not interfering with the season at play, Ziegler hammered the Canucks with a three-hundred-ten-thousand-dollar fine—ten thousand dollars for each day from when the contract was signed to when the league found out about it, as well as for other infractions, like Quinn's in-person meetings with the Griffithses. The Kings were fined one hundred thirty thousand dollars, ten thousand dollars for each of the days that they were aware Quinn had signed the contract with Vancouver and did not notify the league.

But even Quinn's executioner was partially exonerating. In regards to Quinn, Ziegler wrote in his ruling:

> Like Vancouver, Quinn believes and believed that all of his actions and those of his representatives were legal and proper ... however, like Vancouver, Quinn forgot or neglected the most essential aspect of this business, the integrity of the competition.
>
> It may be Quinn would have performed all his duties in loyal fashion up to and including May 31, 1987. He may have chosen his players, changed lines, developed strategy without a thought as to his future responsibilities of making Vancouver a successful operation.
>
> It may be he could have consulted with Los Angeles on May 30 and 31, as to which players to keep, which players to draft, knowing that in two or three days he would have even greater responsibilities for Los Angeles' closest competitor.

Whether he could have or not is not the issue. Neither Los Angeles, the other member clubs, Los Angeles' players, the League, nor most important, the fans of our league and game should have to wonder.

Can any of us really believe that the NFL would not have been the laughing stock of professional sports had it permitted Super Bowl XXI to go forward with the existing coaches if the Denver coach had months before agreed to become the President and General Manager of the Giants and had accepted $100,000 in consideration before?

Ziegler went on to say that regardless of the innocence of intent, it was impossible to ignore the money Quinn took hours before his Los Angeles team was to compete against the team whose total operation he would be controlling within five months. Quinn, Ziegler said, acknowledged some concern when he stated that he wanted the matter to be kept confidential, "Because I had a job to do and I felt it would interfere with my ability to do my job if the public knew about it."

He found that Quinn's "agreement in principle," his execution of the contract on December 24, 1986, and his acceptance of the sum of one hundred thousand dollars on January 2, 1987, were all acts and conduct that were dishonorable, prejudicial to, and against the welfare of the league and the game of hockey.

Quinn was barred from having any contact with the Kings or Canucks during his expulsion, which continued to the end of the season. He was suspended from performing any coaching duties with the Canucks for three years, until the 1990–91 season. He was also suspended from performing any functions at or attending league meetings and drafts, and from conducting any negotiations or transactions with other member clubs, players, draft choices, coaches, assistant coaches, or scouts until the end of the 1987 board of governors' meeting.

Ziegler had smashed his hammer down. The fallout for Quinn was swift and severe. The Canucks hadn't hired him to be their coach, so the ban meant little to Vancouver. The Griffithses refused to acknowledge that they'd done anything wrong. "He wasn't backing down," says Arthur Griffiths of his father, Frank. "The angrier they got, the more he dug his heels in."

But Quinngate would stick with the Big Irishman for the rest of his career.

News trucks surrounded his Laguna Hills house. Quinn offered little, but looked exhausted, his eyes heavy. His hair was streaked with gray. He was clean-shaven but his face looked older, carrying more weight than it had when he first arrived in Los Angeles. After twenty-five years spent in the league building up a reputation for integrity and honesty, Quinn's good name was now associated with deceit. "[I am] looking forward to presenting my side," Quinn said. "When all the facts are presented, I'm confident I'll be exonerated from any wrongful conduct."

Quinn's longtime friend and lawyer, Morris Chucas, stuck to the same message. "The facts will show that Pat behaved honorably, intelligently and legally. He used an overabundance of caution to be well above reproach in order to do what he was allowed to do," Chucas told the press. Of Ziegler, he added, "Obviously he thinks he is acting in the best interests of the league. I certainly have no quarrel with that. Nobody has done anything wrong. The conclusion is wrong and all the facts will prove that. It's very, very unfortunate that a human being can be chopped up like this when he acted so honorably. I have every faith that the league will be honest in its disposition of this case."

Quinn quickly cleaned out his office at the Los Angeles Forum and didn't return. "He became persona non grata," says Mike Murphy, Quinn's assistant coach and close friend, who took over the head coaching position. Murphy spoke with Quinn regularly by phone to get advice on how he should run the team. "I don't think the Kings wanted me to do it … I thought this thing was still in the works and there was a chance Pat would come back. Obviously I was wrong."

Quinn was vilified among Kings fans. "If Pat Quinn can ask his players for commitment, the least he can do is make a commitment," said a man interviewed at the Forum at the time. "They say he's going to be a lawyer. Looks like he'll be a good one. But you gotta learn that there's a difference between the letter of the law and the spirit of the law."

"I blame Vancouver more than anything," said another Kings fan. "They can keep Pat. They're perfect for each other."

At least one summoned sympathy for Quinn. "Good move on his part. He's not selling the Kings out. He loves the Kings," said the young man in a striped blue shirt. To which all the people around him in the Forum concourse vehemently disagreed. "No! No!" several shouted. "He sold out!" another jeered, and others echoed: "He sold out! He sold out!"

The press widely praised Ziegler's ruling, while acknowledging that the league had stumbled into a gray area that Quinn had used to his advantage. Technically, Quinn was within his rights to make the agreement with the Canucks because his contract with the Kings wasn't registered with the NHL head office. (The loophole had been used before. In the summer of 1986, Jacques Demers signed to coach the Detroit Red Wings while the St. Louis Blues claimed they still had an agreement with him, but the contract was not filed with the league.) Even the issue of honesty—of whether Quinn would have done his absolute best with the Kings without being prejudiced by the fat check he took and the deal he made with the Canucks—was discussed more as a matter of perception than actual concern he wouldn't have acted with integrity had he remained the Kings' coach.

"Paddy Quinn would never hurt the Kings to help his future bosses, regardless of what he put his name to," wrote Jim Proudfoot in the *Toronto Star.* "But the whole thing looks terrible and that alone is unacceptable. You know the story. It's not enough that justice is done; justice must be seen to be done."

Alan Eagleson, then the executive director of the NHL Players' Association, charged that Quinn was morally wrong for taking the money from the Canucks. "I feel very sorry for Pat Quinn. He's a hell of a guy and a friend of mine," said Eagleson, whose own egregious sins were yet to be discovered. "[But] to me it doesn't matter whether it's legal or illegal. Justice not only has to be done. The genuine benefit of the situation is that it has to come now.... No matter how you try to do it, you can't serve two masters."

Expelled from the league, Quinn remained in southern California and turned his attention to finishing his legal studies. He finished law school at the University of San Diego that summer, though he received his degree from Delaware's Widener

University because the school, wanting to call him an alumnus, had ensured Quinn had taken his core courses there before heading west. It would be a bittersweet accomplishment, something he'd worked so hard for finally achieved just as his reputation had been tarnished.

The fines against the Canucks were appealed in British Columbia provincial court the following autumn and reduced to just ten thousand dollars—because the offence was committed on a single day, and the league did not have the authority to declare that each day after the contract was signed was in itself a separate offence.

However, the court was powerless to rule on the coaching suspension levied against Quinn (though it did acknowledge that many believed the penalty to be overly harsh). The BC court also noted that Quinn acted on the advice of legal counsel and that the Kings had left him in limbo after the October 1 deadline, and therefore he had good reason to be concerned about his future employment. During the hearing, Quinn said Jerry Buss had offered him a chance to earn one million dollars in bonuses if he remained with the franchise and won the Stanley Cup, but Quinn said he wouldn't renege on his deal with the Griffiths family. He said that he'd been "led down the garden path" into believing that Vachon would eventually be made president of the Kings, making room for Quinn to take over as general manager—and that he was shocked by the expulsion because he believed himself within his rights to sign with the Canucks since the Kings hadn't offered him the general manager's position by the October 1, 1986, deadline.

But Pat Quinn was never the type to be led down the garden path, and the final irony has Quinn's lawyerly fingerprints all

A young Pat Quinn takes up hockey and perfects his trademark glare in east end Hamilton.

Always the tallest in his class, Quinn (back row, middle) excelled at basketball at Sacred Heart junior high in Hamilton.

Quinn (back row, second from left) enjoys his minor hockey days in Hamilton's Police League.

Unless otherwise indicated, all photos are courtesy of the Quinn family

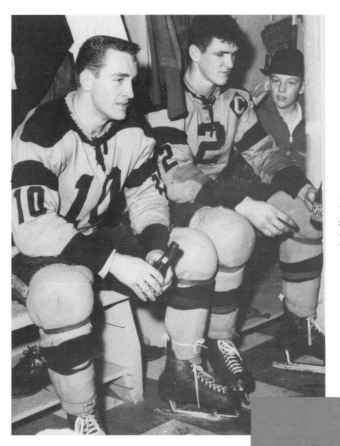

Enjoying a 7-Up after another battle with the Hamilton Kilty Bs.

Quinn poses with the Memorial Cup after winning it with the Edmonton Oil Kings in 1963.

A Quinn-signed action shot from his bruising days in Atlanta. Quinn was a fan favorite with the expansion team, coached by Boom Boom Geoffrion. (Courtesy of Jason Farris)

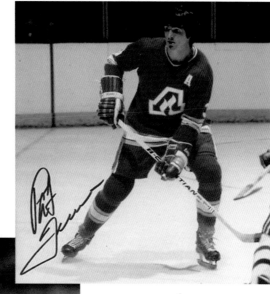

Quinn behind the bench in Philadelphia in 1980. (Bettmann/Corbis)

Quinn and Rogie Vachon enjoy cigars and matching moustaches before the 1984 season in Los Angeles. (Courtesy of Jason Farris)

1984-85 MEDIA GUIDE

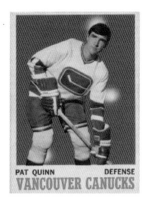

Quinn hockey card.
(Courtesy of Jason Farris)

Quinn lets the referee know how he feels in his first game back as Canucks coach after firing his good friend Rick Ley in 1996. (Chuck Stoody/CP Photo)

Quinn wouldn't score many goals, but he knew how to take care of his own end. (Hockey Hall of Fame)

Quinn and his mentor Tim Horton share a locker-room chat in 1968. The two became good friends, and Quinn even starred in an early commercial for Horton's new coffee-shop chain. (Graphic Artists, Toronto)

Quinn shares his lighter side at Leafs practice with captain Mats Sundin and Gary Roberts. (Rene Johnston/GetStock.com)

Quinn pulled his daughter Kalli into the Team Canada celebration photo after winning gold at the 2002 Olympics in Salt Lake City. (Reuters/Shaun Best)

Pat Quinn embraces Martin Brodeur after Canada beat Finland 3–2 in the 2004 World Cup of Hockey final in Toronto. (Frank Gunn/CP Photo)

Quinn watches over Canada's young stars after John Tavares scores the game-winning shootout goal in a thrilling semifinal game the 2009 World Junior tournament in Ottawa. (Tom Hanson/ The Canadian Press)

Pat and Sandra share their first moments as husband and wife. They were married in Edmonton just before the 1963 Memorial Cup.

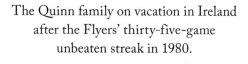

The Quinn family on vacation in Ireland after the Flyers' thirty-five-game unbeaten streak in 1980.

Quinn cradles his granddaughter Kylie. Despite the attention he garnered as a general manager and coach, Quinn was steadfast in his belief that his family was the most important part of his life.

The Big Irishman shows his softer side, giving his granddaughter Kate a ride.

Pat Quinn acknowledges the fans as he walks onto the ice to be inducted
into the Vancouver Canucks Ring of Honour in April 2014.
(Darryl Dyck/The Canadian Press)

over it. It's true that the contract stipulated that Quinn would be promoted to GM. It's also true that it had been left unregistered at his request. He knew what he was doing. "The Kings had a two-year period to evaluate me," he said at the hearing. "I was convinced the [unregistered] contract would not come under the [NHL] tampering laws."

Years later, as Quinngate became an asterisk on an esteemed career, Dick Babush would acknowledge that his friend hadn't gotten the right information from the legal experts they consulted and a lot could have been prevented. "Obviously the thing we should have done in hindsight was we should have gone to the commissioner before we did anything with Vancouver," says Babush. "Pat's legal advice was lacking in that regard."

From Quinn's point of view, he was trying to protect himself and his family. He felt the Kings had not been forthright with him. And when LA ignored the October 1 deadline stipulated in the contract, Quinn was left with no guarantee of future employment. In that case, he felt it was within his rights to look for work elsewhere. All the Kings had to do was honor the agreement.

The perception that he'd acted without integrity would always bother Quinn. There was no doubt in his mind that he would have honored his commitment to the Kings for the remainder of his contract, without his judgment being affected by his future commitment to the Canucks. In the world of gentlemen's agreements settled with handshakes, that logic made some sense. But under the scrutiny of the high-profile, high-stakes business of professional sports, a man's word held little currency. "A man works his whole life to establish a reputation for honesty," Quinn said at the time. "This has been tough on me."

18

Selling Hope

After his exile for the remainder of the 1987 NHL season, Quinn was permitted to officially take over his position as president and general manager of the Vancouver Canucks on June 1.

One night, during a reunion of the 1978 Calder Cup–winning Maine Mariners in Portland, Quinn sat at the bar at the Sonesta Hotel with Brian Burke, the minor league player he'd crossed paths with at the Flyers' training camp a decade earlier. The two had stayed in contact through Quinn's years coaching the Flyers and while he was off at law school. After a single season with the Mariners, Burke had attended Harvard Law School (partially on the recommendation of the Flyers' general manager Keith Allen, who informed him he'd have a better career in law than on the ice). Burke was now a thirty-one-year-old associate at the Boston law firm Hutchins and Wheeler, representing forty-five hockey players—thirty-three of whom were in the NHL. As the Mariners reminisced about years gone by, Quinn spoke with Burke about his new position with the Canucks, asking Burke what he thought was needed to rebuild the Vancouver franchise into something successful. The conversation carried through the evening and into the early morning, as drinks continued to be poured and Burke went through his thoughts on pro and amateur scouting and contracts. By 4:00 A.M., Quinn turned to Burke and asked him if he'd be interested in a job. At first, Burke was embarrassed, worried he'd sounded like he'd been trying to talk his way into a job. He declined the offer. But when he woke up the next morning, he reconsidered the possibility. Despite an already successful career representing players, he saw the appeal of joining Quinn at the top of an NHL franchise.

Burke called Quinn that morning. "If you're serious, I'm interested," he said. Within a couple of weeks, he'd sold his house in Canton, Massachusetts, and moved his young family to Vancouver as the Canucks' senior vice-president of hockey operations (basically serving as the team's assistant general manager).

On their first day together in the team's office, Quinn joked to Burke: "So what do we do now?" And while neither man lacked confidence, they *did* face an enormous task. The Canucks had finished last in the Smythe Division in 1987 with just twenty-nine wins. The team averaged a little more than ten thousand fans a game, and the games were rarely televised. The Canucks were bleeding money—in truth, they were on the verge of failing. When Quinn arrived, the Canucks were taking in about eight million dollars a year, and spending more than twelve million. Frank Griffiths made it clear that he wouldn't be able to keep the team going if they continued with the dismal results on the ice and increasing financial losses off of it.

Shortly after Quinn arrived in Vancouver, he and Burke joined Frank Griffiths for dinner. "We're tired of this," Griffiths told them. "I don't want to lose money. I don't care if I make any money." The media magnate's philosophy was to hire the people he wanted to run the franchise, and to sit back and let them run it. If they failed, they'd answer to him.

As a rookie GM, Quinn relied on the lessons he'd been learning since his early coaching days with the Flyers, under Keith Allen. He looked to build the franchise beyond a one-manager, one-coach operation. He wanted to surround himself with innovative thinkers covering a range of expertise that he could rely on. He set up a management council, headed by himself, with Brian Burke, Glen Ringdal (a remaining vice-president and director of communications), and Carlos Mascarenhas (as vice-president of finance). Arthur Griffiths joined their weekly meetings. He had given his office at the Coliseum to Quinn, and moved offsite to an office in downtown Vancouver to make it clear that Quinn was in charge. Quinn hired Bob McCammon, the man whom he'd replaced and then been replaced by in Philadelphia, to be the Canucks' head coach.

But Quinn's challenge was not only to build a winning team: It was to build a market for that team to flourish in. There was a core of solid Canucks fans (even if they were frustrated), but many more Leafs and Canadiens fans, among others loyal to the original six franchises. The Canucks were still in the growing pains of expansion, despite nearly two decades as an NHL franchise. Vancouverites would joke that if you put two Canucks tickets on the windshield of your car, hoping someone would grab them, you'd come back to find four.

The Canucks embarked on a series of public campaigns to generate hype around the franchise. They tried an off-the-wall commercial series centered around "Chuck" (a large, boisterous man who did all the talking) and "Bobby" (Chuck's brother, who remained silent and sheepish). Quinn and his team thought they were hilarious. One Canucks commercial would have the characters shooting pucks while trapshooting. The commercials ran for two weeks and completely bombed. "People just hated them. They thought they were insulting to fans," says Ringdal. "But everyone in town was talking about these goddamn commercials. They were all talking about the Canucks."

Of course Quinn knew that commercials and public events wouldn't be enough to turn around the fortunes of the Canucks franchise. The trick was in something less tangible, but which he'd cited from the beginning. "We sell hope," Quinn said. As general manager, Quinn believed he needed to give the fans something to believe in again. To do that, he needed to completely rebuild the team's roster.

Quinn's first move was minor, trading away goalie Wendell Young and a draft pick to the Flyers for defenseman Daryl Stanley and goaltender Darren Jensen. He followed that with a blockbuster deal that sent marquee center Patrik Sundstrom to the New Jersey Devils for forward Greg Adams and goalie Kirk McLean. Quinn had coached Adams at the World Championships in Russia. Adams had played college hockey in Arizona, so few scouts noticed him and he went undrafted. In the three weeks Quinn had him during the tournament, he realized Adams had the potential to be an impact player. Jack McCartan, one the Canucks' scouts, who had a long career as a goalie and guided the US Olympic team to gold at the 1960 Olympics, saw a lot of potential in McLean, and Quinn trusted his judgment.

In the Canucks' home opener that season, Adams scored four goals in an 8–2 romp over the St. Louis Blues. But as important as Adams would become for the Canucks, it was McLean who'd prove to be the steal in Quinn's first major deal.

The Canucks' new leadership was full of strong, unique personalities—a combination that led to a few conflicts. The group debated constantly, especially Quinn and Burke, the lawyers of the group. (As heated as discussions would get, however, out of the room, the management group functioned as a unit, says Ringdal.)

Quinn and Burke had a particularly colorful relationship. During one of their early trips together for a league meeting in Toronto, Burke arrived at the airport in a pair of corduroy pants. "Where do you think you're going?" Quinn asked him. "I'm going to Toronto with you," Burke replied. "Not dressed like that," Quinn said. "You look like a bum." Burke protested. "Pat, we're not working today. We're just traveling," he said. "There's no reason to wreck a suit traveling in a plane for four-and-a-half hours." But Quinn's rules were set. "When you travel on team business, you wear a suit," he said.

Burke was a workhorse—he'd often be in the office from 6:00 A.M. to 9:00 P.M.—and as a younger member of the staff, he helped usher in a modern era. Burke transferred the team from typewriters to computers, and helped them get cell phones. At the time, he was raising a young family with four kids. Partway through the season, when the team had a bit of a break, he asked for some time to take a brief vacation up to Whistler with his family, just to get some time away. Unfortunately, Burke's role as the guy who brought in new technology also meant that he was the only person who knew how to fix it. While he was away, Quinn's computer crapped out. When Burke returned, Quinn was pissed off because his computer still wasn't working. Burke said he was sorry, but he had been away. "Well," Quinn replied, "if you didn't take half the goddamn winter off to go skiing we wouldn't have these problems."

The 1987–88 season was another disaster on the ice for the Canucks. Vancouver won just twenty-five games and finished last in the Smythe Division for the third time in four years. Despite the disappointing performance, Quinn was busy in his office making deals at the deadline—trading Craig Coxe to Calgary for centerman Brian Bradley, defenseman Kevan Guy, and minor leaguer Peter Bakovic. Of the three, only Bradley would make a real contribution to the Canucks lineup. He also swapped aging goaltender Richard Brodeur to Hartford for the younger Steve Weeks. None of the deals were blockbusters—if remembered at all—but the flurry of moves showed that Quinn was eager to shake things up in Vancouver.

The Canucks owned the second overall pick in the draft, behind the Minnesota North Stars. There was much debate over whether Trevor Linden or Mike Modano would go first overall, as both players had been compared all season. Linden was a six-foot-four right-winger from Medicine Hat, Alberta—a hometown star with the Medicine Hat Tigers, who had won two consecutive Memorial Cups. In his final season with the Tigers, Linden scored forty-six goals and had 110 points in sixty-seven games.

There was an abundance of talent in the 1988 draft, which included future stars like Jeremy Roenick, Teemu Selanne, and Rob Brind'amour, among many others. All three would easily surpass Linden on the score sheet over the course of their careers. But no *real* Canucks fan would ever argue against taking Linden as the second overall pick.

That spring, Trevor Linden arrived in Vancouver for the first time in his life, to be interviewed by the Canucks. He still hadn't graduated from high school when the team arranged to have him picked up at the airport and driven to the Quinns' house in West Vancouver to meet the family before the draft. Pat, Sandra, and Kalli welcomed him into their home high above the Lions Gate Bridge overlooking a stunning cityscape, and Linden vividly remembers being terribly nervous to be hanging out in Pat Quinn's living room.

Despite Linden's nerves at the Quinn home that day, he left a lasting impression on the Canucks' boss—the shy prairie boy connected with the steel-town Irishman. Quinn believed he had found a player whose true value was in his character, not his ability to score (which, of course, was a huge plus). Linden was simply a "hell of a kid," Quinn thought. He wanted him on his team. And as Linden politely thanked the Quinns and left their house that day, he had a feeling that Vancouver was about to become his home.

At the draft that June, in 1988, Quinn welcomed Trevor Linden to Vancouver. The lanky forward pulled on a yellow jersey with red and black bands around the elbows and an orange and yellow skate logo across the chest. He put on a matching cap and shook hands with a red-cheeked, graying Pat Quinn.

It was the beginning of a new era.

Later that off-season, Quinn added all-star defenseman Paul Reinhart and veteran forward Steve Bozek to the Canucks' lineup in a trade with Calgary. Then he added defenseman Robert Nordmark and picked up a second-round draft pick from the Blues, for Dave Richter. Quinn didn't stop there. He signed towering defenseman Harold Snepsts—a lead-footed tough guy, much like Quinn had been in his playing days—who had been a fan favorite in Vancouver through the late '70s and early '80s. Snepsts had spent the previous three seasons in Detroit. Before the puck dropped for the start of the 1988 season, Quinn had added eighteen new players to the Canucks' roster since he took over a season earlier.

In his rookie season, Linden scored thirty goals—a Canucks rookie record—and finished with fifty-nine points, helping the Canucks sneak into the playoffs for the first time since the 1985–86 season. It was a great accomplishment for Quinn's rebuild. But the Canucks faced the first-place Calgary Flames in the opening round.

The Flames were stacked with talent—led by Joe Mullen, who scored fifty-one goals and 110 points. Calgary's roster boasted Doug Gilmour, Hakan Loob, Joe Nieuwendyk, Al MacInnis, and twenty-year-old Theoren Fleury. Mike Vernon would finish second to Patrick Roy in voting for the Vezina Trophy that season.

It was expected to be a rout. The underdog Canucks, however, managed to win the first game of the series, with a forty-three-save performance by McLean, and an overtime goal by

Paul Reinhart. The Flames won the next two games, but Linden had a goal and three assists to lead the Canucks to a 5–3 win in game four.

The powerhouse Flames managed a 4–0 win to take a 3–2 series lead in game five, and it looked like the Canucks were almost done. But the Canucks dominated game six, scoring four goals in the second period (three of them a little more than two minutes apart), and forced a final game with a 6–3 win.

Headlines had mocked the Canucks' chances going into the series, but now Quinn's team had the Cup-contending Flames on the brink of elimination.

The final game in Calgary was a battle of the goaltenders. McLean faced forty-six shots in the Canucks' net, while the Flames' Mike Vernon saw forty-five. The teams went into sudden death overtime tied at three.

The Canucks had three great chances to score in overtime—including a partial breakaway off the boards by captain Stan Smyl—turned away by Vernon. Then, with less than a minute to go in the first overtime period, a shot from the point deflected off of the Flames' Joel Otto's skate and into the Vancouver net behind Kirk McLean. The series was over.

Despite the scare against Vancouver, the Calgary Flames would go on to win the Stanley Cup. The Canucks were done, but they had the league's attention.

In Vancouver, hope was sold in abundance. And Quinn had a secret shipment coming in.

The Canucks used their eighth overall pick at the 1989 NHL draft at the Met Center in Minnesota to take defenseman

Jason Herter, who would play only one game in the NHL. No matter. Some diligent sleuthing by his staff had set up the best draft-day steal in NHL history.

Vancouver was about to get the Russian Rocket.

Pavel Bure had just finished his rookie season with CSKA Moscow—known as the Red Army—and had clearly demonstrated that he could be an NHL star. But scouts were uncertain if the eighteen-year-old Russian would defect and believed that he wasn't eligible to be drafted into the NHL until the following season, because regulations required that he dress in at least eleven games for an elite-level club sanctioned by the International Ice Hockey Federation. Earlier that year, however, the Canucks' chief scout Mike Penny was on a trip in Finland when he heard that the Red Army was playing on Christmas Day in a remote part of the country. He borrowed a truck and drove through a snowstorm to arrive at the rink in time to see the game. That under-the-radar game would put Bure at eleven. He was eligible to be drafted, even though no other NHL team was aware of it. Penny grabbed the hand-scrawled game sheet as proof and kept quiet.

"This guy is the best guy available by a country mile," Penny told Quinn, urging him to select Bure in the fifth round of the draft. Quinn was apprehensive. This was unchartered territory, and it was unclear how the league would respond. The Canucks knew there would be protests from other teams. They were confident in the information they had—but less confident that the league would honor it. Quinn didn't want to waste a draft pick if it turned out that Bure was ineligible. Worried that another team might have secured the same information, Brian Burke also tried to convince Quinn. He believed the information would likely have been sold to another team. He had reason to believe that Edmonton was also aware that Bure was eligible.

Quinn warned Penny and Burke that he'd be incredibly pissed if the information was wrong. But, trusting Penny, he relented and agreed to make the pick in the sixth round—willing to risk the loss of a lower pick, should any problems arise.

Dan Bylsma went 109th overall to the Winnipeg Jets. Dave Emma went 110th to the New Jersey Devils. The Chicago Blackhawks took Tommi Pullola 111th, and the Minnesota North Stars took Scott Cashman 112th—neither of whom would play a single game in the NHL.

Then Pat Quinn announced that the Canucks were taking Pavel Bure. The sleepy Met Center erupted into shouts of shock and rage, as panicked team executives rushed the stage and declared that Bure was ineligible.

It would take a year to determine who was right.

Shortly after the controversial draft, on July 1, 1989, the Canucks announced the signing of Igor Larionov, the famed Russian center of the Red Army's KLM Line, which included wingers Vladimir Krutov and Sergei Makarov. Quinn coached against the three at the World Championships in 1986. The Canucks drafted Larionov in 1985 and Krutov in 1986—but they had to negotiate to have the Russian Federation release them.

Quinn was at the forefront in trying to come up with a diplomatic solution to bring Russian stars to the NHL. He met with Russian officials in Calgary during the 1988 Olympics to discuss the release of Larionov, Krutov, and Viktor Tuminev, whose rights belonged to Vancouver. In May, Quinn went to Moscow with Frank and Arthur Griffiths to make official contract offers to Larionov and Krutov. Both players were officers in the Soviet army, and would have to be granted leave to be able to join the NHL.

That decision would come down to Viktor Tikhonov, the infamously rigid coach of the Red Army. Tikhonov told Quinn that the Red Army's star player wouldn't be released for at least another season. The following winter, in January 1989, Larionov told the *Toronto Star* he was fed up with waiting and planned to join the Canucks regardless of what the Russian sports bureaucrats said. He was open about his displeasure at not being able to join the NHL and led a revolt against Soviet authorities that prevented Russian players from playing in North America. He was also a critic of the rigid requirements Russian players faced, being kept away from their families and enduring a constant boot-camp training program, immersed in the game on and off the ice.

But Quinn insisted that the Canucks were only negotiating with the Soviet Union Ice Hockey Federation and were not in contact with the players whose NHL rights they had owned. "It's not something we would consider," Quinn said, when asked if they would circumvent the process and negotiate with the players directly.

Regardless, speculation about whether the Russians were coming to Vancouver ran rampant through the remainder of the season and through the spring. In May, high-profile Russian prospect Alexander Mogilny defected during the Ice Hockey World Championship in Sweden, signing a contract with the Buffalo Sabres. The defiant move caused a backlash against Mogilny in his homeland and seriously threatened the ongoing negotiations between NHL teams and Russian hockey officials.

Quinn wasn't sure which way negotiations would go after Mogilny's defection. "I can't read the Soviets' minds," he said. "I've been dealing with them for over two years and it's been awfully frustrating."

In late June, Quinn received a promising fax from the negotiating body of the Soviet Union Ice Hockey Federation. Given the frustrations he had already encountered trying to broker a deal, he tried to stay grounded despite the positive developments. The New Jersey Devils had just signed defensemen Viacheslav Fetisov and Sergei Starikov, though the circumstances of that deal remained cloudy.

"I'm going over for one last try to see if we can get this situation clarified," Quinn said. "The crux of the confusion remains—you can sign anyone, but the trick is getting them out of the country. We have asked them to lay out the terms for us. We want them to say, 'Here it is, here is what we want,' but they've never done that. Last year the Griffithses were invited over, but there was never any intent of making a deal. They hadn't cleared anything with the army, with Viktor Tikhonov, so nothing was accomplished."

On June 27, Quinn boarded a plane for Moscow, cautiously aware that he could return with nothing. Larionov was no longer a member of the Soviet army, but there were still obstacles to clear—namely securing the player's exit visa and negotiating compensation to the Soviet Union Ice Hockey Federation.

Even if they did manage to get the players out, it was unclear just how well they'd adjust in the move over to the National Hockey League. Quinn met his old friend Cliff Fletcher, the Flames' general manager, in the Russian capital. Fletcher hoped to finally sign Larionov's linemate, Sergei Makarov.

Over the course of four days of tense negotiating, Quinn managed to work out a deal with both the Soviet Union Ice Hockey Federation and Larionov's representation. After two years of trying, he returned to his office at the Coliseum with both contracts. (Fletcher also successfully negotiated a deal for Makarov.)

"There was a lot of emotion involved," Quinn said of signing Larionov, who was beloved in his home country. "It was tough for them to say goodbye."

At the time, Quinn was unable to secure the release of Vladimir Krutov, because coach Viktor Tikhonov blocked the move. But Krutov was clear about his intention of playing for the Canucks— and his five-year-old son told Quinn, "I'm coming to Vancouver."

In early September, Quinn again boarded a plane for Moscow, hoping to come back with another signed contract. Quinn had been informed by the Soviet hockey officials that Krutov would soon be released from his duties with the army and that he was free to negotiate with the Canucks. (Quinn had been told this in early August as well, but he canceled the trip when he learned that the army was expecting a cut of the transfer fee that would normally go to the Ice Hockey Federation.)

To help his cause, Krutov refused to play for Tikhonov, forcing the Federation to make a deal. Quinn signed him to a three-year contract, and created a separate deal with the Federation for a transfer fee.

The Larionov and Krutov signings sparked the biggest boost in ticket sales since the Canucks' inaugural NHL season. Season tickets jumped from 6,800 during the 1988–89 season to 10,300 for 1989–90. The average attendance at the Coliseum that year was 15,400—almost 2,000 more than the previous year. Glen Ringdal had to bust up an agreement a small group of gentlemen tasked with pushing season ticket sales had made with previous management—namely that they'd receive commission on every season ticket sold, regardless of how that sale came about. "If I hadn't changed it, every one of those four salesmen would have made more money than Pat Quinn made and they wouldn't have had to get out of their pyjamas," says Ringdal.

The marriage with the Russian stars didn't go quite as planned, however. The Canucks were a disappointment on the ice through the 1989–90 season. Even with the addition of Larionov and Krutov, Vancouver managed just twenty-five wins and finished last in the Smythe Division. Krutov scored eleven goals and had thirty-four points in his first season with the Canucks. Coach Bob McCammon regularly benched him because he wasn't physically fit to play.

As the hype and hope began to fade, Quinn tried to engineer deals that could bring some life back into the lineup. In January, he brought in forwards Dan Quinn, Andrew McBain, and rookie Dave Capuano from Pittsburgh for veterans Barry Pederson, Tony Tanti, and Rod Buskas.

At the deadline, he retooled further by picking up Adrien Plavsic and a couple of draft picks from St. Louis for Rich Sutter and Harold Snepsts. Quinn flipped one of the draft choices from the Blues to the Montreal Canadiens for defenseman Jyrki Lumme—a huge move for the Canucks, as Lumme would become a fan favorite and the team's all-time scoring leader on defense.

The Canucks failed to make the playoffs, but fans still appeared to be buying into what Quinn was trying to create in Vancouver. The 1990 NHL draft was held at BC Place Stadium that June. The night before, the Canucks' brass were sitting in their room preparing for their upcoming picks, when they were called to come up to commissioner John Ziegler's suite. Quinn and Burke went into the suite, where Ziegler was sitting with Gil Stein, who'd completed the league's investigation into Quinngate just a few years earlier.

This time, he brought better news. Stein handed Quinn a press release stating that the NHL was officially acknowledging that the Canucks' claim to Pavel Bure was legitimate and would be upheld. After a year of uncertainty, the risky pick had paid off. And they still had the second overall pick in the current draft. "It was like Christmas, we were so excited," says Burke. They returned to the hotel room to tell the team's scouts, and proceeded to celebrate with the customary consumption of several beers.

The next day, more than nineteen thousand fans showed up at BC Place to watch the draft live. Owen Nolan went first overall to the Quebec Nordiques. Quinn went up to the podium to make the next pick for the Canucks and the stadium thundered with cheering fans. "The Canucks are proud to select from the Seattle Thunderbirds and Czechoslovakia, Petr Nedved." Nedved, eighteen years old, had left home for the first time eighteen months earlier. He was a six-foot-three center who had just broken the record for rookies in the Western Hockey League with 145 points.

With Larionov, Bure, Adams, Linden, and Nedved, it looked like Vancouver's middling decade was finally over. Quinn didn't make any trades in the off-season (a lack of moves that received some criticism).

The only major bust on the part of the Canucks appeared to be Krutov, who had been nicknamed "Tank" before he arrived in Vancouver, but was now often referred to in the press as "Crouton" because of his excessive weight gain. The thirty-year-old had trouble adjusting to life in North America. He and Larionov, once good friends, had grown apart during their first season in North America. "We wanted Vladimir Krutov to come here and show up in condition ... like he committed to in his contract," Quinn said at the time. "That didn't happen.... We believed he was a world-class player who'd come here and play like a world-class player. We gave him every opportunity to do that."

Krutov was cut from the team in early October with two years remaining on his $375,000 contract. The standard buyout figure was two-thirds of the contract—so five hundred thousand dollars in his case. The deal also provided for Sovintersport (the Soviet Ice Hockey Federation) to receive four hundred thousand dollars for each season Krutov played. But Quinn had no intention of paying it.

Krutov and his representation would push for full buyout, while Quinn maintained that the contract was never filed with the league—and was therefore invalid. Krutov's lawyers argued that his contract had an addendum stating that he could not be sent to the minors or traded without his permission. The league rejected that, because it did not allow no-trade clauses at the time. His lawyer, Bill Faminoff, argued that the league had suggested an addendum overriding the no-trade clause, but the

Canucks simply deleted both the no-trade and no-minors provisions, even though the no-minors provision was valid.

While the Krutov legal battle was playing out off the ice, the Canucks were once again disappointing on it. At the end of January, Vancouver was last in the Smythe Division with a 19–30–5 record.

During a 3–3 tie with the Rangers (in which New York goalie Mike Richter made fifty-nine saves), Quinn decided he needed to fire Bob McCammon. He had the perfect replacement in mind—someone who had spent three years in exile from the bench, learning how to run a franchise.

His time now served, Pat Quinn—the coach—was back.

19

Superboss

Quinn's first game on the bench after his three-year ban from coaching was, as though scripted, against the Kings in Los Angeles. His return to the Forum was a juicy story line that was sure to dominate the sports pages. Although a few seasons had passed—and the greatest player in the game now wore a black and white jersey with a number 99 on the back—the Kings' faithful still viewed Quinn as a traitor for his inelegant exit from the franchise. But the relative insignificance of Quinn's sins was thrust into perspective before the Canucks even made it to the Forum.

On the evening of February 1, 1991, the Canadian Pacific commercial flight the Canucks were on touched down at LAX just ahead of USAir Flight 1493—a Boeing 737-300 carrying eighty-three people. A mistake by air traffic control sent a small commuter plane, SkyWest Flight 569, onto the same runway where the 737 was set to land.

As the Canucks' plane was taxiing off the runway, the 737 crashed into the runway and smashed into the smaller commuter plane, crushing it. All twelve people on SkyWest Flight 569 were killed.

The crash happened about one hundred yards from the Canucks' plane, which jolted to an abrupt stop as the pilot hammered on the brakes as the barreling 737 veered in his direction before hitting an airport fire station. The pilot of the Canucks' plane came onto the speaker system and said he was going to get away from the problem, before speeding his plane into nearby grass to distance his passengers from the explosion.

On the opposite side from the crash, Quinn saw a ball of fire that filled four windows from where he sat. The passengers from the crashed 737 leapt desperately from the tail and wings. Fire inside the plane blocked two of the front exits and one of the overwing exits.

Twenty-three of the eighty-nine passengers on the 737 died in the crash, many of them as a result of asphyxiation in the fire. In the end, thirty-five people lost their lives that night.

"Everyone was pretty quiet after that," said Steve Tambellini, then the Canucks' media director.

"We might have been the ones," Quinn said. "It makes you think how vulnerable you are when you see those poor people killed like that."

The next night, still grappling with the disaster, the Canucks lost 9–1 to the Kings at the Forum—the team's worst defeat of the season.

In Quinn's first ten games as coach, the Canucks won just two games, lost six, and tied another two. It was a rocky start, but after that the team started to turn around, making an unlikely push for the playoffs as the season wore on.

As general manager, president, and coach, Quinn had two offices at the Coliseum. One on an upper floor was more elegant, befitting his position as the team's "superboss." His other office—the coach's office—was at the ice level. Above his desk he hung a sign: "A total commitment is paramount to reaching the ultimate in performance." It was a quote from football coach Tom Flores, who won two Super Bowls with the Raiders.

From his upstairs office that spring, Quinn engineered another trade that would help turn the Canucks' fortunes around. At the trade deadline on March 5, he sent defenseman Garth Butcher and center Dan Quinn to St. Louis for center Cliff Ronning, forwards Geoff Courtnall and Sergio Momesso, and defenseman Robert Dirk.

Quinn believed in giving second chances to players that other teams had overlooked or dismissed—perhaps a carryover sentiment from his playing days. He took a big chance on Ronning, a diminutive forward whom many thought to be too small to have a decent career in the NHL. He saw the potential in Ronning. "He gave me the opportunity when no one else would give me the opportunity," says Ronning.

The deal was an immediate victory for Quinn. Quinn put Ronning at center, on a line with Linden and Courtnall. It immediately bolstered the Canucks' offense.

Vancouver managed to move up a spot in the Smythe Division standings and snuck into the playoffs. (An overtime goal against the Jets by Courtnall—the guy Quinn had traded for—in the last game of the season put them a point ahead of Winnipeg.)

Naturally, Vancouver faced the first-place Los Angeles Kings in the opening round. The Canucks managed to take two games in the series but fell to the Kings in six. Still, it was a modest gain on what had looked to be another lost season for Quinn's team.

A day after being eliminated from the playoffs, the Canucks officially announced that Quinn had inked a lucrative four-year contract extension (the terms of which had been agreed on when he took over as coach in February). In Quinn's first four years as the Canucks' general manager and president, Vancouver finished nineteenth, fourteenth, twentieth, and seventeenth overall—certainly less than stellar results on the ice. The franchise hadn't made it past the first round of the playoffs and had extended its string of consecutive losing seasons to fifteen, an NHL record.

Quinn's record in the draft was filled with hits and misses, but he had pulled off some valuable trades. Primarily, he looked to bring in players that he knew he could rely on. He bolstered his team with a gritty, shut-down defensive core with guys like Gerald Diduck, Dana Murzyn, and Dave Babych. All three played the game much like Quinn did, and he went out of his way to pick them up. Quinn traded for Diduck in January 1991, bringing him over from Montreal.

Like Quinn, Diduck was a reliable mucker on the ice—and also the locker-room intellectual. He liked to read up on the markets and often had a copy of *The Wall Street Journal* with him. ("You're still reading that same fucking paper," Quinn chirped at Diduck when he saw him with a copy of the *Journal* a decade later.)

Shortly after trading for Diduck, Quinn picked up Murzyn at the trade deadline. In the off-season he traded for Babych.

Though Quinn was respected by the entire room, he connected most with his rugged defensive core. "He identified with them," says Linden.

At the helm of the team he built, Quinn was a natural leader. Loyalty followed him. His damn-the-critics attitude with the press reinforced the feeling that it was Quinn and his boys versus the world. They'd follow him anywhere. It didn't matter how loud he yelled or how hard he slammed his fist on the ping-pong table in the middle of the locker room. Quinn's boys were with him. The loyalty they saw in him inspired loyalty to each other. The Vancouver Canucks teams from the early '90s would maintain an unusual sense of connection through the years. "It was a unique bond, a unique experience," says Diduck. "Everybody was playing with and for each other."

Fans had also bought in. By 1991, the seats at the Coliseum filled to capacity on most nights. By that measure, arguably the most important one, Quinn's first four years in Vancouver had been a success.

The question was, just how long would those seats stay filled if the Canucks didn't start winning?

A few years earlier, Quinn had hired his close friend and former Leafs teammate, Rick Ley, to run the Canucks' International Hockey League affiliate, the Milwaukee Admirals. After a season in Milwaukee, Ley took the head coaching job with the Hartford Whalers, the organization he'd starred with as a player through the 1970s, when the New England Whalers were part of the WHA. When Ley was fired in Hartford after two seasons, Quinn immediately called him up to offer his condolences, and to say, "Hey, how would you like to come out here and work with me? How would you like to be my assistant?"

Ley jumped at the offer and joined Quinn on the bench for the 1991–92 season. Quinn also hired Stan Smyl, the Canucks' former captain who had retired that July, to be an assistant coach along with Ley and Ron Wilson, who had joined the Canucks the previous year.

That season turned out to be a turning point for the franchise.

Through the off-season, the Canucks had been working to secure the release of Pavel Bure from the Red Army. He had been a star on his Russian team, once playing on a line with Alexander Mogilny and Sergei Fedorov, both of whom were now in the NHL after Mogilny defected in 1989 and Fedorov defected and signed with the Detroit Red Wings the following season. The Russian officials forbade the Canucks from speaking with Bure directly. Bure was, reportedly, afraid to defect because it would make things difficult for his younger brother Valeri, who was a promising player.

In early September 1991, Bure's agent, Ron Salcer, got in touch with the Canucks to let them know that he had managed to get Bure to California, along with his father and brother. The Canucks hadn't expected to be able to negotiate for Pavel Bure for at least another year, but Quinn sent Burke to speak with them right away. He called Salcer and told him he was flying to LA that day, and would bring a good book to read. But Salcer didn't make him wait. He invited Burke to his house in Manhattan Beach. They went for a two-mile walk along the coast down to Hermosa Beach. Burke told Salcer the Canucks were determined to sign Bure. They didn't care about outstanding issues with the Russian Federation. The Canucks were prepared to fight for Bure in court. Over the course of their two-hour stroll through the sand, Burke and Salcer hammered out Bure's first deal in principle. Of course, there was still the messy matter of securing his release from the Central Red Army. The NHL wouldn't allow the Canucks to negotiate with Bure until they had permission from the Red Army.

But Burke had discovered that Bure signed his contract with the Red Army before turning eighteen years old, and that his father had signed as his guardian. The Canucks thought they had discovered a loophole to get around Bure's obligations to the Soviet army team. Burke researched which states had the most favorable laws in regard to contracts with minors and discovered that Michigan was likely the team's best bet. He flew to Detroit and hired a law firm, while Quinn remained in Vancouver quarterbacking the action, says Burke. The Canucks sued the Russian hockey federation in Detroit, hoping that they would file a response. The Russian hockey federation responded—and so Pavel Bure's NHL future would be decided in Detroit.

Both sides met with a judge, who mediated the negotiations between them. The Russians wanted three hundred thousand dollars to release Bure, but Quinn refused to go over two hundred thousand. The judge tried to get both sides to meet in the middle, but neither would budge. They wrangled back and forth for three days. Bure had yet to agree to terms with the Canucks, so even if they did manage to come to an agreement with the Russian hockey federation, the Canucks still had to negotiate with him.

The Canucks had resolved to tell the judge they couldn't reach a deal, which would send Bure back to Russia for another year, after which they'd all come back to the table. But as the judge again informed the Canucks that they were offering too little and the Russian ice hockey federation was asking too much, Pavel Bure stood up in the courtroom and said that he'd pay fifty thousand dollars of his signing bonus to split the difference. As soon as Bure started talking, Burke thought, "Sit down and shut up!" because of course, at that point, there was no signing bonus to take the fifty thousand from—the Canucks and Bure hadn't started to negotiate. The judge thought that was a perfect idea, and asked the Russians if they agreed. They did.

Bure was free to play for the Canucks. On October 31, 1991, he and the Canucks agreed to a four-year deal reported to be worth $2.7 million, with an eight-hundred-thousand-dollar signing bonus, including the extra fifty thousand dollars the Canucks coughed up after Bure took matters into his own hands.

He was worth every cent.

During Bure's first practice with his new team, two thousand fans showed up just to watch him skate. Up to that point, no player of Bure's game-changing caliber had worn a Canucks sweater. While the team had boasted many beloved characters— Kurtenbach, Snepsts, Smyl, and Linden—the franchise now had the kind of talent that could seemingly score at will. Bure was an instant star in Vancouver.

In Pavel Bure's first game, at home against the Winnipeg Jets, he went coast-to-coast three times, dazzling Canucks fans even though he failed to score a goal. Trevor Linden, now the Canucks' captain, received fan mail that said, "Dear Trevor: You have always been my favorite Canuck. Can you get me Pavel Bure's autograph?"

Even though Bure started the season a month late, he still managed to lead the Canucks with thirty-four goals in sixty-five games, playing on a line with Igor Larionov and Greg Adams. Bure's efforts won him the Calder Memorial Trophy as the league's top rookie—the franchise's first ever award for on-ice performance.

Trevor Linden, who had become the Canucks' youngest captain when he was twenty-one, led the team in points with thirty-one goals and forty-four assists. Cliff Ronning proved that Quinn's assessment of his ability was bang on, finishing second in team scoring with twenty-four goals and adding forty-seven assists—just ahead of Larionov, Bure, Adams, and Geoff Courtnall.

Kirk McLean had a standout year in goal, winning thirty-eight games—a team record—posting a 2.74 goals against average and earning a nomination for the Vezina Trophy. (And Gino Odjick, a Quinn favorite, broke the team's single-season penalty minutes record with 348, in just sixty-five games.)

With the exception of Larionov—whose looming departure would be a mark on Quinn's record as a GM—those names were about to become etched in Canucks lore.

Vancouver won forty-two games—taking the top spot in the Smythe Division, finishing twelve points ahead of the Los Angeles Kings, and coming second in the Campbell Conference. They faced the Winnipeg Jets in the playoffs for the first time ever.

After splitting the first two games of the series in Vancouver, Quinn hoped to pick up a key victory in game three in Winnipeg. But in front of a wild crowd at the Winnipeg Arena, with more than thirteen thousand dressed in white, the Jets barreled over the Canucks. Vancouver trailed Winnipeg 3–0 heading into the second intermission—a score that could have been more lopsided had Kirk McLean not stood on his head.

Quinn was furious with his team's effort. He stormed into the locker room and slammed the door. Then he launched into his speech. It was relatively calm at first. But the heat started to rise. Quinn's face grew redder and redder as he rhymed off the reasons his team was blowing the game. His voice got louder. The rage continued to boil. Two large jugs of Gatorade sat on a table in the middle of the room. Quinn smashed his massive fist into one of the jugs, knocking it off the table and flooding the floor with orange Gatorade and ice. Quinn didn't flinch. He just turned and walked out of the room while his players sat there stunned. Vancouver lost that game 4–2 and were outplayed again in the next game, losing 3–1.

Afterwards, the Canucks coaching and management staff gathered in a bar. Quinn and the others were upset about a call the referee had made, which might have cost the Canucks the game. Glen Ringdal, unfortunately forgetting that his role was with the business and marketing side of the team, offered that he felt the right call was made. Quinn stopped him immediately. "When I want your fucking opinion about fucking hockey I'll fucking tell you," he snapped. "When he was mad, you knew it," says Ringdal. "I've never forgotten it and to this day before I say anything, I say, 'Well, I know nothing about hockey....'"

But despite being down three games to one, Quinn eventually cooled his temper and tried to find a tactical counter to the Jets game plan. During an off day before the fifth game back home in Vancouver, Quinn calmly outlined the plan the Canucks would follow to get back into the series. The players were dejected. "I thought, we're going to lose this series," says Linden. "We were done, down 3–1, nothing was going our way." But Quinn broke the series down to a tactical level—explaining exactly how the Canucks were getting beaten, and exactly how they were going to fix it. "We're going to stretch the right winger, we're going to come underneath, we're going to get skating," Linden remembers Quinn saying. "I was so low after game four," Linden says. "I left that day, and I remember thinking *wow*—I bought in. *That's the way we're going to win.*"

The Canucks stormed back and took three straight games to win the series. "He changed our mindset," Linden says. "He didn't panic." In the second round, unfortunately for the West Coast faithful, the Canucks fell to the Edmonton Oilers in six games and were eliminated from the playoffs.

But, for the Canucks' remarkable turnaround, Quinn was awarded his second Jack Adams Award as the NHL's best coach. A year earlier, his decision to move behind the bench while remaining the team's general manager had been viewed with skepticism in the press. Many scribes derided the decision as panicked and ill-advised. Now, Quinn was being hailed as the first-ever coach to win the Jack Adams with two different teams.

But the year had also marked tragedy for the Quinn family.

In the late eighties, Pat's youngest brother Phillip became gravely sick. Jack and Jean Quinn cared for him at the house on Glennie Avenue where their children had grown up. Pat called them often, and made sure his parents were provided with anything they needed as they tried to care for their youngest son.

In times of pain and tragedy, the Quinns came together as though they had never grown up and left that humble home on Glennie. The support would help them through the most difficult times. For two years, as Phillip grew weaker, the family bond remained steadfast. Faced with the shattering reality that there was nothing to be done but to pray and love, the Quinns held on and did both together.

On October 4, 1991, a call came through to the Canucks' office while Pat was coaching. A member of the team staff came and found Sandra in her seat to let her know that Phillip had passed away. Sandra waited until after the game, then went into his office, closed the door, and told Pat.

Phillip's death hit Pat and Sandra hard. Sandra had often helped Jean take care of him when he was a boy. Later, when they were chasing Pat's dreams through the minors and often found themselves back on Glennie, Phillip was always there, while the other siblings had grown up and moved out. During NHL training camps, when Pat had finally arrived, Sandra and the girls would often stay with Pat's parents. Phillip would frequently look after Valerie and Kalli and dress them up. The girls adored him. "He was a young, fun uncle," Kalli says.

The family flew to Hamilton and stayed for a few days to attend the funeral. The service was the first time Kalli saw her father cry.

Quinn's lieutenant, Brian Burke, left the Canucks that spring to take a new position as the general manager of the Hartford

Whalers. "I have very mixed emotions," Quinn said of Burke's decision to leave. "Brian and I worked very closely. I don't think I'll ever have that type of relationship with a member of the management team again. I'm very proud and happy for him. But I'm also unhappy to see him go because he's a workhorse." Quinn had leaned on Burke to handle most player contract negotiations, oversee the farm system, and deal with player development. Quinn readily admitted that he'd have a hard time filling his three important roles with the club.

"I felt I got spread too thin last year, to be honest," he said. "I don't think I did as good a job as I wanted to in any of the phases of responsibilities I had as president ... and general manager and coach for that matter." Now, without Burke beside him, Quinn had to find a way to fill the void.

The summer of 1992 delivered a new list of challenges for Quinn to deal with in his upstairs office. The team's second overall pick in 1990, Petr Nedved, was unhappy with his situation in Vancouver and asked to be traded. At the same time, Igor Larionov became a free agent and was hoping to re-sign—but a clause in his initial contract said the Russians would receive an additional transfer fee, equal to his contract, if he re-signed in Vancouver. He had reportedly made three hundred seventy-five thousand dollars for each of his first three seasons with the Canucks, and Sovintersport received the same.

The problematic stipulation complicated the situation. Larionov was tired of the control the Russian ice hockey federation had on his career, and wanted the Canucks to break the agreement to pay them for his services. He was tired of the

Russian bureaucrats making money off of him, and it had become a matter of principle to him. "I don't want to talk about even a small amount of money going to Russia," Larionov said. "They received over a million dollars for three years. Now they want more money. It's unfair. Lots of young people came to the NHL this year to escape from Russia and nobody got any money. For me, they were paid a huge amount of money for three years. They never used this money to develop players. They used this money to put in their own pockets and travel around the world."

While he was waiting to find out what would happen, Larionov was offered a contract to play the upcoming season in the Swiss National League. "All my thoughts are about Vancouver. I don't think about any other teams," Larionov said. "But I have to make a response in the next couple of weeks to Europe. First, I want to stay in Vancouver and sign with Canucks again and be happy. But if they don't work it out with the Russians, I have to make another choice. It will be bad for me. This is ridiculous. It is unbelievable. It makes me angry. It is like another war with the Russian bureaucrats. I'm like a hostage."

The clause seemed ludicrous to begin with, but had been part of the negotiations between Calgary's Cliff Fletcher and the federation to get Sergei Makarov.

"I had closed my book and was prepared to leave without Igor," said Quinn. "Then Cliff made his deal and I said 'Alright, I'll match it.' It would have been a public relations nightmare for us if Cliff had come back with Makarov and I had come back without Igor."

The Canucks tried to circumvent paying the Russians by arguing that the initial three-year contract had expired, and therefore the clauses were no longer applicable. The Russians eventually offered a $150,000 buyout of the clause, but Larionov refused to agree to any deal that gave them more money after they had already received $1.2 million for his first contract.

In the end, the Canucks weren't able to get around the clause legally and in July Larionov signed a three-year deal with HC Lugano of the Swiss National League. The deal included a clause that would allow him to return to the NHL at the end of the Swiss season. Larionov was emotional when he announced that he was leaving Vancouver, a place he had come to think of as home and where he hoped to return with his family one day. He called the Canadian birth of his daughter Dianna the biggest achievement of his time in Vancouver.

That August, Quinn brought in George McPhee to join the Canucks' front office. Just as he had with Burke, Quinn showed a preference for hiring college men over friends he had played or coached with. McPhee won the Hobey Baker Award while playing collegiate hockey at Bowling Green University. He was also a wild tough guy in his playing days with the New York Rangers through the 1980s. In addition, Quinn moved scrappy head scout Mike Penny to the front office. Penny was a well-established hockey mind who had no trouble sharing his opinions. The moves were intended to fill the hole left by Burke's departure, and to provide the confidence Quinn needed to allow himself more time to focus on coaching—which he'd realized he loved too much to stop doing. At the same time, he intended to rely more heavily on his three assistant coaches—Ley, Smyl, and Wilson—giving him the ability to delegate authority in his roles as president, general manager, and head coach.

"We finally came to the decisions about the front office and I'm comfortable with those," Quinn told reporters. "And I've now decided, perhaps selfishly, I want to coach the team. If [I] had to pick a job that was the next best to playing, I think coaching's it. It has that emotional gamut you run through as a player. I love that feeling."

Before the season, Quinn moved Linden to center from the wing. The coach and young captain had grown close, personally and professionally, over the previous five years since the Medicine Hat kid had sat nervously in Quinn's living room. Now, Linden saw his coach as the best teacher he knew. "He made sense of things," Linden says. "He did an amazing job with our group, not just from a managerial standpoint but then from a coaching-on-ice standpoint. He taught us the right way to play and why. That's what he was great at."

Quinn knew how to use a six-foot-four, 210-pound power forward like Linden, and a five-foot-nine, buck-sixty Cliff Ronning in a way that optimized their talents. He knew how to get the most out of an enforcer like Gino Odjick and a Russian superstar like Pavel Bure (who became close friends). "You have to understand the gifts that are given to you," Linden remembers Quinn telling him. Of Quinn, Linden says, "He had the ability to get the most of each player and understand where their strengths are and how to use them. He made it understandable for people."

"He was a great motivator.... His stories were intriguing, they were inspiring. A lot of times, they included past wars or battles," says Garry Valk, the kind of marginal player Quinn liked to give opportunities to. "He was a lot like a schoolteacher. Just a really good social studies teacher. You didn't skip his class when the guy was teaching.... He knew how to inspire you."

Cliff Ronning, who again finished second in scoring on the team in 1992–93 with twenty-nine goals and fifty-six assists, took note of all the books Quinn would read on different army generals and war tactics. He was always thinking, Ronning says, looking for the best ways to utilize a range of talents—the finesse, the muscle, the small guys.

But beyond Quinn's ability to bring unique talent together, he made sure his players knew he had their backs no matter what.

"He gave you a chance," says Gino Odjick. "Everybody played, everybody had a chance to do something special."

"He was a smart coach who used the strong side of each player," says Pavel Bure. "When you looked at Pat, you felt you could trust him."

Quinn could be a cantankerous presence with the press, however, especially if he felt his players were being unfairly criticized, or if he needed to direct the attention away from the team and put it on himself.

"If he didn't really respect a writer or a broadcaster, they knew it," says Tom Larscheid. But his often-gruff presence with the press never told the whole story. "That demeanor could change with the snap of your fingers, that little smile would come out and that little twinkle in those blue eyes. People felt very comfortable around him even though he was so big. That handshake would swallow your hand but there was a real tender, warm side of Pat I came to love and know about him."

The 1992–93 regular season proved to be another success for the Canucks, as they won the Smythe Division for the second straight year, with forty-six wins and 101 points. In his sophomore season, Bure led the team in scoring with sixty goals and 110 points, becoming the first Canuck ever to score more than fifty goals.

But despite the season's success, Vancouver again ran into trouble in the playoffs. Once again, the Canucks met the Winnipeg Jets in the first round—and again they struggled to get past them. It took an overtime win in game six to get to the second round.

In the division final, Vancouver faced Wayne Gretzky and the Los Angeles Kings. The outmatched Canucks fell in six games. The second-round departure came with a fresh set of questions about whether Quinn should continue his role as the Canucks' superboss, or if he'd be more effective either hiring a new coach or replacing himself as general manager. Quinn was criticized for not benching twenty-one-year-old Petr Nedved during the playoffs when he wasn't producing. It was clear that Nedved still wanted out of Vancouver, and was now a restricted free agent. Quinn was criticized for being too loyal, too stubborn, too old-fashioned, and ill-equipped to match lines effectively.

"OUT played OUT coached," read one Vancouver headline.

"Quinn hit brick wall of worn-out philosophy, uninspired players," charged another.

The hope Quinn had peddled through six seasons appeared to be running out.

20

Dreamland

Despite the calls for Quinn to streamline his superboss responsibilities, he retained all three positions in the fall of 1993, and continued in the role as the season looked to spiral into disappointment. In the off-season he did little to change the team, which brought on the nickname "Stand Pat Quinn" from the media. The Canucks appeared to be ill prepared to start the season and were hammered by injuries throughout.

The matter of Petr Nedved continued to fester, with the center opting to sit out instead of returning to Vancouver. "I don't care if it takes one week, one month or two years, I'm not going to play in Vancouver anymore," Nedved said from his home in the Czech Republic. "I have a lot of friends on the team and I wish them very well. I have a problem with the management there and a personal problem with Pat Quinn."

Nedved was upset with the negotiations over his contract, saying he'd received one offer from the team, had asked for another, and it came back fifty thousand dollars less than the first. "And then when it's convenient for them they go to the public with figures," Nedved said.

Making matters worse for Quinn, Igor Larionov had returned to the NHL—for the San Jose Sharks. Quinn had faced criticism for refusing to pay the one hundred fifty thousand dollars the Russians had demanded to keep Larionov a season earlier (even though Larionov himself was against making the payment), and now he'd returned with a rival team. Had Larionov returned to Vancouver, the hole left by Nedved wouldn't have been a problem. Instead, every move, or nonmove, that Quinn made was put under a microscope. Quinn's relatively weak record in the draft was often cited: Rob Murphy, Leif Rohlin, Jason Herter, Rob Woodward, Alek Stojanov, Libor Polasek—all were first- or second-round picks under Quinn's regime who had done nothing for the club. He had, however, picked up Mike Peca fortieth overall in 1992, which would prove to be a pretty smart move.

The Canucks floundered through the season, hampered by injuries. Before the New Year, Vancouver had twelve wins and sixteen losses—the season looked to be running away from them. Linden looked around the Canucks' locker room. "Back-to-back division champions—one hundred points," he thought. "What happened to our team?"

That January, Quinn picked up former junior-hockey phenom Martin Gelinas off waivers from the Quebec Nordiques. Gelinas had performed well below expectations since his first season with the Cup-winning Oilers in 1989–90, but Quinn hoped that in Vancouver, he might rediscover the offense that had made him a star in junior, where he scored 101 goals and 107 assists in 106 games. In February, Quinn also picked up journeyman defenseman Brian Glynn off waivers, hoping to add some depth to the blue line.

In late March, when the Canucks were in Texas playing the Dallas Stars, Quinn found himself holed up in a hotel room. He spent the whole weekend on the phone, puffing cigars, and ordering room service, as he tried to orchestrate a deal as the trade deadline loomed. Earlier in the month, the St. Louis Blues had come to an agreement with Petr Nedved, which would end his holdout with the Canucks. Vancouver was awarded center Craig Janney as equalization for Nedved, but Janney refused to report. Quinn worked out a deal to send Janney back to the Blues for defensemen Jeff Brown and Bret Hedican, along with rookie center Nathan LaFayette. (To make space for Brown and Hedican, Quinn had to deal defenseman Robert Dirk to the Blackhawks for a fourth-round pick.)

"It's a grade-B movie plot," Quinn said, exhausted after the deadline, in bare feet and wearing a golf shirt. "We weren't presented with the best scenario in this situation, but we have acquired a quality defenseman in Brown and up-and-coming young players. We didn't have Petr and we didn't have Craig, but we do have some players that can come in and help us now."

Late that season, as Vancouver limped toward a seventh-place finish in the Western Conference, the Canucks were practicing at the Agrodome at the Pacific National Exhibition grounds.

It didn't go well. During a breakout drill, Geoff Courtnall kept dropping the puck instead of dumping it in deep like Quinn instructed. The coach was upset because the team was continually turning the puck over at the blue line. When Courtnall did it again, Quinn lost his mind. He called the team to center ice—and erupted. Quinn smashed his stick on the ice. Red-faced, he yelled at his players until he could find no more words. He canceled the practice. Just called the whole damn thing off. Then he stormed toward the gate to leave the ice, stopping to smash his stick against the boards, taking several swipes until it broke into pieces. Quinn disappeared down the hallway, into the coaches' room.

The players stood at center ice, stunned and silent.

Broadcaster Jim Robson watched it all from the stands. He was supposed to interview Quinn after practice for a regular segment. "What's *this* going to be like?" he thought, as he sheepishly made his way toward the coaches' room. He walked in and found Quinn sitting on a chair taking off his skates, which had the sides cut out to fit his wide feet comfortably. He seemed relaxed.

"What was that all about?" Robson asked him.

"Ah, you gotta wake 'em up," Quinn said, smiling. "They're not into it."

Perhaps taking a page from the coaching manual of Punch Imlach, Quinn had put some fear into his lackluster roster. He'd pulled tactics like that before—once kicking a garbage can so hard he broke his toe, and then limping away hoping no one would know he'd hurt himself.

On April 7, 1994, Frank Griffiths died after a lengthy struggle with several health issues, cancer among them. He was seventy-seven.

Griffiths—a chartered accountant who'd made his fortune building TV and radio stations, not sports teams—was a competitive owner who seldom made himself a publicly visible part of the team. He hired people he believed in. Since he'd taken over ownership of the Canucks in 1974, Griffiths had hoped to bring the west coast a Stanley Cup, but his team had had only middling success on the ice, including the unexpected and unlikely Stanley Cup Final appearance in 1982. Since moving to Vancouver in 1987, the Quinns had grown very close to the Griffiths family. Pat and Sandra had vacationed with the Griffithses, sailing aboard their family yacht off the west coast. Quinn loved working for Frank, a man he knew he could trust. He did not have to pander to a boardroom full of people who knew nothing about running an actual hockey team.

Family came first for Quinn. And he felt the Griffiths family brought the same values to the franchise they owned.

"Mr. and Mrs. Griffiths were a great couple; even in their olden days, they'd walk holding hands. We always called them Mr. and Mrs. G. And I think Pat liked that. They were good people," says Glen Ringdal.

Frank Griffiths didn't want the franchise to lose money, but never cared if it made him another fortune. He wanted to give Vancouver something to get excited about. Quinn had certainly put paying fans in those seats. The Canucks averaged more than fifteen thousand fans each game at the Coliseum in 1993–94— five thousand more than they brought in before Quinn arrived. But the numbers had dipped slightly from the two previous seasons, when the Canucks won the Smythe Division and looked like serious Cup contenders.

After a difficult season, as the Canucks struggled to reach the playoffs, it didn't look like all that hope Quinn had sold Vancouver would pay dividends anytime soon.

The day of Frank Griffiths's death, the Canucks wore a patch on their sweaters that said "2 pts for FG"—a tribute to the owner's common request that all he wanted from his team was the two points in the standings that came with each win. "That's how he ended every conversation we ever had," Quinn told reporters after the Canucks beat the Sharks at home 3–2, on two goals from Pavel Bure, who led the league in goals with sixty. "All he ever wanted for this community was to have a strong team and he was willing to do anything to support that," Quinn said. "Without Frank Griffiths, Vancouver would not have a hockey team."

The Canucks faced the Calgary Flames in the first round of the 1994 playoffs. The Flames finished first in the newly formed Pacific Division, ahead of the Canucks in second. Despite having just one fewer win than Calgary, the Canucks finished with eighty-five points, while the Flames had ninety-seven. The gap was built entirely on the ten more ties Calgary had over Vancouver, and meant that the Flames were seeded second in the Western conference, while the Canucks ranked seventh.

It was already a heated rivalry, reaching back to the 1989 play-offs when the Canucks took the eventual Stanley Cup–winning Flames to the brink of elimination in the first round. Before the first game of the teams' 1994 meeting, Quinn charged that the Flames were the dirtiest club in the league—a point he'd made earlier in the season, referring to the opponents' chippy stick work.

The Canucks looked to be outmatched against a team that still boasted talent like Robert Reichel, Theo Fleury, Gary Roberts, Al MacInnis, and Joe Nieuwendyk—holdovers from the Cup-winner five years earlier. While Bure had just tied his

own club scoring record, Vancouver's other top guns had struggled of late. Geoff Courtnall hadn't scored in eleven games.
Trevor Linden had a rough second half of the season and hadn't
scored in nine games.

Quinn looked to rework his offensive schemes and defensive
systems, knowing that his previous plan hadn't been panning out
through the final stretch of the season. He decided to pair Linden
with Bure, hoping the combination of size and speed would jam
up the Flames' defensive strategy. And he intended to use the
heated history between the clubs to spark a physical series.

"I think our guys respond in a physical game," he told reporters. "I would like to see a good, strong physical contest. That's
the way hockey is best anyway. Last year we faced two clubs that
didn't play physically, necessarily, and we struggled against
Winnipeg and lost to Los Angeles. So this may be a series that
plays towards things that we have that need to be awakened once
in a while."

The Canucks surprised their detractors in the first game of the
series, blanking the Flames 5–0 at the Saddledome in Calgary.
Kirk McLean made a lopsided score possible, blanking the Flames
on eight power plays and making thirty-one saves for the win.

The Flames found a way past McLean in the second game—
mostly after Gary Roberts ran him twice, knocking the goalie
off his game. It was a 7–5 win for Calgary. The Flames went on
to take games three and four, riding the hot play of goalie Mike
Vernon, winning 4–2 and 3–2 at the Coliseum and leaving the
Canucks one game from elimination.

Quinn didn't panic. In front of his players, he didn't reveal a
hint of doubt that they would come back and win the series.

"He was very good at keeping the guys loose and focused, telling a joke or something, before a game," says Kirk McLean. "He kept the guys patient and sticking to the game plan." Quinn told McLean: "You shut the door and we'll win this one for you."

He also constantly told his players to "believe." It didn't matter how unlikely a comeback seemed, he said. If they knew in their hearts that they could turn the series around, they would. "I think he always believed," says Rick Ley. "And he knew he needed them to believe and he could do that with just a few words.... We found a way."

The day before game five in Calgary, the Canucks found a pool hall to take their minds off the game. "We weren't a cliquey team," says McLean. "We did a lot of stuff together." Shooting pool before each playoff game was soon to become a team tradition.

After the pregame skate, before game five in Calgary, Quinn boarded the team bus to head back to the hotel, sitting in the second seat on the right-hand side, like he always did. Broadcaster Tom Larscheid sat behind him, catching a ride back to the hotel. "Well, the boys will get it going," Larscheid said, offering some encouragement. "You know, I really believe in this team," Quinn replied, as Larscheid recalls. "I thought they could do it. If we don't get the job done I'm probably going to have to tear it apart."

That night, the Canucks and Flames went into overtime tied 1–1. Every play had the potential to end Vancouver's season. With the Flames' commanding series lead, most had already penciled them in as winners, moving on to the second round. But in overtime, Geoff Courtnall sprang loose on a breakaway and fired a snap shot past Mike Vernon to win the game.

The series was headed back to Vancouver—and just one win at home would give the Canucks the advantage heading into game seven. But again, one loss, and it would all be over. Quinn sat in the locker room after the press had scurried off to write their reports about the Canucks' sudden gasp for life. He sipped a beer, sitting on the bench next to George McPhee. "They won't beat us now," he said quietly.

Back at the Coliseum, fans had allowed themselves to indulge in some hope. The arena rocked with support as the Canucks took the ice, looking for one more win to keep the series going. Once again, the game went into overtime. During the extra period, the Flames were called for a too-many-men penalty. On the man advantage, Linden picked up a rebound off a shot from Bure and scored on a fallen Mike Vernon. The Canucks stood on the edge of achieving an improbable comeback over the favored Flames.

Back at the Saddledome for game seven, the Canucks found themselves trailing the Flames 3–2 with just minutes remaining— when Greg Adams deked around a poke-check from Mike Vernon and tied the game at three, forcing overtime for the third straight game.

Through the first overtime period, McLean made several spectacular saves for the Canucks. At the halfway point the Flames broke in on a three-on-one, and Theo Fleury made a perfect pass to Robert Reichel who fired at a seemingly wide-open net. But McLean kicked the puck out with his left leg just as it was about to cross the line. The goal judge behind the net turned on the red light. The play had to go to video review to determine it hadn't been a goal. In Vancouver, McLean's stop became known simply as "the save."

A few minutes into double overtime, Pavel Bure cut in on a breakaway on a perfect blue-line-to-blue-line pass by Jeff Brown. The Russian Rocket faked a backhand, went to his forehand, and slipped the puck past Vernon.

Bure tossed his stick and gloves while leaping into his teammates in one of the most electrifying moments in Canucks history. Vancouver had done it.

After the game, as the Canucks soaked in a first-round victory, Quinn walked up to McLean, who had saved the season with his toe. He punched his goalie in the shoulder, proudly. "You did it," he said.

In Vancouver, Canucks fans went wild after Bure's goal, invading Robson Street, singing out "We are the champions!" and chanting "Calgary sucks!"

Even though the Canucks were again considered underdogs against Mike Modano and the Dallas Stars, they carried the momentum of round one into the Conference semifinals. Vancouver took the first game 6–2 in Dallas. Throughout that game, the Stars tried to knock the Russian Rocket off his game by hammering and hacking away at him. When the Stars continued to take shot after shot at Bure in the second game, he decided it was time to send a message. After being knocked down by Craig Ludwig, Bure took another shot from Stars enforcer Shane Churla while he was still down on the ice. On the same shift, the puck went down the ice into the Canucks' end. While Churla drifted toward the net, Bure flew in on his blindside and rocked him with an elbow to the head, knocking him unconscious. (Despite being known for his finesse, Bure was one of the strongest players on the Canucks.) The hit was vicious and calculated. And effective. Bure didn't receive a penalty on the play—and scored two goals in the Canucks 3–0 win.

The league was considering suspending Bure after reviewing the hit the next day. Quinn fumed at the suggestion that his star player should be suspended for protecting himself. "This is the playoffs for crying out loud, and I'm tired of teams crying," he said. "This kid has taken so many illegal hits. We should talk about their tactics. Put the focus where it belongs.... If the referees don't do their job, any human in the world would take a swing back at someone who tried to hurt him. This kid has taken a pounding from Calgary and now these guys. It's almost like the referees want to see the Russian get beat up."

Brian Burke, now the man in charge of handing out punishments for the league, gave Bure a $500 fine for the hit. The Rocket was unrepentant. "I had to do it. Otherwise they try to kill me all the time," Bure said, relaying a sentiment that would make the Mighty Quinn proud. "I got to give it back—and I will."

The Canucks went on to dominate the Stars, winning the series 4–1 and moving on to the final four. (Churla refused to shake Bure's hand as the teams lined up when the series was over.)

During the series against Dallas, the Canucks welcomed a new addition to the family as Sergio Momesso's wife gave birth. The Canucks came off from a practice between games, and Momesso handed out a bunch of cigars. All the players and staff lit up, in Pat Quinn fashion, puffing in celebration before the doors were opened to the press—who were greeted by a pungent cloud of cigar smoke, wondering what the hell the Canucks were up to.

The idea of "family" was central to Quinn's Canucks. Quinn took the time to make sure that staff—from his assistant managers to the security guards at the doors—knew they were part of a larger family. He learned names. He remembered meaningful details. At Christmas, Sandra would get gifts for everyone in the Canucks' office. After home games, win or lose, Quinn always arranged a dinner to be shared with staff family and friends.

Moving past the second round of the playoffs for the first time in Quinn's tenure with the club, the Conference finals were uncharted territory for the club. The Canucks had to wait to see if they'd play the San Jose Sharks or the Toronto Maple Leafs. Asked which he'd prefer, Quinn quipped in media-grumble mode: "If you want to ask that question you can expect a crappy answer: It doesn't matter who we play ... our coaching staff is preparing for both teams." Pavel Bure, however, did allow: "I'd like to play San Jose just because it's closer...."

It took more than a week before the Canucks would find out which team they'd face in the Conference final. While the time in between would undoubtedly put a little bit of rust on their skates, it did provide a valuable rest and the opportunity for a few players to spend some time in the team's hyperbaric chamber—a cutting-edge oxygen therapy unit that helped wounded Canucks heal more quickly. The players called it the "space shuttle."

After nearly a week in orbit, the Canucks were Toronto-bound. The Leafs had ousted the Sharks in seven games. The matchup would be a west-versus-east rivalry, a battle for bragging rights. It would be the first time Vancouver and Toronto had met each other in the playoffs.

It was also a return for Quinn to the team he'd watched as a boy, and that gave him his first chance to play in the NHL. A team that, on top of everything else, was run by one of Quinn's close friends, Cliff Fletcher, who had been Toronto's president and general manager since 1991.

"There's going to be a lot of intimidation this series—that's how Toronto plays," Quinn said before the series started. "They zero in on your key guys and go after them, and infringe upon the rules doing it. They run the goalie."

Quinn charged that Leafs pest Bill Berg, who'd injured Cliff Ronning earlier in the season, was a "cheapshot" player. "I don't respect a kid like that," he said. "He's exactly the type of player that comes about when they say 'No fighting' because he never has to pay the price."

Cliff Fletcher knew the clash with his old friend would turn into a bloody war. "This is going to be the most physical series of the Stanley Cup playoffs," he said. "I just talked to Pat Quinn. I told him I don't want to talk to him again until it's over."

It was over quickly.

The Pat Burns–coached Leafs won the first game 3–2 in Toronto at the Gardens, on an overtime goal by Peter Zezel. The Canucks evened the series with a 4–3 win in game two, also in Toronto. Then Kirk McLean took the spotlight. In game three, the Canucks goalie stopped twenty-nine shots in a 4–0 win. In game four, he went save for save with Leafs netminder Félix Potvin through two periods—and nearly a third—before Cliff Ronning scored with just over two minutes remaining. An empty-net goal by Bure sealed the 2–0 win and put the Canucks a win away from the Stanley Cup final.

In the first eight minutes of game five, the Leafs scored three goals. Toronto just had to protect their head start to force a sixth game back at the Gardens. But they couldn't hold off the surging Canucks. Vancouver scored three times in the second period, tying the game with goals from Murray Craven, Nathan LaFayette, and Greg Adams.

After a tense but scoreless third period, the game went into overtime. The first extra frame was scoreless too, and the Vancouver fans prepared to endure another sudden-death period.

Just after the opening draw in the second overtime period, Adams forced a turnover at the Leafs' blue line. Linden picked up the free puck and cut into the Leafs' end along the left-wing boards. He passed it back to Dave Babych, who fired the puck on net. Felix Potvin misplayed the rebound, leaving the puck a few feet in front of his left pad. Adams got there first, shoveling the puck over Potvin's right shoulder.

The Coliseum erupted. Vancouver shook. The Canucks were in the Stanley Cup Finals.

Jack Quinn and his son Barry were on a tour through Ireland throughout the NHL playoffs that season. It would have been a safe bet, had the Canucks remained as mediocre as they seemed throughout the season. As Vancouver continued to get closer to the final, Jack and Barry tried to find updates at pubs they visited, but seldom found hockey highlights on the tube. Jack didn't know his son had coached the Canucks to the Cup final until the plane touched down in Toronto. The next day, he and Jean were on a plane to Vancouver.

The proud parents had plenty of time to get there, because

the Canucks still had to wait to find out which team they'd meet in the Cup final. The New Jersey Devils and the New York Rangers were grinding out a physical Eastern Conference final. The Rangers eventually took it with a thrilling overtime win in game seven.

When the series opened in New York, the Canucks relied again on the incredible play of goalie Kirk McLean. He stopped fifty-two shots, including seventeen in overtime, before Greg Adams—the man Quinn brought to Vancouver in 1988—once again scored to win the first game with just over thirty seconds to go in the first overtime period.

The Canucks left knowing their goalie had stolen a game they should have lost. Mike Keenan and the Rangers knew it too.

McLean was run several times by New York's Adam Graves in the second game of the series—at least from Quinn's perspective. "The embarrassing thing for our officials is they [Rangers] said they were going to do it and it wasn't stopped," Quinn said about the net crashing, after the Canucks lost 3–1 in game two. "There's three ways you can handle it: You pound the hell out of the guy who did it—but you can't do that anymore—or you run their goaltender ... or the official does his job. If you don't pound the crap out of somebody, then you're relying on number three. But if the official isn't [stopping it], then I guess you go to number two and run their goaltender."

The series swung back to Vancouver for game three, but the Canucks didn't do much better with the crowds at the Coliseum behind them. Pavel Bure was ejected for a high stick on Glenn Anderson early in the game, and the Canucks crumbled without him, losing 5–1. In game four, Bure was robbed by Rangers goalie Mike Richter on a penalty shot in the second period. It looked like the Canucks' Cinderella spring was over. The Rangers won the game 4–2 and were just one win from defeating Vancouver to hoist the Stanley Cup.

The Canucks flew back to New York, looking for one more miracle comeback.

At the Quinns' home in Vancouver, Jack and Jean stayed with Sandra to watch the game on television. All through the series Jean had sat on the edge of her seat, hollering at the refs with the passion she'd instilled in her son. "She didn't suffer fools," says Ellen Ley. Still, Jean would cringe when the camera caught her son cursing at referees. While in Vancouver during the finals, Jean went to Sunday mass, as always. While she was there, the priest made a comment about praying for the Canucks. As Jean left the church with Ellen Ley, she turned to the priest and said, "You know, my son's the coach." The priest didn't know what to say. "She was very, very proud," says Ellen.

For road games during the playoffs, friends would come over to the Quinns' in West Vancouver to watch the games. Ellen Ley would make her lucky spareribs—which were discovered to bring good fortune to the Canucks when she first made them during the team's comeback against the Flames way back in the first round. Jack and Jean added spaghetti and chili to the list of superstitious food that had to be included on game days. They were as essential to the Canucks' chances of winning as the perfectly arranged sticks of gum on Pat Quinn's desk, and the faded black-and-pink tie he wore. "That was his lucky tie," says George McPhee. "It was the funkiest thing I've ever seen."

But even Quinn knew that it would take more than a funky tie to beat the Rangers—especially trailing three games to one. Quinn needed to make sure his players knew that the series wasn't over. He needed them to believe that the outcome belonged to them. "If we're going to lose this series, make them beat us," Quinn said during a team meeting before they faced elimination. "They're not beating us right now; we're beating ourselves. Make them beat us."

Back in New York for game five, it looked like the Rangers had *in fact* decided that they would beat the Canucks, taking a decisive 3–1 lead in the first period. Through those first twenty minutes, one could practically imagine the New York headlines declaring that the team's fifty-four-year championship drought was finally over. "Tonight's the night," one paper had splashed across its front page that morning. "The Cup stops here," it wrote on the back. New York was ready to celebrate.

"If you're human and read all that stuff, it makes a difference," said Pat Quinn, who knew he'd have plenty of headlines to read in Vancouver if the Canucks didn't rally. Quinn had done little to address a lineup that didn't seem to be working against the Rangers, and would be sure to hear about it from the vocal west-coast scribes. The only switch he made was to move Linden back with Courtnall, instead of playing him with Bure as he had through most of the playoffs. If the Canucks dropped four straight, Quinn would be criticized for not managing his lines properly. But Quinn had always been the kind of coach to stick to his plan.

With time running out, the switch Quinn did make paid off royally. In one of those playoff moments that seems ripped out of a *Mighty Ducks* screenplay, the underdog Canucks responded with five goals in the second period, with two from Pavel Bure and two from Geoff Courtnall.

Vancouver won 6–3. Quinn's Canucks had done it again— they were coming home, with a chance to force a game seven.

Momentum had shifted. Back in front of a thunderous crowd at the Coliseum, the Canucks fired fifteen shots on Mike Richter in the first period of game six. They went into the second inter- mission with a 1–0 lead. They'd score twice more in the second, answered by a single goal from New York, to take a 3–1 lead into the third period.

With 1:32 remaining in the third, Jeff Brown appeared to score off the crossbar, but the goal light didn't go on. The Rangers rushed down the ice and Mark Messier scored with fifty-eight seconds remaining. Quinn and the Canucks appealed, and the play was reviewed. Brown's goal counted. The Canucks were up 4–1. They had survived.

In the wild final minute of the game, Trevor Linden fought to keep the puck out of the Canucks' zone. He was knocked down and, while crawling to his bench, was hit again by Messier—"Linden has struggled to the bench," announced *Hockey Night in Canada* broad- caster Jim Robson. The fans at the Coliseum were delirious as time wound down. "There is going to be that seventh game. We'll hope they can patch Linden up and get him in that one. He will play. You know he'll play. He'll play on crutches. He will play— and he'll play at Madison Square Garden on Tuesday night."

Quinn had stood by with a Canucks team that many believed should be dismantled and rebuilt, and brought them to within a single game of winning the Stanley Cup.

That accomplishment would be enough to entrench his place as one of the most beloved figures in the history of the franchise. Now he had the chance to get what had eluded him years earlier in Philadelphia and what he'd never come close to touching as a player. It took sixteen wins to get there. Quinn had gotten to fourteen in 1980—and now he stood at fifteen. But the Stanley Cup is one of the hardest trophies to win in pro sports, with playoffs being a grinding test of endurance and will. And that last win was always the hardest.

But if Quinn was nervous about coaching in the most pressure-packed situation in the NHL, he didn't betray any fear. During a two-day break before game seven (which Quinn lamented because it cut into Vancouver's momentum), he took aim at his coaching counterpart, Mike Keenan. Iron Mike had complained that the refereeing was unfairly targeting the Rangers.

"He's a guy that's afraid right now," Quinn told reporters. "I guess he's going to the toolbox to try anything to give his team an advantage. All of us chip away at the referees. You moan and bark at them once in a while, but in this case, he's gone beyond normal credible stuff. It's been clear since game four he's trying to manipulate them.

"Keenan doesn't have his facts right," Quinn continued. "It's pure smoke." Leave it to Pat Quinn to call out Iron Mike.

It would be hard to argue that the 1994 Canucks lacked anything when it came to will. Each player bore the wounds of playoff hockey. Cliff Ronning was playing with a broken hand. The twenty-five-year-old captain, Trevor Linden, suited up for game seven with cracked ribs and torn cartilage. As his teammates dressed, Linden could be heard in a room down the hall screaming as a needle was injected into his rib cage. Linden was Quinn's guy—a captain who refused to quit, who never complained. He was the kind of old-school character who could inspire a team to victory.

So it was fitting that Quinn's guy—the boy he drafted and made captain at age twenty-one—willed the Canucks back into game seven after the Rangers took a 2–0 lead in the first period. Linden, like lightning, ripped toward the Rangers goal on a partial break with Brian Leech on his back and flipped the puck over a sprawling Mike Richter to put the Canucks within a goal in the second period. Back at the Colesium in Vancouver, a full house of rabid fans watching the game together whipped around white towels and roared.

The Rangers took back the two-goal lead on a goalmouth scramble tapped in by Mark Messier before the end of the second.

The Canucks sat quietly in the locker room before the third period, facing a two goal deficit and just twenty minutes left. They were a team of underdogs that was never supposed to be there—not this year, when everything had gone wrong before the playoffs. But here they were, underdogs together, a miracle away from the Cup. Dave Babych broke the silence, addressing what many were already thinking: This group would probably never play a full game together again. Contracts and moves would take them this way and that, but this was a team and this was a time that none of them would ever forget. So this was it, with no certainty that any would be this close to the Cup again. It was twenty minutes for everything with anything they had left to give.

Again it was Linden who gave them hope—scoring off a beautiful pass from Russ Courtnall on a powerplay five minutes into the third. Down a single goal, Vancouver had life. And they had plenty of chances. Mike Richter dove to stop a wide-open shot by Martin Gelinas that shook the earth in Vancouver. Later, with six minutes left, Nathan LaFayatte got behind the Rangers defense and took a pass from Courtnall. He fired the puck at the open net as Richter stretched across in desperation.

The puck clanked off the post. The Canucks were an inch away from tying it. The final minutes wound down too quickly, as dreams do when they are ending. Vancouver couldn't will itself to another goal.

Quinn's men had become close in the ways that most teams aren't—through their underdog status, the come-from-behind wins, constantly facing elimination, and always finding a way to stay alive. Broken and battered, they did it together as a family. And together they watched as Mark Messier and the New York Rangers charged toward Mike Richter to celebrate the team's first Stanley Cup in over half a century.

There would be time for reflection, time to consider just how great the accomplishment had been. After the long, dark—nearly silent—flight home that night, there would be a mob of fans waiting at the airport to greet them. They would be remembered, and adored.

But in the gutted aftermath of being so close and losing, there was only dejection. The Canucks sat in the locker room in near silence. No one on the team knew if they'd ever be this close to winning a Cup again. Murray Craven had been to the final three times, and never hoisted the prize. He fell to the ice and wept. Most on the Canucks roster that day would never get close again. Bret Hedican would be the only player to go on to win a Cup, which he did in 2006 with Carolina.

Quinn left the locker room and made his way to the press podium to say all the things coaches say at times like that. "Obviously, to be in a series like this and come so close without winning, it tears your guts out," he said and hinted that he wouldn't be back on the Canucks' bench the next season. Then, still wearing his lucky tie, Quinn walked down a hall beneath Madison Square Garden, as another team's celebration poured through the city.

There, he found his family waiting—Sandra, Valerie, and Kalli—who'd made the trip to New York hoping for a different kind of ending. The Mighty Quinn, to them just a big teddy bear, wrapped his arms around all three of his girls.

It was the second time Kalli Quinn saw her father cry.

21

The End of an Era

The phone rang in Pat Quinn's hotel room in Landover, Maryland. It was early in the morning on Tuesday, November 4, 1997. He wasn't expecting a call, and the voice on the other end surprised him. It was Stan McCammon, CEO of Orca Bay Sports & Entertainment, owner of the Vancouver Canucks ever since an overextended Griffiths family had been forced to take on partners the previous year.

McCammon was in the lobby. Quinn knew he was done.

Since taking his team to the Stanley Cup final in 1994, Quinn's grip on control of the Vancouver franchise had been slipping.

He had appointed assistant coach Rick Ley to head coach the following season, allowing himself more space and time to focus on his role as president and general manager. But that didn't prevent him from standing up for his players. In late March 1995, Don Cherry used his *Coach's Corner* pulpit to criticize Pavel Bure for a report that he had threatened to sit out game seven of the Stanley Cup final if the Canucks didn't get a new $6-million-a-year contract.

"What kind of a guy is that!" Cherry charged, while co-host Ron Maclean questioned how he knew the story was true. "It happened! It's all over...." Cherry continued, accusing Bure of blackmail. "The owner says sign him because they have a new building coming up and they need a superstar."

Bure had been in negotiations with the Canucks all season, but both sides adamantly denied that there was any truth to the report. Sergei Fedorov and Alexander Mogilny had both recently signed three-year deals for $3 million a season. Bure would sign a five-year deal for $5 million. The contract was agreed to before the playoffs began, but was executed before game three of the Cup final. Still, the rumor persisted and was reported to have started inside the Canucks' front office.

The story goes that Quinn stormed the *Hockey Night in Canada* set looking to use Cherry as a punching bag after he heard about the remarks. Instead, he settled for an on-air interview with Maclean to address Cherry's rant.

"It's been reported to me that comments were made about Pavel Bure—in fact, very disparaging comments," Quinn said calmly. "I know there's some prejudice in his game ... but he slandered this young man. This boy didn't threaten to walk out on this hockey team in the seventh game, the first game, or anything else last year. I don't know where that got started"— Quinn grew agitated as he spoke, his voice rising and his jaw clenched—"I know what point Don was trying to make, but—"

Maclean jumped in to clarify the accusations. Quinn was heating up.

"It's absolute untruth," he said, angry now. His massive hand was folded into a fist on the desk of the *Hockey Night* set where they sat.

"There was some confusion about it. And I have never heard an official declaration from you that that didn't happen," Maclean said.

"Well, it was made last year," Quinn snapped back, tilting his head down toward Maclean like a bull ready to charge.

"Okay …" Maclean said, backing down a touch.

"And [that] I have to make it again here half a year later is a bunch of crap," Quinn steamed.

In a later *Hockey Night* segment, Cherry defended his statement by saying he had done nothing but praise the Canucks: "But no one ever came up to me and said, 'Good job, Don.' But let me say one thing wrong, and I'm going to get punched in the head. If you're going to give it to me one way, give to me the other way," Cherry said. "No, I don't back down at all, and I don't blame him for being upset, because that's what Irishmen are. He's sticking up for his own player, and that's the way it should be."

The dustup quelled the rumors for a bit, but reports that Bure and Quinn didn't get along persisted for years afterward. Bure had once asked Quinn for a trade because he didn't like the scrutiny that he faced in Vancouver. Quinn told him it wasn't going to happen. Bure later said in an interview that he felt Quinn didn't want to sign him to his lucrative contract in '94. The false rumor of the blackmail incident was often cited as proof of a rift between Quinn and the Russian Rocket. Another television interview in which Quinn seemed to be critical of Bure for not defending an injured teammate was also recalled often.

It was all nonsense, according to Ron Salcer, Bure's agent at the time. While the blackmail rumor did start in the Canucks' front office, he says it had no effect on Bure and Quinn's long-term relationship.

"He really respected him. As a player you get a good sense of what a guy is about—in his soul, his heart," says Salcer. "Pat had a soft heart. He was very intimidating, but he was very compassionate. He really loved Pavel and the way he played."

As a GM, Quinn could be a tough negotiator, but he never played games or tried to downplay the talent a player had, says Salcer. In his negotiations over Bure's contract, Quinn was always reasonable. "He was a man of his word," Salcer says. "Everything with him was black and white."

The Canucks had struggled through the lockout-affected 1994–95 season. Under Ley, they won eighteen games, the same number they lost, and tied twelve. After finishing sixth in the Western Conference the team managed to get by the St. Louis Blues in seven games in the first round of the playoffs, but then got swept by the Chicago Blackhawks to close out the Pacific Coliseum era.

Quinn had been an important part of the development of the new GM Place in downtown Vancouver, first championing the need for a new arena, then adding his input and insight into the design of the rink. Entering the new arena in the 1995–96 season, Quinn made a bold move to bring more star power to the Canucks. He traded Mike Peca, Mike Wilson, and a draft pick to the Buffalo Sabres for Alexander Mogilny, hoping to pair him with his junior teammate Pavel Bure. (Bure, though, would miss most of the season with an anterior cruciate ligament injury.) The same day, Quinn traded Sergio Momesso, a tough guy with Stanley Cup experience, to Toronto for Mike Ridley, a skilled forward who was past his prime. The deal would turn into a bust for Vancouver.

But the Canucks new era came with some heavy baggage. Arthur Griffiths, at the helm of the company his father built, was taking on massive debts as he pushed to construct a new $100-million arena, GM Place (now Rogers Arena), with private financing. On top of that, the plummeting Canadian dollar and the decision to buy into the NBA expansion with the Vancouver Grizzlies weren't making matters any easier.

In order to truncate the losses, Arthur had brought in John McCaw Jr., a Seattle billionaire who made his cash in a cell phone service company, as a minority owner. With costs mounting, Griffiths was forced to give up more and more control of the franchise that had been considered the jewel of his family for two decades. By 1995, McCaw had the controlling interest in their company, Orca Bay Sports & Entertainment, which included both sports teams and the arena. McCaw's affairs with the team were mostly taken care of by CEO Stan McCammon. Griffiths was still involved, but had less and less sway.

Quinn had a heated relationship with the new ownership group from the start. As team president, he was deeply involved in the design and development of the Canucks' new home. But it was growing apparent that he might not be part of the team's future. Quinn's upstairs office at the new GM Place was across from Griffiths's, and one afternoon Arthur heard the unmistakable thunder of Quinn arguing with someone behind a closed door. The voices grew louder and louder, until there was a loud slam—and then a moment of silence. Stan McCammon quickly left Quinn's office. The Big Irishman and he had engaged in one of many disagreements about how the team should be run. Quinn ended this one by whacking his massive hand on his desk.

Griffiths stood in his doorway, somewhat stunned, until Quinn appeared with an enormous smile on his face. Neither said a word. They just started to laugh—Quinn, with a deep belly howl. Afterward, Quinn recounted the story to his deputies in the coaches' room. "I don't think I did myself any favors," Quinn said. "I threw him out of my office." "*That*'ll get you a lot of friends," chirped Mike Penny.

The perception among Quinn's men was that McCaw didn't have any actual interest in the Canucks—that he cared more about the Grizzlies side of the company. "He didn't give a shit about the team," says Penny. "He never came to any of the games." McCammon, who was known among them as McCaw's henchman, simply didn't have any feel for hockey, says Penny.

Quinn missed the freedom and trust he'd had under the Griffiths family. That was never going to happen under Orca Bay, which looked to exercise control in player acquisitions and contract negotiations.

Despite Mogilny's 107 points, the Canucks struggled through the rest of the 1995–96 season.

Quinn was criticized in the press for being loyal to a fault, sticking with the players on his roster and keeping his friend behind the bench when it was clear the situation wasn't working. Orca Bay management made clear at the beginning of the season that Ley needed to go, but Quinn refused. "That's my call," he said defiantly. He took a stand on principle, but Quinn knew it was hopeless. He may have been president and general manager, but the Canucks were in someone else's hands now.

Rick Ley remembers that the rumors began in the press on November 2, his birthday. "It was on TSN," he recalls. But the axe didn't fall until nearly five months later, when there were just six games left in the season. In the gap between the rumors and the actual firing, Ley knew that Quinn was fighting with ownership to save his job.

On the NHL trade deadline, Quinn traded Alek Stojanov to Pittsburgh for Markus Naslund, in what still stands as one of the ugliest muggings in NHL history. But the haul wasn't enough to satisfy the concerns of the Canucks' new owners. With the team once again fighting to keep a playoff spot, the Orca Bay ownership made clear to Quinn that he was to fire Ley.

On March 28, the fight was over. Quinn walked into Ley's office at the Canucks' practice rink, a day after losing 6–2 to Toronto. Quinn looked like he hadn't slept. "I knew as soon as I saw him," Ley says. "You don't have to say anything," Ley told Quinn. "I know. You don't have to say a word." Ley left Quinn in his office, walked down the hall to the Canucks' training room, and grabbed two disposable cups and a bottle of fifteen-year-old Lagavulin he had in a drawer. He poured them both a drink. "I'll have both of my offices cleaned out by the end of the day," Ley said.

Two days later, Quinn was back on the Canucks' bench as they took on the Chicago Blackhawks. After the game, he called

Ley and told him he'd arranged for a two-year pro scouting contract for him with the Canucks, based in Hartford, where he'd
spent several years as both a player and coach. Ley took the job.

Quinn finished the season on the bench, but the Canucks
were wiped out of the playoffs in six games by the Colorado
Avalanche.

The example most commonly cited of Quinn's frustration with
Vancouver's new ownership group is the botched signing of
Wayne Gretzky in the summer of 1996.

When Gretzky became available, Quinn made contact with
his agent Mike Barnett, who also represented Alex Mogilny.
Quinn was about to go on vacation in the Far East but offered to
cancel it to get the deal done. Barnett and Gretzky told him not
to worry. But while on the trip, Quinn said he received constant
calls from Stan McCammon, asking him how the negotiations
with Gretzky were going. Then Quinn got a call from Arthur
Griffiths, asking him to come back because John McCaw and
McCammon didn't think he was really interested in getting
Gretzky signed. Quinn cut his vacation short and flew back in
time for a meeting that had been arranged in Seattle.

Was the Great One *really* about to become a member of the
Vancouver Canucks? "Yup," says Wayne Gretzky. "One hundred
percent."

As Gretzky recalls it, he flew to Seattle with his agent
Barnett to meet with the Canucks to negotiate a possible contract
with Vancouver. John McCaw, Stan McCammon, George
McPhee, and Quinn met with Gretzky and his group at their
hotel in the late afternoon. At this point, Gretzky was very

interested in coming to Vancouver. Several teams had shown interest in signing him, but the Canucks were the first team Gretzky spoke to as a free agent. His wife, Janet, was researching possible schools for their kids to attend in Vancouver.

While Barnett negotiated a potential deal, Quinn and Gretzky spent several hours together, chatting about hockey and the direction of the franchise. Negotiations dragged on late into the evening, but Quinn was certain he had convinced the greatest player in the game to join the Canucks. Between the two of them, the deal was pretty much done.

At around 10:00 P.M., Gretzky says, McCaw asked if he wanted to go to grab dinner, while the others continued the negotiation. (The two were friends then, and still are, Gretzky says.) At the time, it looked like the deal was pretty much done and the fine details were all that remained. But when the others broke for dinner, Quinn said, McCammon said he was worried that Gretzky's camp was going to use their offer to get a better one from another team. They already knew that the New York Rangers had interest too.

Around midnight, Quinn was comfortable that a deal was in place and that Gretzky would sign a contract in the morning. It was going to be in the ballpark of a $6-million-a-year contract for five years, Quinn later said.

But when everyone else left, Stan McCammon stayed behind with Barnett to discuss the bonuses that would be included in the contract. At around 1:00 A.M., Barnett told McCammon that he felt they were very close to a deal that Gretzky would agree to and that he'd present it to him first thing in the morning. McCammon told Barnett that the Canucks needed to know that night, or the offer was off the table.

Barnett objected to waking Gretzky up, he says, but McCammon insisted that there was too much at stake to wait until the morning. It was that night or nothing. So Barnett went to Gretzky's hotel room, knocked on the door, and woke him up. Gretzky told Barnett that he wouldn't make a decision without speaking with his wife first, and he wasn't going to call her in the middle of the night. He asked if they could just wait until morning.

"Apparently not," Barnett said. He called McCammon and told him that Gretzky wouldn't make the deal that night. McCammon stuck by his position. The next morning, Barnett says, the Canucks rescinded their offer.

Quinn was furious, believing that ownership had blown a deal that would have been done had they just waited. Gretzky says he was "100 percent" prepared to become a member of the Vancouver Canucks, but has never brought the incident up with anyone from the Canucks organization, even McCaw. He signed with the New York Rangers instead, and scored ninety-seven points in the 1996–97 season. "Everything seemed to be copacetic. I honestly don't know how it fell apart," says Gretzky. "Sometimes that's how it happens in business. It's one of those things that fell through the cracks."

That fall, Arthur Griffiths would sell his remaining shares in Orca Bay and McCaw would acquire full ownership of the company. The Canucks struggled through the 1996–97 season under new coach Tom Renney, who had been a standout junior coach with the Kamloops Blazers but had no NHL experience. Vancouver finished ninth in the Western Conference and missed the playoffs.

Having missed out on Gretzky a year before, Orca Bay made a strong play for high-profile free agent Mark Messier in the summer of 1997. At thirty-six, Messier was long past his prime, but certainly carried cachet as one of the biggest names in the game since his days with the Oilers' 1980s dynasty. Quinn didn't think it was an investment the Canucks should pursue. Regardless, that July, Quinn dutifully flew to Hilton Head Island in South Carolina with Canucks executive John Chapple (who he got along with) to meet with Mark Messier and his father and agent, Doug Messier. They met with the Messiers at a local pub and bonded, talking about golf, fishing, and hockey. The next day, they spoke about a potential deal and the numbers it would take to get it done. After Quinn flew home, Chapple convinced the Messiers to fly to San Francisco to spend some time with McCaw on his yacht.

Quinn wasn't aware this was happening. He called McCaw. "Who's doing this deal?" Quinn asked. "I want to know who's doing this contract."

"That's what I want to know," McCaw replied, as Quinn would later recall. "Who's doing this contract?"

"It better be me," Quinn said.

It wasn't.

The deal was struck that afternoon. McCaw offered Messier $5 million a season for three years, plus an additional $1 million a season for team promotions and marketing. The deal also included bonuses that pushed the deal's value to close to $20 million. Messier flew from San Francisco to Vancouver for a press conference announcing the deal. Quinn was asked if he felt the Canucks had overpaid for the thirty-six-year-old. "That's a difficult question to answer," he replied diplomatically. "But we believe he's the player we need."

Truthfully, Quinn felt McCaw had gone around him to get the deal done—and committed to too many years and too much money in the contract. "I knew then that it was only going to be a matter of time, because the ownership can't operate that way," Quinn later said. "They might as well not have a manager if that's the way it works."

Quinn's gut was right.

A month into the 1997–98 season, the Canucks had just three wins in fifteen games. During an east coast road trip that saw Vancouver lose to Chicago, Pittsburgh, and New Jersey before taking on Carolina, it was clear something needed to happen to save face in Vancouver. At that point the Canucks had dropped six consecutive games.

Before they played Carolina, Quinn asked Mike Penny what he thought he should do to shake up his listless team. "Can him," Penny said, referring to coach Tom Renney. "Right after the game. Take over." Quinn wasn't sure if he was ready to pull the trigger so early in the season. "Let me think about it," he said.

The Canucks lost 5–3 that night, and Quinn knew he had to make the change. Still at the rink in Carolina, Penny asked Quinn what he was going to do.

"We're going to go to Washington," Quinn said, referring to the next game against the Capitals on the Canucks' road trip. "I'll do it in the morning. You and I will have breakfast at 7:00 A.M. I'll call him to my room, I'll do it in the morning, and I'll take over the team."

"You've got a window, right here, right now," Penny said.

"Tomorrow," Quinn replied.

That night, Quinn called John McCaw and said he planned to fire Renney the next morning.

It was sometime after 6:00 A.M.—he wouldn't remember exactly—when the phone rang in Quinn's room. Stan McCammon was in the lobby and wanted to come up to speak to him.

Mike Penny's phone rang at 6:45 A.M., just before he was supposed to meet Quinn for breakfast. Penny answered.

"Mike," Quinn said. "I just got fired."

The news of Quinn's firing quickly spread across the old Iceplex arena before the Canucks' pregame skate that morning. The players were cramped together in the rink's dingy visitors' room when McCammon came in and delivered the news. "That took a piece of my heart away," says Linden, who had given up his captaincy to Messier. "Deep down I think I knew that was going to be a kind of end for me as well." (The feeling was prescient. Linden was traded to the New York Islanders a few months later.)

One of the Canucks' trainers, Pat O'Neill, came out of the locker room and told the reporters, who huddled around and then rushed to get the news out. Tom Larscheid, who was still broadcasting for the Canucks, wanted to get back to the hotel as quickly as possible to try to interview Quinn before he left. Ironically, he shared a ride back to the hotel with McCammon. "How did Pat take this?" Larscheid asked. McCammon thought for a moment. "Stoic," he said. "He was very stoic."

At the hotel, Larscheid rushed into the lobby and had reception call up to Quinn's room. Quinn told him to come up. Larscheid walked into Quinn's luxury suite lugging a massive tape recorder. It was a fitting bookend—that the reporter who broke the news of Quinn's coming to Vancouver would conduct his first exit interview.

Before the tape went on, Quinn confided in Larscheid, a journalist with whom he'd always had a good relationship, that he felt McCammon had always been out to get him.

Partway through the interview, tape rolling now, there was a knock on the door. Quinn got up to answer, and Pavel Bure and Gino Odjick walked in. "They had the saddest look on their faces," says Larscheid. Both men hugged Quinn and told him how upset everyone was at the news of his firing. When they left, Quinn sat back down and tears filled his eyes. "That's why I love this business, Tommy," he said. "That's why I love this business."

After the interview, as Larscheid ran off to cut his clips and file his interview, Quinn packed up his bags to head home. He walked out of the lobby, wearing his game-day suit, carrying a large garment bag over his shoulder. Quinn was fifty-four years old now—his hair mostly salt with shades of pepper. He carried more heft on his frame than he ever had, and he struggled with constant pain in his hip. It was difficult to get around. A decade had passed since he'd first been given the daunting task of bringing Vancouverites a hockey team they could be proud of. Whatever your thoughts on his coaching or management, there was no taking away the fact that he had accomplished what he set out to do—the seats were full, the team wasn't going anywhere. He had saved the Canucks and nearly won a Cup doing it. No owners or boardroom managers could take that away from him.

But these weren't laurels the Big Irishman was inclined to rest on. Quinn's massive hands still lacked a certain ring.

Quinn was one of the best-paid coaches in the game, and wouldn't find himself in the unemployment line for long. He'd be fine. But when Larscheid looked out his window as Quinn tossed his bag into the back of an old station wagon taxi with smashed-up fenders, he realized—as Linden had—that an era was ending for hockey in Vancouver.

Quinn angled his massive frame into the back of the station wagon and closed the door. The cab pulled onto the street and drove away.

Pat Quinn was gone.

22

Back to Where It Began

ired from the Canucks, Quinn briefly considered just
moving on from the game—as he had two decades earlier
when he'd contemplated life as a car salesman, and later when
he decided to move into law. He wasn't angry, he said. He was
disappointed at the outcome. "I've had enough of this," Quinn
thought. "I'll try to find something else."

With a year left on his contract, he still collected his healthy
salary of a reported $1.2 million (though an early lump-sum
buyout at a discount rate was eventually agreed on). Even with
that cushion, he didn't take an extended vacation. Quinn was a
member of the management group for the Canadian team that
won gold at the World Championships in Finland in 1997, and a
couple of months after being fired by the Canucks, he signed
on to be the general manager of the Canadian team for the
1998 tournament in Switzerland. He was in his mid-fifties now,
and his large frame was showing the lasting effects of long-gone
battles. While piecing together the national team, Quinn had

hip-replacement surgery to take care of a painful injury that had bothered him for years.

Team Canada floundered at the World Championships that May, finishing sixth. That result came shortly after Canada's flameout at the 1998 Winter Olympics in Nagano, where the team lost to Finland in the bronze medal game—and unleashed nationwide panic about Canada's supremacy in the sport.

The game was never the end for Quinn. There was always another venture to consider. So when the possibility of taking over as the Maple Leafs' head coach was first floated in front of him in the spring of 1998, Quinn initially had little interest. Toronto was coming off of two straight seasons without an appearance in the playoffs. Quinn's good friend Mike Murphy—his assistant coach in Los Angeles and Vancouver—had struggled as the Leafs' head coach. Ken Dryden, the team president and general manager, was openly shopping for a replacement while Murphy still had a year remaining on his contract. (Murphy *could* be back, the press was told—an embarrassing ordeal for Murphy to endure publicly.)

Quinn also received a call from the Chicago Blackhawks, but wasn't interested in that position either.

But while he was in Toronto to attend the wedding of Cliff Fletcher's daughter, the Leafs convinced him to meet with assistant general manager Mike Smith. The meeting sparked some intrigue.

There is one job for a coach to take in the NHL that, if ultimately successful, would forever carve their name in hockey lore: Win a Stanley Cup with the Tampa Bay Lightning? *Great!* Guide the Toronto Maple Leafs to victory? *Bedlam.*

There was no position more challenging, more demanding, or more appealing to Quinn than becoming the bench boss of the Leafs. The timing of his firing from Vancouver was perfect, really. As much as he loved the franchise and the city—and he did, and always would—the situation with Orca Bay had become untenable for Quinn. He needed to have control. He needed to be free to make decisions and know they wouldn't be undermined.

Quinn had no interest in the superboss position he had held with the Canucks. He already had enough gray hairs—he didn't need the stress of working on the management side of an organization like the Leafs. But he still loved to coach. He *wanted* to coach. It was the closest to the action a person could get without actually being on the ice. The idea of being with a team every day, being part of that kind of larger family, moving together in a common pursuit—Quinn was intrigued. The game was calling him back.

The phone rang at around 10:00 P.M. one night later that June at Dick Babush's house in Georgia. The man who had negotiated all of Quinn's previous contracts was known for retiring early of an evening, and his wife now had to drag him out of bed. "You've got a call from Toronto," she said. "They said they need to talk to you right away."

It was Ken Dryden, then the president and general manager of the Maple Leafs. He wanted to get Pat Quinn to Toronto, and he wanted the deal done soon—Dryden was under pressure to make a change. Babush flew in from Atlanta the next day to meet Quinn, who made the trip from Vancouver and participated in the negotiations that could make him Toronto's next coach.

It was a grueling process. Both sides went back and forth for two days. The sticking points were money and power.

Quinn insisted that there not be any interference from management about what players to use and when. Quinn had faced that with Ed Snider in Philadelphia, and had a similar experience in Los Angeles, Babush says. And his recent experience in Vancouver remained a sore point. If management or ownership started going around him, Quinn felt he wouldn't be able to do his job. Dryden bristled at some of Quinn's stringent provisions regarding his control, Babush says.

At the end of the long debate, the chain of command within the organization was clearly defined. As coach, Quinn would answer directly to assistant general manager Mike Smith, who would consult with Dryden on final decisions. But Quinn would have complete authority over how he used his players, and autonomy in selecting his own coaching staff. Decisions regarding player trades, recruitment, and drafting belonged to management, but Quinn would be consulted on all decisions.

The other matter was money. Quinn had been very well compensated throughout his coaching career, and expected no different in Toronto.

"I negotiated the highest-paid coaching contract in the history of the NHL when he got it. It was with the Maple Leafs," says Babush. "It was over seven figures.... There was a point when he was the highest-paid coach, when you count all the incentives."

Those incentives—bonus for a certain number of points, how far into the playoffs the team went, and other measures—took a long time to hammer out, Babush says. Exhausted, both sides agreed on a deal at 2:00 A.M. after two days of negotiations.

Quinn lit a cigar as he sat at the podium next to Ken Dryden, being announced as the Leafs' new head coach the next day. When it was official, one of Quinn's first moves was to pick up the phone and dial Rick Ley. Ley was in talks about a coaching role with the St. Louis Blues at the time, but Quinn quickly put that option out of his mind. "I'd like you to come to Toronto with me," Quinn said. A few days later, Ley's contract was signed.

Pat and Sandra kept their place in Vancouver—a city that now felt like home, and to which they always intended to return. Looking back at a long list of short-lived Leafs coaches, they decided to rent in Toronto instead of buy. The Quinns leased a massive penthouse suite at 33 University Avenue, just a few blocks up from where the finishing touches were being put on the brand-new Air Canada Centre. Rick and Ellen Ley moved into a smaller condo in the same building, several floors down.

Over the summer, Quinn consulted with Mike Murphy about the team he was taking over. Pat and Sandra went over to the Murphy house for dinner and spent the evening talking about the difficulties Mike had faced with the team and his concerns with the lineup. The Leafs had struggled on offense, with the only real first-class production coming from captain Mats Sundin, who scored thirty-three goals and had seventy-four points the season before Quinn arrived. Quinn laid out a plan to try to turn Toronto into a winning team with the pieces he had. He planned to develop a reliable second line, and to pull some secondary scoring out of Darby Hendrickson and Alyn McCauley. He sought to fix the Leafs' impotent power play—and built a plan around the team's speed (which, aside from diminutive winger Steve Sullivan, many argued was limited), while ditching its trap-focused defensive system.

Now in the role he'd first watched Punch Imlach hold thirty years earlier, Quinn sought to reach back into the franchise's storied history—creating an open policy for Leafs alumni to come down to the locker room and be part of the team anytime they wanted.

The Leafs would close down the historic Maple Leaf Gardens. The rich history encased in the white-domed, gold-bricked cathedral on Carlton was important to Quinn. In a way his former teammates weren't quite able to be, he was back under the glow of the Gardens' lights—a bigger star now, as a coach, than he'd ever been as a player.

Quinn was no longer the young dark-haired Irishman who had diligently watched Fred Shero and Keith Allen run the Flyers. Quinn was the veteran now—two decades on from deciding whether he wanted to be a coach or a car salesman. At fifty-five, he would be the third-oldest coach in the NHL, behind Scotty Bowman and Roger Neilson, both sixty-four. And now, he was a grandpa—his daughter Valerie had given birth to her first child, Quinn, in 1994.

He was also one of the most famous faces in the NHL. With his size and distinctive appearance—always in a suit, always with polished shoes (the Jack Quinn way), and always dangling a cigar from his lips—Pat Quinn was noticed everywhere he went. He couldn't walk down a street in Toronto without being recognized. And each time he was, he'd stop to chat or sign an autograph. Quinn was almost unfailing in that regard. He never seemed annoyed or put out by a fan's request.

If they wanted a photo, no problem. If they wanted to chat, he'd love to.

The press, of course, was another matter entirely. Quinn felt he'd been unfairly treated by some of Vancouver's ink-stained wretches. He tended to make up his mind about reporters quickly, to decide on the ones he liked and the ones he didn't.

But any question a reporter had about the game—any desire to talk strategy, and to learn more about specific systems— Quinn was happy to entertain. He'd talk on and on, if the questions were good and genuine. But if Quinn detected bait, *good luck.*

In Quinn's first season on the bench, the Maple Leafs moved from the Western Conference to the Eastern Conference. It marked the arrival of goalie Curtis Joseph, who came to the team while Felix Potvin was still playing very well for the Leafs. During the season, Potvin would be traded to the New York Islanders for defenseman Bryan Berard, who had won the Calder Trophy as the league's top rookie just a few years earlier. Meanwhile, Joseph posted a 2.56 goals against and a 0.910 save percentage, and quickly became a fan favorite with his acrobatic, highlight-reel saves.

The Leafs engineered a remarkable turnaround that season. Toronto led the league in goals scored, with 268—an almost unbelievable feat, considering they were the third-worst offensive team the season before, with just 194 goals. Mats Sundin led the team with thirty-one goals and eighty-three points, followed by Steve Thomas and Sergei Berezin.

And while the Leafs came equipped with talent, Quinn also reached into the list of players who had earned his loyalty over the years. Before the season started, he called veteran Garry Valk and offered him a tryout with the team. At thirty-one, Valk was in career limbo. He had a deal waiting for him in the Swiss league, and he was prepared to make the move from the NHL to finish out his career in Europe. Valk had always been Quinn's kind of player—not necessarily a guy who scored goals, but a guy who understood his role and was willing to play the part. He asked Valk to come to training camp to try out for a spot. "That's just typical Pat," says Valk. "His first year in Toronto—what does he do? He makes a spot open."

Valk took the red-eye in from Vancouver to the Leafs' training camp being held at Copps Coliseum in Hamilton. A few days earlier, he had been playing in a beer league, prepared to leave the NHL world behind him. Now, he was playing an exhibition game with the Leafs against the Oilers in front of seventeen thousand fans. Quinn told Valk he'd made the team after a training camp practice at Maple Leaf Gardens. "Go find yourself a place," Quinn said. Valk had been staying at the Delta hotel nearby. "I was shocked," says Valk. "Thinking your career is over and the next thing you know, you're still playing. I played another five years after that."

In Quinn's system, Valk became a key part of the Leafs' success, adding some grit on the fourth line while also being used regularly with Sergei Berezin and Igor Korolev on the third line.

Todd Warriner, a fringe player on the Leafs' roster, regularly found himself in the press box as a healthy scratch. Trying to find his way back into the roster, Warriner nervously went into Quinn's office and asked his coach what he needed to do to get back on the ice. Quinn respected that. They sat in his office and talked about the team and about the game for a while. Quinn's door was always open to anyone who wanted to talk puck.

As the season went on, Warriner continued to try to earn a regular spot on the roster. He worked at points Quinn had mentioned to him. As Warriner was skating around before practice, Quinn would come up and say, "Hey, I like what you're doing down the middle," and would point out a few small things he could do better. Quinn was like that with most of the players in the lineup, Warriner says. He didn't yell often. And if he did, during a game, it was never at a specific player.

The Leafs connected as a team that season. They were a close group off the ice, hanging out regularly, and the connection translated to results. Toronto finished with ninety-seven points, and sat third in the Eastern Conference. The Leafs knocked off the Philadelphia Flyers and Pittsburgh Penguins in the first and second rounds of the playoffs, but fell in five games to the Buffalo Sabres in the Conference finals.

Despite the disappointment of falling just short of the team's first berth in the Stanley Cup finals since before he had even laced up his skates for the team, Quinn had Toronto fans believing that it wouldn't be long before there was another parade down Yonge Street. For his efforts, Quinn was again named a finalist for the Jack Adams Award.

He was back in the business of selling hope.

After the season, Ken Dryden announced that he was searching for someone to take over his own position as general manager and decided not to renew the contract of associate general manager, Mike Smith.

The search didn't last long. That July, freshly tanned after a yachting trip off the coast of France, Quinn accepted the vacant general manager position. Though he had insisted after being fired in Vancouver that he only wanted to coach, Quinn said he couldn't pass up the opportunity to run the Leafs. At the time the "superboss" position that he held with Vancouver was going extinct. A day earlier, Jacques Demers had been fired as coach and GM of the Tampa Bay Lightning. So the additional duties made Quinn the only coach/GM in the league. But Quinn was confident that he could still handle the job.

"In Vancouver, I spent so much time on the presidential duties and the business side of things that it took away from my duties towards the hockey operation," he said. "I'll be much more effective wearing just the two hats this time around ... I know the job can be done because I've done it."

After his success that season, Valk worked up the courage to walk into Quinn's smoke-clouded office at the Air Canada Centre and ask for an extension on his one-year deal. (Quinn's office was cloudy despite the $50,000 air-ventilation system MLSE executive Tom Anselmi had built into it when he learned Quinn was coming to Toronto. Anselmi had worked with him in Vancouver and knew the new ACC needed to be Quinn-ready.) Valk had scored the goal that pushed Toronto into the Conference final. "It doesn't get any better for me. He must be pretty happy with me right now," Valk decided. "I'm going to go in and talk contract with him." Valk opened up his pitch, the coach chuckled. "You know what, Valk?" Quinn said. "The only reason you were on the fourth line a lot this year is because I didn't have a fifth." (Valk eventually re-signed on a three-year deal.)

As coach, Quinn surrounded himself with people he trusted. After hiring Ley that first season in Toronto, Quinn gradually added more people he knew he could trust. As a boss, he was known to stay committed to the people he brought in—from his equipment managers to his assistant coaches. Sometimes he was criticized for being too loyal, allowing his fondness for some to cloud his judgment about the positions he put them in.

Reid Mitchell, who had been a young member of the Canucks public relations staff in the early 1990s and was steadily promoted through the ranks, knew the path to Quinn's heart. At Christmastime during his first season with the Canucks, Mitchell pulled Quinn's name for the staff's Secret Santa. There was a twenty-dollar limit. "What the hell can I get for twenty dollars that can impress Pat Quinn?" he thought. So he walked into a Vancouver cigar shop and told the owner: "I've got Pat Quinn in a Secret Santa. I'm supposed to spend twenty dollars, but I'll up it to thirty, I don't care," Mitchell said. The owner took pity on the young Canucks staffer and offered to set him up with a gift if he'd include the store's card and make sure Quinn knew where it came from. They gave Mitchell a cigar that he swears must have been a foot-and-half long. He put the twenty dollars back in his pocket. Quinn unwrapped the gift a few days later. "Son," he said, "you've gone over the limit, I think." Mitchell had a place in Quinn's good books from then on.

In August 1999, Quinn called up Mitchell in Vancouver, where he still worked for the Canucks. "What do you know about video?" Quinn asked him. "I can change the flashing clock on the VCR," Mitchell said. "Good enough," Quinn replied. "You're our new video coach." Mitchell took the gig and moved his family east.

Just as he had back when he started with the Flyers, Quinn was always looking for ways to find small advantages for his team. As video coordinator, Mitchell sat down with the coaching staff daily to analyze both the Leafs and their upcoming opponents. If Toronto had a game against Tampa Bay, Mitchell would take tapes of the last five games the Lightning played and break them down into clips, showing Quinn and the other coaches how their opponent executed on its breakouts, on power plays, in shorthanded situations, and on the forecheck. "It's a misnomer that people think he wasn't into the X's and O's of the game." Mitchell says. "He was." Under Quinn's orders, Mitchell taped all of the games happening in the NHL every day, on televisions in his office, creating a massive library of content to sort through.

During the Leafs' games, Mitchell sat in the locker room logging clips as they happened. During intermissions, Quinn wanted to watch all of the other team's scoring chances over again. Mitchell had them cued up when coaches walked into the office during the fifteen-minute break, but he wasn't allowed to push play until Quinn and Ley had their cigars lit. "The smoke would be wafting through the coaches' room," says Mitchell. "My clothes would smell every night." Sometimes there were only a few mistakes to show Quinn; other times, there were more than a dozen. "Two dozen if we were horrible," says Mitchell. After watching every mistake Mitchell had pulled from the video, Quinn would put out his cigar and go to the locker room to address the team. This was always his routine.

Routine was important, and Quinn was famous for his superstitions. He chewed long sticks of Juicy Fruit or Doublemint gum during every game, and kept sticks of it arranged neatly on his desk. If the sticks lay askew by the slightest angle, Quinn would know. Several people in the Leafs' organization incurred Quinn's wrath by accidentally messing with his gum. Assistant general manager Bill Watters popped a stick in his mouth one game. "What the hell?" Quinn said. "What are you chewing?" Watters swallowed the gum immediately. During a game against the Rangers at Madison Square Garden, Pat Park, the Leafs' media relations director, watched the final few minutes of the period in the visitors' coaches' room, and absentmindedly took a piece of the forbidden Juicy Fruit. The Leafs lost the game in overtime. When Park went into Quinn's office to bring him to the postgame media scrum, the coach stopped him. "You know why we lost, don't ya?" Quinn said, angrily. "Sorry, what's that?" Park replied. "You took my gum," Quinn said. Somehow, Quinn had found out that Park was responsible for the single piece of gum missing from the table he was using as a desk. He was serious, says Park. Very serious. Quinn apologized to Park the next day. But he didn't laugh about it. "It was short and sweet."

The Leafs finished first in the Northeast Division in the 1999–2000 season, with one hundred points. Mats Sundin led the team in scoring again, with thirty-two goals and seventy-three points. Steve Thomas was second on the team with sixty-three points. Tie Domi led the team in penalty minutes while Curtis Joseph was great in goal, with a 2.49 goals against average and thirty-six wins, a team record. The season also marked the return of fan favorite Wendel Clark, who had been released from the Chicago Blackhawks. The Leafs picked up the beloved thirty-three-year-old former captain off waivers.

Partway through the season, Todd Warriner was in the Platinum Lounge at the Air Canada Centre on the morning of a game, when Pat Park came and told him Quinn wanted to speak with him. Warriner walked into Quinn's office, unaware that he was about to get traded. Quinn told him, "Listen, I had this on my desk for almost a year. Cliff Fletcher has been trying to get you in Tampa since last Christmas." The Leafs had just picked up forward Dmitri Khristich, Quinn said. "I'm not sure how much I'm going to be able to play you, so I traded you to Tampa. I appreciate the way you played last year in the spring— you played really good for us." Quinn stood up and shook Warriner's hand. "Good luck," he said. And that was it. Warriner wasn't happy to be on his way out of Toronto, but the way Quinn had handled the situation left him with a lot of respect for the coach—and the GM. It was matter of fact, Warriner says, but it was honest. "That's who he was," says Warriner. Quinn treated him like a person, not just a name taking up a roster spot. "I liked it."

The Leafs knocked out the Ottawa Senators in the first round of the playoffs—the start of several heated battles with their rivals in the capital. In the second round, Toronto was beaten by a New Jersey Devils team that included heavy-hitter Scott Stevens and agitator Claude Lemieux. The Devils' stifling defense deflated the Leafs, who managed just six shots on Martin Brodeur in game six, as New Jersey eliminated Toronto. The Devils went on to win the Stanley Cup.

Although it marked another year without putting his name on the Cup, the turn of the millennium presented a new opportunity for Quinn to put his name into the hockey history books. Through his experience with the World Hockey championships, Quinn had become good friends with Bob Nicholson, the president of Hockey Canada. It was a relationship that would ultimately give Quinn the biggest challenge of his career. The pressure that came with coaching the Toronto Maple Leafs was small compared to the expectation and scrutiny that came with leading a team that would represent the entire nation.

After Canada's embarrassing defeat at the Olympics in Nagano in 1998, Hockey Canada looked to Salt Lake City in 2002. Nicholson knew they would have the players, but needed a coach who could take them to gold. At the recommendation of Bobby Clarke, he reached out to the recently retired Wayne Gretzky and asked if he would serve as Canada's general manager. Gretzky accepted, knowing how much pressure the job carried. Nothing but gold in Salt Lake would be accepted by Canadian hockey fans.

His first task was to find a coach who could handle that kind of pressure. During a round of golf at Sherwood Golf Club, just outside Los Angeles, with Bob Nicholson and Russ Courtnall (who played for the Canucks from late in the 1994 season through 1997), Gretzky listed off the coaches he was considering for the Team Canada job and asked Courtnall what he thought. "Are you kidding me?" Nicholson remembers Courtnall saying. "There is only one head coach, and that's Pat Quinn." "You're sure you're not just biased here?" Gretzky said. "We need to win or our heads are going to be on a platter—and I'll throw your head on with us." Nicholson laughed, because he had Quinn at the top of his list too. After the round of golf, Nicholson flew back to Hockey Canada headquarters in Calgary, and when the plane landed he had a message on his phone from Gretzky.

Gretzky had made up his mind. There were two people he definitely wanted involved in Team Canada: Kevin Lowe, his former teammate, whom he knew he could work with. "And there's no question," Gretzky said. "We want Pat Quinn to be the head coach."

23

Glitter and Gold

He sat in the same spot every night, puffing his cigar in the February chill. A year from sixty, hair full white, Pat Quinn faced the most daunting task he'd experienced in a quarter-century of coaching. It had been fifty years since Canada had won the Olympic gold medal in the sport the nation claimed as its own. Quinn had been just a kid skating at Mahoney when the Edmonton Mercurys brought home gold from the 1952 Olympics in Oslo, Norway. He had barely noticed it then, when the tournament was played by amateurs. But every day leading to Salt Lake, Quinn was reminded of the great gap between the last gold and now. Canada's claim to hockey supremacy had been severely damaged by the 1998 Olympics in Nagano, where the nation's best finished fourth. Salt Lake was about righting that wrong. Nothing but gold would atone for what wasn't won four years before.

Every night, Quinn sat on that bench in front of the Canadian Olympic team quarters, puffing clouds of smoke into the dark sky as the nation's finest athletes stopped to confide in him their fears and anxieties. His evening chats with the athletes who passed by became so common that volunteers put a "Pat's bench" sign over the spot where Quinn always sat. He'd ask them questions about their lives, and share stories of his own. Mostly, though, he'd listen. Quinn had great respect for the young athletes representing their country, who battled to achieve their dreams with little financial reward, if any. The Big Irishman was a figurehead for the entire country at the Olympics. Heroes like Wayne Gretzky were certainly an inspiration, but Quinn was something different—he was a force of stability and confidence. He reflected a Canadian ideal: not necessarily the most talented, but nevertheless unrelenting in the pursuit of greatness.

While he could be hard on his own players, Quinn didn't have the expert knowledge of the sports the other athletes played. And so he just listened and learned, offering some of the philosophical and physiological advice he'd gathered through a lifetime in sport. He sat with snowboarder Jasey-Jay Anderson—who knew nothing about hockey and didn't follow the NHL. When freestyle skier Steve Omischl sat next to him, they spoke for more than an hour. The twenty-three-year-old had just crashed in the first round of his event and placed eleventh. He was devastated. While his own coaches only wanted to talk about what had gone wrong, Quinn just told him that all the hype and stress were just distractions. He told Omischl not to worry about the media, not to worry about his coaches—not to worry about the expectations that come with a nation expecting success. "Don't worry about what other people think," Quinn told him. "Just do what you need to do to get the job done."

The sparkles on Quinn's socks were evidence that he'd taken his own advice. Quinn had been chosen by the greatest hockey player in the game's history to lead a team stacked with some of the best players of a generation—Mario Lemieux, Joe Sakic, Rob Blake, Martin Brodeur—into a tournament where a single game could forever put an asterisk of failure next to your legacy in the game. If Team Canada failed to win gold—even if it won something less, even silver—the disastrous outcome would be pinned on Quinn. "How could Quinn lose with a lineup like this?" the radio hosts and columnists would bray. Others would certainly feel the wrath, but as head coach, every move Quinn made would be dragged out and judged, endlessly. Quinn was the captain of this ship. He knew it. But he wasn't bothered by it.

Quinn was used to the outsized overreactions of both Toronto and Vancouver, among fans and in the press. And he knew *this* was an incalculable exponential of that. Despite that, sparkles fell from Quinn's slacks as he walked. They were affixed to his lucky socks and briefs—a gift from his grandkids, decorated with love and glitter glue. Along with his six-year-old grandson, Quinn, he now had two granddaughters—four-year-old Kate and Kylie, who was just six months old. While some knew about the lucky socks that Quinn wore for every game he coached at the Olympics, only a few would learn of the shimmering tighty-whities beneath his suit.

From the moment the names of Team Canada's executive group were announced, their every move was analyzed by the nation. Quinn's coaching staff included associate coach Wayne Fleming and management assistant Kevin Lowe—who had been named on the same day as Quinn, on November 8, 2000. Ken Hitchcock and Jacques Martin were later added to the coaching staff. The early stages were easy. The executive group announced the first eight members of Team Canada in March 2001: Mario Lemieux, Rob Blake, Scott Niedermayer, Paul Kariya, Joe Sakic, Steve Yzerman, Chris Pronger, and Owen Nolan. Lemieux was named captain. As big as the names in the top eight were, what was even more impressive was the talent pool Canada still had to choose from: Eric Lindros, Brendan Shannahan, Jarome Iginla, Joe Nieuwendyk, Adam Foote, Al MacInnis, to list just a few. Over the months, the executive debated how the remaining spots would be used. But while Canadians daydreamed about how strong the men's Olympic team would be, Quinn had to get back to his duties managing and coaching the Toronto Maple Leafs. And there was much to manage.

The Leafs struggled through the 2000–01 season and found themselves fighting to hang onto a playoff spot. There were rumblings in the press that Quinn would have to give up his GM job if the Leafs didn't make it past the first round of the playoffs. There was pressure to get results. Quinn felt his team had been pushed around too much the previous year and promised they wouldn't be roughed up this time around. Toronto had picked up Gary Roberts and Shayne Corson, two tough forwards who wouldn't back down from anyone. The Leafs lineup already included Darcy Tucker, Brian McCabe, and of course, Tie Domi.

Late in the season, Domi sprayed a water bottle at a Flyers fan who was chirping him and throwing trash while he sat in the penalty box in Philadelphia. The fan took a swipe at Domi over the glass, and the panel buckled and sent the fan tumbling into the penalty box and into the clutches of the league's heavyweight champion. The fan managed to escape with his life.

They finished seventh in the Eastern Conference and, once again, faced the the number-two-ranked Ottawa Senators.

But despite the Senators success in the regular season, the Leafs made quick work of Ottawa in the first round. Curtis Joseph posted two straight shutouts to start the series. He made thirty-seven stops in game two. The Leafs snuck away with a 3–2 overtime win in game three before finishing the Senators off with a 3–1 win in game four.

For the second straight season, Toronto faced the New Jersey Devils in the second round—a matchup Quinn had in mind when he added gritty vets Corson and Roberts to the lineup in the off-season. The Conference semifinals promised to be bloody. And it delivered.

The Devils carried a 2–1 series lead in game four—a must-win for the Leafs. Quinn juggled his lines to put Corson, Tucker, and Domi together in an attempt to shut down Devils hot-hand Scott Gomez, who had four points in the last two games. It worked. The Devils had just twenty-four shots on net, and Toronto had a 3–1 win secured with less than twenty seconds remaining when Tie Domi unleashed a vicious blindside elbow to the head of Scott Niedermayer. The star defenseman lay on the ice for almost ten minutes before being carried off on a stretcher.

In the aftermath Quinn stuck by his player, saying his pugnacious Domi didn't intend to hurt his target and charged that he was only reacting to a butt-end from Scott Stevens on a previous play. Domi was called to a hearing at the league head office in Toronto the next day. He arrived with Ken Dryden and

Quinn beside him, with a mob of photographers snapping pictures. As they entered the elevator, Quinn's temper found an ill-advised target. "Get out of my way," he shouted at *Toronto Sun* photograher Stan Behal and grabbed him by the neck, shoving him aside. Later, Behal reportedly went to Toronto's 52 Division and filed an assault charge and made a formal complaint to the league. He dropped his complaint after Quinn apologized for the incident—but it wasn't enough for the Big Irishman to avoid a $10,000 fine from the league. Meanwhile, Tie Domi was suspended for the rest of the playoffs for his brutal hit on Niedermayer, who was sent to the hospital and suffered a concussion. He offered a tearful apology for his actions and called Niedermayer to make amends.

But the tone was set. The defending Stanley Cup champs came out looking for blood in game five but instead only spent time in the penalty box. Scott Stevens and Scott Gomez went to the box together for cross-checking Darcy Tucker. The Leafs scored on the two-man advantage. But the Devils regained composure, and the teams battled until Tomas Kaberle scored with thirty seconds remaining to give Toronto the win—and put them a game away from winning the series. Through all the smoke, Quinn had somehow coached his seventh-seeded Leafs to being within a game of the Conference final.

But New Jersey wasn't about to be backed into a corner. Even without Niedermayer, the Devils were too deep for the Leafs to contend with. The Devils took the next game in New Jersey, winning 4–2. The game ended with Randy McKay crashing into Curtis Joseph, setting off yet another melee. The Leafs and Devils had gone gash for gash through the series, and game seven was expected to be a passionate finale in New Jersey. But Quinn's Leafs took a knockout punch in the second period, allowing four straight goals, and they couldn't get back up. The Devils stepped over the battered Leafs with a 5–1 win.

Quinn was optimistic in defeat: "We've just got to learn to win at playoff time," he said. If Toronto was going to have a shot at winning—and if Quinn was going to have a shot at keeping his GM position—he was going to have a busy off-season.

And, of course, there was still that other matter to take care of.

The Team Canada coaching staff of Quinn, Fleming, Martin, and Hitchcock spoke once a week through the summer. They got along very well, and Hitchcock became the butt of Quinn's jokes. They used three events to get a better sense of the talent available to Canada—the World Championships in 2001, an Olympic training camp in Calgary that September, and the first few months of the NHL season leading up to Salt Lake City.

It was clear who the top lines and defensive pairings would be. But the last seven spots, rounding out a roster of twenty-two, were the most difficult and the most important decisions the executive had to make. The final decisions fell to Quinn, as Gretzky wanted to be sure his head coach was confident in the players he'd have to rely on. "I'm a really big believer in 'Okay, you're the coach, there's a minute to go in the game. Two guys are hurt, two guys are in the penalty box, so who are you going to send out if we're down a goal or up a goal?'" says Gretzky. "So Pat was really instrumental in picking the final few pieces of the team." Quinn championed the inclusion of Ed Jovanovski as the team's seventh defenseman. He also made a strong push to have Ed Belfour included as the team's third goalie behind Martin Brodeur and Curtis Joseph. (When they called Belfour, they told him that if he didn't want to come nobody would ever know, sparing him any potential embarrassment if he didn't want to be the third-string guy. No one would know—Quinn was adamant about that. But Belfour didn't care. He offered to sharpen the team's skates, if it would get him there.)

The goaltending equation would be difficult to solve. Leading up to the Olympics, Joseph was arguably the best goaltender in the game. Along with Mats Sundin, he was the most essential player on the Leafs' roster. Martin Brodeur—who would be remembered as one of the best goalies of all time—had just been to two Stanley Cup Finals in a row.

Quinn clearly faced a conflict of interest. The decision was made that Joseph would start the tournament, against Sweden. If Canada won, Brodeur would play the second game, and regardless of the outcome, Joseph would play the third. But if Canada lost the first game with Joseph in net, Brodeur would play the second—and if he won, he'd keep playing until Canada lost. The decision was made by the entire executive group, Gretzky says. Quinn wanted to make sure he wasn't going to allow a bias toward his own player to affect his decision-making.

Because of the NHL schedule, most of Team Canada didn't arrive in Salt Lake City until Tuesday night, two days before the opening game against Sweden. They had a team meeting on Wednesday, followed by a light skate. That first practice started on an off-key note, as Quinn had forgotten his whistle at the hotel and had to get Keith Hammond, head of Team Canada's security and a longtime friend, to run out and find one to use (Hammond managed to borrow one from an officer outside the rink). The skate was rough. The players looked exhausted. Canada was set to play Sweden Thursday afternoon. "My goodness, we're in trouble tonight," Gretzky thought.

He was correct. Mats Sundin scored twice, helping Sweden beat Canada 5–2 in the opening game, sending a wave of panic across the country. Joseph was off his game, allowing five goals on twenty-five shots—while Tommy Salo stopped thirty-three for Sweden. As the game was ending, Bob Nicholson found Keith Hammond and asked him to find some beer for the coaches—knowing that they'd be in need of some libation to calm themselves before speaking to the press. The liquor laws being very strict in Utah, patrons of the arena were allowed to buy only one beer at a time, and the only place beer was available in abundance was up in the suites. So Hammond put on his winter coat and ran up five flights of stairs to the NHL suite—where he knew the security team— and filled his pockets with as much beer as he could grab. He ran back down the stairs in time to find Quinn and the coaches huffing into their makeshift office. Hammond handed Quinn a beer and cautioned, "I wouldn't open that for a while." After a beer and a cigar, Quinn was ready for the press. Critics questioned whether Quinn should have included Salo's Edmonton Oilers teammate Ryan Smyth in the lineup, suggesting he might have had more knowledge of how to score on the goalie (as Sundin had on Joseph). "We elected to go with experience today," Quinn told the press after the loss. "Ryan will play Saturday. Would he have been a factor today? I don't know. Hindsight is terrific."

Canada's second game, against Germany, was a ninety-minute drive from Salt Lake City in Provo. It was a cold rink, which sat a little more than two thousand people—like somewhere the Canadian stars might have skated during their minor hockey days. Gretzky was nervous. In the tiny locker room before the game, Quinn lightened the tense mood by unveiling his home-made "Big Ol' Can of Whoop-Ass"—an aerosol can of deodorant or maybe air freshener, no one can recall, which Quinn had wrapped in hockey tape inscribed by hand with "Whoop-Ass." (It was a play on a Molson Canadian commercial that had Canadian fans heading to Salt Lake City with a can of "whoop ass.") "If all else fails, we've got this," Quinn said, making the can spray. The light gag earned some chuckles and took the tension out of the room.

The Canadian execs were sore after that opening flop. Quinn reminded them to relax. "It's one thing to be able to do that and make everyone comfortable and feel at ease, and it's another thing to turn the switch and have everyone respect and look up to you," says Gretzky. "That's leadership."

But the game against Germany didn't put anyone at ease. With Lemieux sitting out to rest his troublesome back, Quinn shuffled his lines, but the moves failed to generate any offense. After a scoreless first period, Canada scored three goals in the second but looked anything but dominant doing it. But Germany scored twice on Brodeur in the third period, again sending a jolt of panic through every Canadian watching the game.

Canada won 3–2 and looked terrible. Quinn gave his players an earful after the game—reminding them that they came to the Olympics to win a gold medal, and nothing less. "We seemed pretty tight early on. Our guys were too ready if anything," Quinn told reporters after the win. "That's what caused all the tension."

That night, driving back to Salt Lake City with Kevin Lowe, Steve Tambellini, Bob Nicholson, and Lanny McDonald, a team executive, Gretzky worried whether they had selected the right group. "We beat Germany 3–2. We can't beat Germany 3–2!" Gretzky remembers saying. "No disrespect, but it should have been 8–1!"

McDonald dismissed concerns that the team was a dud. "We're going to win a gold medal in ten days," he told Gretzky as they rolled through the Utah night. "Don't worry about it."

The next afternoon, Canada faced the Czechs back at the E Center in Salt Lake City. The teams exchanged goals in each period, in a back-and-forth thriller that saw Canada tie the game with a goal from Joe Nieuwendyk after an incredible saucer pass from Theo Fleury with less than five minutes to play. Moments later Roman Hamrlík laid a vicious cross-check on Fleury from behind. The game ended in a 3–3 tie.

After the game, Canada was fuming about the hit. Quinn hinted at hockey justice: "If something like that happens in the NHL, a guy can respond by beating the crap out of him," he said at the postgame press conference. "I tell my guys not to respond out there. There will be a more appropriate time. One week from now, we'll get payback."

Gretzky also went on a tear about the Hamrlík hit, lashing out with a rant that would be praised as a rallying point for Team Canada. "If that had been a Canadian player doing something like that to a European, the first thing I'd be asked by you guys was whether he should be suspended, how Canadian players are hooligans," Gretzky said at a press conference. "But the other way around, no one says anything. I'm so tired of people taking shots at Canadian hockey."

After Gretzky came down from the podium, Quinn laughed: "Oh, did you have my can with you today?"

"No," Gretzky said. "But I should have brought it."

Away from the arena, the executive team spent a lot of time together. Even with the single win to show for Canada's first three games, Quinn seemed relaxed and confident between games. He and McDonald insisted that everything would be okay. It was difficult for the coaches to get away to talk strategy because there were no designated coaches' rooms where they could meet to talk privately—and it was hard to find a restaurant to meet at in town because there'd be thousands of Canadians wanting to know what was wrong with the team—so the coaches often met in Quinn's or Hitchcock's room in the Canadian Olympic village. Sometimes Gretzky and the other executives would be involved, but often it was just Quinn, Martin, and Hitchcock.

As Canada's bench boss, Quinn deferred to his assistant coaches Hitchcock and Martin in the team's technical strategy. "He signed off on the technical side of the game—we just had to pass everything by him, whether it was special teams, five-on-five play, whatever," says Ken Hitchcock. "He did the managing of the people after that. His focus became getting people to buy into the technical program we wanted the players to play with."

There were many internal debates among the coaches of the Olympic team, but Quinn listened to every opinion. "He would let us talk it through, argue it through, and when he thought it was time to make a decision, he would halt the proceedings and say, 'OK, this is what we're doing.' That's the way he did business," says Hitchcock. "He let everybody have their say, everybody have their opinion, and then he made the final decision. He never curtailed any debate or discussion or argument—he let it play out. But then, when it was time to make a decision, he made it."

The one clash they did have was when Hitchcock grabbed a stick of gum that was sitting on Quinn's shelf. (Reid Mitchell had arranged to have a box sent down for the coach.) "Who took my gum?" Quinn boomed. "Who moved this piece?" It was the last time Hitchcock ever went near Quinn's gum. "He about had a heart attack," Hitchcock says. "I learned very well ... if I ever touched the gum again, I wouldn't be getting up off the mat."

Canada finally played to its potential in its next round-robin game against the Finns, holding them to just nineteen shots. The team played an NHL-style game—abandoning concerns about defending against or using stretch passes on the open ice with the red line out of play. Canada dumped the puck in and controlled the tempo of the game. Quinn benched the mighty Eric Lindros for the second half of the game. "We got into a groove with the people we were using and went with those players," Quinn said, explaining the decision to cut back Lindros's playing time. Canada won the game 2–1, a score kept close by the play of Finnish goalie Jani Hurme, who stopped thirty-three shots.

On February 21, the Canadian women's hockey team played the United States in a heated gold medal game. The men's team was in attendance, cheering their counterparts on. The women played with incredible grit and resilience, battling through eleven U.S. power plays to hang on for a thrilling 3–2 win. Quinn was moved by their performance. The women kept fighting even though the advantage was clearly stacked in the Americans' favor, and the penalties kept piling up.

In the semifinal, Canada would have sought vengeance on the mighty Swedish team that handed them defeat in the first game—but Sundin and company were stunned in a 4–3 loss to Belarus in the quarterfinals. The unexpected win for Belarus was compared to the "Miracle on Ice" win by the United States over the powerhouse Soviet Union at the 1980 Olympics in Lake Placid. Belarus goalie Andrei Mezin stopped forty-four of forty-seven shots, while Swedish goalie Tommy Salo bobbled a shot from outside the blueline, which bounced off his mask and into the net for the game-winner. But there would be no such miracle for Belarus against Canada, who beat them in an easy 7–1 rout. After a stuttering start, Quinn's team was living up to exactly what it had been expected to do.

The night before the men's gold-medal final against the rival United States, Quinn called a team meeting, in a small room at the end of the mess hall in the Canadian quarters. The players squeezed to fit into the room. The coach's message was simple. "Your best will be good enough," Quinn told the room, packed with the greatest players of a generation. "If you play your best, it'll be good enough to win—our best beats everybody."

Back in southern Ontario, Jack and Jean Quinn had watched every game wearing Team Canada sweaters, sitting in their reclining chairs in the back bedroom at the house on Glennie.

Pat called his mother before and after every game. For the gold medal game, they gathered at Barry Quinn's home in Burlington. Jean wore a red-knit Canada sweater, while Jack wore a white one. They had just celebrated their sixtieth anniversary.

The Canadian executive met in a small weight room, to have a private discussion before the gold medal game. It was there Quinn revealed that the sparkles following him everywhere he went during the Games were not solely the result of the glitter glue his grandkids had used to decorate his lucky socks. He untucked his shirt and pulled down his suit pants, revealing that the grandkids had decorated his lucky briefs too. If there was ever a time for Quinn to reveal the sparkles on his briefs, it was then.

Canada fell behind early on a goal by Tony Amonte in the first period, but fought back to take the lead before the second. In one of the most magnificent examples of pure hockey intelligence, Mario Lemieux allowed a pass from defenseman Chris Pronger to pass through his legs to a streaking Paul Kariya, who zipped past two frozen American defensemen and scored on a sprawling Mike Richter. Later in the first, Joe Sakic sent a perfect pass across the net to Jarome Iginla, who tipped the puck past Richter, giving Canada a 2–1 advantage.

In the second period, Lemieux hit the post on an open-net chance during a five-on-three power play. A few minutes later, the Americans tied the game on their own power play, with a goal by Brian Rafalski. It looked like the score would be drawn at two heading into the final period, but on another man advantage Sakic banked the puck off a cluster of players in front of the

American goal and it bounced past Richter to give Canada a one-goal lead.

Across Canada, people were fixed to their television screens or listened to the play-by-play on the radio. Though it had been fifty years since the country had won a gold medal in men's hockey, it was only the last four that really mattered—this was about correcting the loss in Nagano. This was about demonstrating hockey supremacy. Canada—the nation, not just the team—had twenty anxious minutes to go.

In the third period, Canada played suffocating defense on the Americans. Sometimes protecting a lead brings out the worst in a team, but the Canadians completely dominated the Americans. Canada's shifts lasted no more than thirty seconds, as Quinn cycled through fresh bodies to keep the Americans exhausted and unable to execute an effective attack. With four minutes left, Jarome Iginla scored on a breakaway to put Canada up by two. The E Center rocked with chants of "Go-Canada-go," now overpowering the "U-S-A" chants that had rivaled them earlier in the game. Fans across the country started to celebrate when Joe Sakic scored with a little more than a minute remaining to make it 5–2.

Canada was moments away from a gold medal.

In the stands, Sandra Quinn watched as the final seconds ticked away toward the end, just as she had almost forty years before when her newlywed twenty-year-old husband was about to win the Memorial Cup. The Canadian fans in the crowd bellowed out celebratory renditions of "O Canada."

Before the game, Quinn had turned to Keith Hammond, who sat behind the bench for security, and asked him to make sure he could bring Sandra, Kalli, and Valerie down to the ice if the team won. When Canada's victory was clear, Hammond ran up to the concourse to find them waiting at a security check-point, unable to pass. Hammond pulled them through security and raced with them down to the ice to watch the final seconds tick away. As the players piled onto the ice, Sandra and her daughters climbed onto the bench and embraced Pat. They stayed on the bench while the gold medals were presented and the national anthem played.

Back in Burlington, the friends and family gathered at Barry Quinn's place started a celebration of their own. They were cheering and clapping and laughing, as the announcer called out the last moments of the game. In the revelry, Jack Quinn got out of his chair and walked over to Jean and hugged her close.

When the players crowded in to take a team photo with their gold medals, Quinn shuffled over to the bench and grabbed Kalli to be part of the picture. (He always told her to make sure she was in the center of photos, so she couldn't be cut off the ends.) When the flashes went, Kalli was right there in the middle next to her dad, with his puff of white hair, bright-red cheeks, and an enormous smile.

A few minutes later, as Jack and Jean Quinn gathered their things, put on their winter coats over their Canada sweaters, and made for their green van, the phone rang in Barry Quinn's kitchen.

"Is mom there?" It was Pat.

The cordless was rushed outside to Jean, just as she was about to climb into the front seat. He'd called. Of course he had. Patrick always did. Jean took the phone and spoke to her boy. The words were brief, but full and complete—and proud Jean Quinn started to cry.

No reporters were allowed in the locker room. The players and the team staff were free to celebrate on their own. But the room was very quiet. Most of the players for Team Canada just sat in their stalls staring at their gold medals, shaking their heads at what they'd just accomplished. The best hockey players in Canada, the best in the world, seemed astonished by the feeling.

Pat Quinn sat in the corner, with that huge smile still stretched between his round cheeks. Wayne Gretzky and Bob Nicholson sat down beside him. After all the pressure, all the planning, all the concerns and doubt—the players had done it. "It felt like it was the first time I won the Stanley Cup," says Gretzky. "It was almost surreal." The three sat there and cracked open a few beers. Quinn thanked Gretzky for giving him the chance to be Canada's coach. Then they just sat there, drinking it in, and didn't say much at all—as Quinn's socks twinkled beneath them.

24

Last Dance

"Pat wanted that Stanley Cup more than anything. He'd won everything else."
                                                      —*Reid Mitchell*

Quinn returned from Salt Lake City to a hero's reception in Toronto. But despite the ovations, it appeared that one of the team's key players didn't hold the same affection for him. During a celebration at the Air Canada Centre to honor the gold-medal win, Curtis Joseph put his blocker out to tap Quinn's hand instead of shaking it—unleashing wild speculations about the coach's fractured relationship with him after Joseph sat on the bench through the Olympics.

But the whole ordeal was a media-fueled misconception, said Joseph, who was playing for the first time in a couple of weeks and was just trying to focus on the game he was about to play. "I put my blocker out, and everybody mistook that as not shaking his hand," says Joseph, who insists he felt no animosity over his lack of playing time in the Olympics. "I didn't play great, and Marty [Brodeur] played awesome. He made the right decision."

The Leafs finished second in the Northeast Division with one hundred points in 2002. Mats Sundin finished fourth in league scoring with eighty points. The Leafs had the third-best offense in the league, with 249 goals.

The playoffs opened on April 18 with a 3–1 win at the Air Canada Centre against the New York Islanders. That day, Jean's birthday, she and Jack visited the doctor and were told that X-rays of Jack's lungs and other tests revealed that he had cancer. It had advanced in his liver and lungs, and was terminal. Jack had a difficult time accepting the diagnosis. He asked about the possibility of chemotherapy. "I'm sorry, Mr. Quinn," was all the doctor could say.

Toronto beat the Islanders in a thrilling seven-game series that opened with Darcy Tucker's low hit on Mike Peca that injured his knee and took him out for the series. Toronto faced Ottawa in the second round, surviving another seven-game series to reach the Conference final. Mats Sundin was injured for much of the playoffs.

In the Conference finals, the Leafs faced the Carolina Hurricanes. Toronto won the first game 2–1 in Raleigh, but dropped the second game by the same score in an overtime loss.

To that point, Quinn had lived a large life—enjoying big meals with several glasses of wine, and smoking a seemingly endless supply of cigars. But at nearly sixty, it was clear the life-style had caught up with his aging body. Quinn was over three hundred pounds. After the Leafs lost game two, Quinn had trouble sleeping, and felt a pain in his chest. He went down to the lobby and waited for the team's trainer to come out. Quinn was rushed to the hospital and diagnosed with heart arrhythmia.

He'd survive, but his life was about to undergo a major change.

Somehow doctors managed to keep Quinn in the hospital as the series went on without him. Rick Ley took Quinn's place on the Leafs' bench as they again lost 2–1 in overtime in game three, back at the Air Canada Centre. Quinn watched the game from his hospital bed. He managed to get out for game four, but the Leafs lost 3–0 at home to Carolina. Continued complications with his irregular heartbeat meant that Quinn couldn't travel back to Carolina for the fifth game. Once again, he was stuck in his hospital bed as the Leafs pulled out a narrow 1–0 win—and were one win away from forcing the Leafs' third game seven in the 2002 playoffs.

Back in Toronto for game six, Quinn was released from Toronto General Hospital and made it to the rink in time for the pregame skate. He showed up in a dark-blue tracksuit and watched his team from the sidelines, allowing Ley to run the drills while he occasionally pulled players over to give them instructions.

When he spoke with the press, Quinn grumbled about the poor play-by-play commentary he'd had to endure while watching the games from his hospital bed. The press bombarded him with questions about his health and the state of the team. "Are you trying to make up for the three games I missed, you guys?" he asked dryly, with a wink to the fact that he'd only missed two games, but perhaps wasn't fully present when he coached the Leafs to a loss in game four.

But despite his apparent return to form, in crusty spirit and health, Quinn was unable to pull his team past the Hurricanes. The Hurricanes' Martin Gelinas—whom Quinn resurrected off waivers nearly a decade earlier—capitalized on a giveaway by Alex Mogilny and scored with eight minutes remaining in overtime, sending the Hurricanes to the Stanley Cup and ending the Leafs' run to make the final for the first time since 1967.

It would be the closest Quinn would get to another chance at raising the Cup.

That summer, Quinn trimmed down and committed to getting healthy. He swore he'd give up cigars, which he called his crutch. It'd be difficult to reverse his unhealthy habits, but over the next year Quinn would lose almost seventy pounds.

Meanwhile, Jack Quinn's condition got worse. Despite the long odds, they had tried chemotherapy. His family surrounded him through the difficult times, pulling together to make sure he was cared for and Jean wasn't overwhelmed. His grandkids would try to get him to take his pills, but he'd often refuse, saying, "If they're so good, you take them!" Eventually Jack was unable to stay steady on his feet, and had to be in a wheelchair. The decline was devastating for Jack Quinn. When family came to help, he'd say, "Come to *visit* me. Don't come to do *this* for me."

The whole family gathered in mid-July for the upcoming wedding of Barry Quinn's daughter. On a Tuesday evening, they congregated at the house on Glennie Avenue—Pat, Carol, Barry, Guy, and their parents. They sat around the table in the same kitchen where Jack had quizzed them on their homework and lectured Pat about needing to *skate, skate, skate* instead of messing around with the puck. The living room where Jack had wrestled with each of them was the same but for the woodstove heater, long gone like the handmade bunks upstairs. The rafters in Jack's workshop in the basement he'd excavated by hand with Pat were lined with stickers he'd collected from his son's teams over the years—the Atlanta Flames, the Maine Mariners, the Vancouver Canucks—next to one that read "Go Navy." The coal bin he'd carved out with Pat was now hidden behind a wooden door, blocked by a workbench. The house was painted white now—the green paint long gone. So much had changed, but so much was the same.

The Quinn family visited with each other and remembered, knowing that these small moments shared together would soon change forever. Captain Jack didn't have much time left. An IV dripped morphine into his veins to ease the pain. No, there wasn't time left. But he had them there, together, and that was enough. And as Pat and the boys cracked open another can of beer, Jack said, "Well, what about me?" This was all he wanted, to share a drink with his boys. To be there, with family—it's what the story of his life had always been about. And so they poured out some beer in a glass for their dad. The Quinns shared a toast, and Jack had one more drink with his boys, although he didn't even raise the glass to his lips. He sat there, his drink in front of him, and just watched. When they were done, Jack said it was time to sleep and his sons carried him to bed.

Jack Quinn passed away a couple of days later. He was eighty-six.

Heavyhearted, the Quinns carried on with the wedding a few days later. Jack would have wanted it that way. A celebration of something new. A party, full of songs. At the wedding, Pat and his daughter Kalli danced to "The Tennessee Waltz"— as requested by Jack, who loved that song, and who thought it was funny because Kalli was working in the Nashville

Predators front office at the time. Jack had told them he didn't know if he'd be there to see it, but he wanted them to dance anyway. And so they did. One last dance for Captain Jack—*"I remember the night and the Tennessee Waltz. Now I know just how much I have lost"* ... Pat and Kalli took soft steps on the floor, together ... *"Yes, I lost my little darling the night they were playing the beautiful Tennessee Waltz"* ... They turned and turned and twirled, for him.

That spring the Leafs and Joseph—who was playing some of the best hockey of his career—were in talks for a new deal but couldn't agree on how long and how much the new contract would be for. Quinn was prepared to pay the thirty-five-year-old goalie $9 million a season, as much as team captain Mats Sundin was making, and more than any other goalie in the league at the time. Joseph was looking for a four-year deal. Quinn wasn't prepared to give him that. "He was worried about my age," says Joseph. "And rightfully so."

Both sides went back and forth several times but were unable to come to an agreement before July 1, when Joseph officially became a free agent. The first caller to his agent Don Meehan was Ken Holland, the general manager of the Detroit Red Wings, the Stanley Cup champions. Dominick Hasek had retired and the Red Wings needed a replacement.

To the dismay of most Leaf fans, Joseph signed with the Red Wings for three years and $8 million a season. It was less money than Toronto offered, which poured fuel on further speculation that Joseph was upset with Quinn for being benched in Salt Lake City and for balking at a longer deal. Both sides denied that it was anything more than business and what Joseph perceived to be his best chance at winning a Stanley Cup.

Joseph says the decision had nothing to do with any animosity he had for Quinn—and still regrets not taking the deal the Leafs offered him. He played through injuries most of his first season in Detroit and was then relegated to a backup position when the capricious Dominick Hasek returned after a year in retirement. Joseph found himself watching Leafs games on television, knowing his heart was still with the city he left. "In hindsight, I should have stayed in Toronto," he says. "It was home for me."

Quinn took heat in the press for letting the team's MVP walk. That spring, he had signed his own three-year extension to continue coaching and management duties with the Leafs. But with Cujo gone, Quinn's acumen for the job was questioned by some—especially when a few hours after Joseph's tearful farewell press conference, the Leafs announced that they had signed thirty-seven-year-old Ed Belfour to replace him. Despite being the third-string goalie for Team Canada at the Olympics, Belfour was coming off his worst season in a decade and had had clashes with the coaching staff of his former team, the Dallas Stars. He also had well-documented run-ins with the police, which included his attempt to bribe them with a billion dollars when he was arrested for allegedly assaulting a hotel security guard.

Looking at Quinn's track record, though, the Belfour signing was far from surprising. Throughout his career he had picked up players who seemed to be out of chances and managed to get good value out of them. Indeed, in his first season in Toronto, Belfour won a franchise-record thirty-seven games, posted a .922 save percentage, earned a spot in the all-star game, and was a runner-up for the Vezina trophy.

So the loss of Curtis Joseph didn't ruin Quinn in Toronto. But another departure in the summer of 2002 helped set up his end with the Leafs. Quinn lost his biggest ally in the Maple Leaf Sports and Entertainment (MLSE) boardroom when longtime chairman Steve Stavro stepped down as he sold his majority stake in MLSE to the Ontario Teachers' Pension Plan. Quinn got along very well with Stavro, who would often come down to the coaches' room after a game, win or loss, and have a couple of glasses of Scotch with the coaches.

"Mr. Stavro was a dream," Quinn later said. "He was the face of that organization in my opinion. He was just supportive in so many ways. He was a great guy to work for or with and so I had a lot of luck as far as owners are concerned in my management roles."

But without an owner like Stavro, Quinn feared, MLSE investors would be able to gain control and would attempt to start making hockey decisions, thinking they were smarter than the general manager or coach—which is what Quinn believed happened in Vancouver when Orca Bay took control of the Vancouver Canucks and Grizzlies. Quinn believed ownership got in the way of success when it didn't allow the general manager to have complete freedom to do the job. He felt the same way about managers interfering with the way coaches ran the room and their benches. All of this, of course, showed that Quinn liked to have control. And with Stavro gone, Quinn's control was again slipping away.

The respect he had in the locker room never truly wavered, though. Despite rumors of players' disgruntlement following

Quinn everywhere he went, players themselves would rarely admit to anything but respect and a healthy dose of fear when it came to Quinn. Darcy Tucker marveled at the way Quinn brought together a roster with so many unpredictable parts—including Tie Domi, a magnet for controversy, among several other characters—Quinn turned them into a team that could win. Quinn always had a handle on the room. When he spoke, they listened, though sometimes amused at the verve with which he delivered his game plans. When he drew on the whiteboard to illustrate and punctuate his speeches, he hammered the dry-erase marker so hard that the felt would break off. It happened constantly. "Get me a goddamned pen," he'd yell to one of the trainers. Other times the cap would fall off the back of the marker and roll around at his feet. Quinn was at his largest then, and he'd looked a bit like a teapot being poured as he'd bend to pick up the cap. The Leafs would share glances, thinking he might tumble, and try not to chuckle.

But his players knew better. When Quinn was steaming, you didn't mess around with him. In lighter moments, though, he did have a sense of humor. He had no problem laughing at himself. In Toronto he still wore his old Mircon plastic-molded skates, which would squeak as he skated. "They must have been thirty years old," says Curtis Joseph. "We thought they were going to come apart at the seams.... You looked at his skates, and you thought, this man is old-school—he's not changing those things for anything."

That mix of hard-ass seriousness and his damn-what-they-say uniqueness endeared Quinn to his players. They could laugh at him, but he sure as hell had their respect.

"You walk into a room with Pat Quinn and it's almost as if you turn into a twelve-year-old boy," says Darcy Tucker, one of the more fearless guys in the NHL. "You lose almost all function of being a man and turn into a kid. It's nothing he says or nothing his does. It's just his presence.... No matter what you feel like, you're twelve talking to a teacher."

During pregame talks with his players, Quinn regularly brought up shift workers, the guys who had to punch in and out every day. "You guys have got to sign your name to your work at the end of the game," Quinn would tell his players. "So leave it all on the fucking ice. Don't shortchange yourself, your teammates. Be proud."

Throughout the 2002–03 season there were reports of division within the Leafs locker room, which primarily centered around Shayne Corson's dissatisfaction with his ice time. There were suggestions in the press that he had complained about the minutes Jonas Hogland and Tom Fitzgerald were receiving over him. Players on the team vehemently denied the reports. Despite the apparent distractions, the Leafs finished second in the Northeast Division in 2002–03 behind the Ottawa Senators. With ninety-eight points, they were seeded fifth in the Eastern Conference and faced the Philadelphia Flyers in the first round of the playoffs.

Corson suffered from a flare-up of colitis, which caused his playing time to diminish down the final stretch of the regular season. But few people knew that there was much more to the story. Corson played a little more than nine minutes in the first two games of the series against the Flyers, which the teams split, but was a healthy scratch in the third game. After the Leafs beat the Flyers 4–3 in double overtime that game, Corson walked into Quinn's office and told him he was leaving the team. He told the media he was leaving so he wouldn't be a distraction for his teammates. Quinn provided few details about how his conversation with Corson went. He simply stressed that his team needed to move on.

"It's there. It's done. He's gone, and we have to treat it like it might be an injury or anything else," Quinn told his players. "Go forward and get ready to play. It doesn't matter. The only thing that matters is being ready."

Toronto lost the fourth game of the series 3–2 in triple overtime, despite a remarkable seventy-two-save performance from Ed Belfour. (The seventy-five shots Toronto allowed were the most in Leafs playoff history.) The Leafs lost the fifth game 4–1 in Philadelphia but rallied with a 2–1 double-overtime win in game six. But the thrilling series ended with a dud in the seventh game, as Toronto fell 6–1 to Philadelphia and was eliminated from the playoffs. It was the first time the Leafs had been knocked out in the first round since Quinn took over as coach.

After the season, stories about the Leafs divided roster continued to persist. Quinn refused to entertain them. But Shayne Corson publically criticized the way the coach had dealt with the speculation that he had complained about ice time. "He's our leader. It's up to him to stand up and say to the people or the players or the media, 'That's a bunch of crap,' and put his foot down, and it would have ended right there," Corson told radio station Fan 590. "But instead he didn't deal with it, and it just sits there and boils and boils and boils, and people keep talking about it."

However, Corson would later admit that he left the team because he was suffering debilitating anxiety and panic attacks, but had blamed his struggles on colitis. When Corson left the Leafs that spring, only those closest to him knew the true extent of the issues he was facing. During one severe bout of anxiety before the season, Corson didn't leave his house for twelve days. He didn't seek the help he needed because he was afraid how the hockey world would react. "Your brain's a powerful thing. It took over my body and my life for a long time," Corson says. "I fought it and battled it, but the worst thing I did was fight it and battle it—and not get the proper tools I needed to get through it."

When he quit the Leafs in the middle of the playoffs, Corson says he walked into Quinn's office and said, "Pat, I just can't do it anymore … I can't keep going."

Quinn was unaware of the extent of Corson's illness. Corson says he could tell from his coach's reaction that he understood there was something more severe going on, but he didn't pry. "Okay," Quinn told him. "You have to do what's best for you."

Looking back, Corson says Quinn was in a difficult position because he didn't really know what was going on with him. Corson was upset with his lack of ice time, but that was only a surface issue. Regardless of what happened with the team or individuals, Corson says, Quinn would take the blame, deflecting it away from his players. Today, Corson regrets that he didn't tell his coach the full extent of his personal struggles. "He was a family man, and he cared about his players as people," Corson says. "He'd give us shit when we needed it, trust me … [but] he'd stand up for his players. That's something I'll always respect him for."

When Quinn agreed to take on the general manager's position in Toronto a year after he started as coach, he made it clear that he would do it for a short time to help Toronto get through its transitional period. He intended to go back to just coaching, and when he did, he wanted to have a say in who would assume the general manager's position. In the summer of 2003, Quinn suggested people he thought should take over the job—Bob Nicholson, Steve Tambellini, and Mike Penny were all names he brought up.

That August, however, Quinn was on a golf course in Vancouver when he received a call on his cell phone from Larry Tanenbaum, the new MLSE chairman. Tanenbaum told Quinn that he was hiring John Ferguson Jr. to be the Leafs' new general manager. Quinn was blindsided by the decision.

"He was not a happy man," says Ron Toigo, a close friend who co-owned the Vancouver Giants WHL franchise with Quinn, and was with him on the golf course that day in August 2003. It wasn't so much that Quinn was against Ferguson—it was that he didn't really know anything about him, and that he'd been told he'd be part of the selection process for the new general manger, but really wasn't.

Quinn hoped to mentor Ferguson, who was just thirty-six and would be the youngest general manager in the league. However, several sources say that Quinn felt completely cut out of decisions being made about the team—and having meaningful input had been essential to his initial agreement to come to Toronto. Under Ferguson, Quinn felt he learned more from reports on the radio or television about the moves the Leafs made than from internal discussions. Looking back, Quinn would view the decision to hire Ferguson as the end for him in Toronto.

In 2003–04, the Leafs finished second in the Northeast Division with 103 points. The success came with experience— the Leafs roster had five players over the age of thirty-five, including Brian Leech, Joe Nieunwendyk, and forty-year-old Ron Francis. Alexander Mogilny was thirty-four. Mats Sundin was thirty-two.

Toronto faced the Ottawa Senators in yet another battle of Ontario. Once again, it was a thrilling, heated series. Thirty-nine-year-old Ed Belfour was exceptional in goal for Toronto, posting three shutouts. He had a 1.57 goals average and a .950 save percentage—once again making Quinn look like a genius for signing him. And once again—for the fourth time since 2000—the Leafs knocked the Senators out of the playoffs. This time it took seven games, on the back of their goaltender, before an anti-climatic game seven in which Toronto scored three goals in the first period and walked away with a 4–1 win.

The aging Leafs again faced Philadelphia in the second round and hoped to avenge their seven-game loss from the previous season. But after exchanging wins and losses in the first four games, Toronto was embarrassed 7–2 in game five. In game six, Jeremy Roenick broke in on a two-on-one in overtime and fired a wrist shot past Belfour, ending the Leafs season.

"I guess you have hopes and dreams," Quinn said after the loss. "I was convinced that this team had a little bit of destiny in it."

It was the last time Toronto would make the playoffs for nearly a decade.

Quinn teamed up with his Olympic coaching staff—Ken Hitchcock, Wayne Fleming, and Jacques Martin—to lead Team Canada at the World Cup of hockey, in September 2004. The tournament took place over the course of two weeks in a number of cities in North America and Europe, with the finals being held in Toronto.

For Hitchcock, the World Cup was even more of a magnifying glass on Quinn's unique ability as a leader in the sport. "It was a different animal," Hitchcock said of the 2004 tournament. "He had to manage the team and manage the business side of it. He took care of a lot of things around the game and around the competition that allowed us to coach."

Kalli Quinn recalls the mass hysteria that came with hosting the final in Toronto, where her father already couldn't walk down the street without being stopped for an autograph or just to talk hockey. With Team Canada being involved, the attention blew up. After Canada beat Finland 3–2 in the final, she went with her parents to a team party at Wayne Gretzky's pub a few blocks away from the Air Canada Centre. They had stayed behind at the arena and therefore missed the team bus and security escort to the party. When they pulled up in a cab, a massive crowd outside the restaurant mobbed Quinn, trying to get to him. "This is crazy," Kalli thought. Police officers had to push the crowd back and make a path for the Quinns to get into the restaurant.

Quinn was used to the attention—though usually it was nothing quite that aggressive. He was known to go out for drinks with his staff at Toronto bars along the Esplanade or Front Street, where his three-piece-suit-wearing, cigar-puffing presence immediately became the talk of the evening. Patrons would buy Quinn and his party drinks, and snap photos with the beloved Leafs coach. During one of his St. Patrick's Day celebrations, Quinn dressed in that year's Irish getup, complete with shamrock socks and a matching tie, and went to a post-practice lunch at Fionn MacCool's on the Esplanade, near the Air Canada Centre, with Mike Penny, Ricky Ley, and Bill Watters around noon. At 8:00 P.M., Mike Penny's wife came through the doors, having searched all of the nearby bars for them. By that time, Quinn's getup had been augmented by a green hat with blinking lights, which had been given to him by one of the many Leafs fans who sat down and bought him a beer.

Returning from the lockout, the Leafs struggled in 2005–06. The team signed thirty-two-year-old Eric Lindros in the summer, but though he played well to open the season with Sundin injured, he was no longer the same player who once ran rampant in the league. Toronto enjoyed a five-game winning streak through Christmas, right up to the New Year—but then won just five of their next twenty games through January and February. They made a last-minute push for the playoffs on the surprise heroics of third-string goalie Jean-Sebastien Aubin, and the offense of Mats Sundin, who had thirty-one goals and seventy-eight points. Darcy Tucker scored a career high twenty-eight on the season. But it wasn't enough. The Leafs ended up with ninety points— two behind the Tampa Bay Lightning, finishing ninth in the Eastern Conference and missing the playoffs for the first time in seven seasons with Quinn on the bench. Before the last game of the season, against the Pittsburgh Penguins, Quinn told the press that he felt the team didn't have success because there wasn't enough cap room to sign free agents. "We had a tough job to build on the group we had," Quinn said, while adding that he felt the team was good enough to make the playoffs. "Either you misread your capabilities or underachieved. You try to find where the differences come from between your expectations and reality."

Speculation had grown through the final months of the season that the Leafs would part ways with Quinn if the team didn't make the postseason. Reports at the time said the MLSE board was conflicted over whether to can Quinn, but ultimately they had approved the hiring of Ferguson and decided to back the decision of the general manager they'd put in charge: Quinn was fired the next day, April 20, 2006.

Rick Ley got the news from his wife, Ellen, as he was on his way to the Air Canada Centre. When he arrived at the arena, Quinn was sitting alone in his office. Ley went up to Ferguson's office and walked right in, asking, "What's going on?" Ferguson said he would tell him after the press conference but Rick insisted, saying, "I want to know now." Ferguson told him he was fired too. Ley shook his hand and went back down to the coaches' room in the Air Canada Centre where, together, he and Pat cleared out their desks. Staff came down and removed their computers right away. "They had to guard Pat," Ley says. "They were worried about him taking their stuff, I guess. I don't know. It wasn't a very cordial send-off, that's for sure."

Quinn had always been kind and generous with staff throughout the Air Canada Centre, regardless of their station. News of his firing upset a lot of people used to hearing his voice and seeing his smile every day. He had learned their names. He had learned their families' names—he treated them as though they were as important as anyone named Sundin or Roberts.

He soon received a call from strength trainer Matt Nichol, equipment manager Scott McKay, and his video coordinator Reid Mitchell, who were down at P.J. O'Brien Irish Pub and Restaurant, a place they all frequented regularly, drinking away a lost season and toasting a fired friend. There was a very clear sense that the success of the past seven years was done. (As the NHL moved into its new salary-cap era, the hope that Leafs fans felt in flashes through the early years of the millennium would dissipate. Indeed, it'd be seven years before Toronto would even see the playoffs again.)

Quinn told them he'd try to come out to the bar, but McKay didn't think the Big Irishman would show. He was the largest news story in the city that day—and the man who was always recognized was sure to be spotted and questioned about the firing.

But, after a few more pints were had, the door at the end of the low-lit bar opened and in walked Quinn. "Sorry boys," he said. "I'm a little late." He pulled up a chair and sat down beside them. It was one more with the boys, before the story found its end.

25

A Song for Paddy Quinn

P at Quinn sat alone on the bench, watching his players skate by. There were no fans in the Rogers Arena on that night in 2014. Just his '94 Canucks—the team that pushed and pushed, so close to winning the Cup. The team he'd cried for two decades before. Quinn was weak now. He'd lost the heft in his frame and his face was thin. He was seventy-one years old.

Before parting ways with the Leafs, Quinn had taken Canada back to the Olympics, but the team failed under a spell of injuries. The exact same group that coached Canada to its first gold wasn't able to reach the medal round in Turin in 2006. After being fired in Toronto two months later, he and Sandra had moved back to their home, with the view over Vancouver. And Quinn had waited. He had waited for another chance to stand on an NHL bench— another chance to get that one thing still missing. But the call never came. The game was changing, they said. He was too old now. He was retired. But Quinn never wanted that title. It was involuntary.

Quinn didn't ask to quit. He became more involved with his Vancouver Giants, recruiting players, evaluating talent. He sat in a box above the old Coliseum, where fans had once filed in to watch the first Canucks team play, and later where they leapt from their seats as their team, Vancouver's team, nearly pulled off the impossible. From his seat, he watched the future of the game he loved.

When the phone did ring, it was Hockey Canada on the line. They asked him to coach the future he was watching—to guide the national team in the IIHF World U18 Junior Hockey Championships in Russia in 2008. And so he climbed on rickety airplanes and flew to Kazan—and told old war stories to boys who could be his grandchildren. They listened, enthralled, like he had to Grandpa Snooze. It would be the time of their young lives—a tournament on the brink of their dreams— before time decided where it would take them. Taylor Hall, Jordan Eberle, Tyler Myers, and Matt Duchene—they were just boys, giggling at stupid things and wide-eyed to the world around them, but would attain adulthood in the NHL. Quinn led his staff—Guy Boucher and Jesse Wallin—teaching them about the intangibles in the game. "Our boys are nervous for sure," he told Boucher and Wallin before the tournament. "It can't be about the X's and O's right now. It has to be about how they feel."

Quinn showed them how to relax. Showed them how to have fun with the game. He taught them how to chirp opponents the good old-fashioned way: "Hey, you can't swim down there, the water's too tick," he'd shout in a vaguely European accent every time a player on the other team dove. His players on the bench just looked at each other and laughed. "It was like your grandfather shouting in traffic," says Matt Duchene, who holds Kazan as one of his most cherished memories.

The Russians thundered in the rink in that gold medal game—with more than ten thousand fans roaring for Canadian blood—but Quinn kept the boys steady and steered them to a 5–0 lead in the first period as they coasted to victory. "That will be one to remember," he told Guy Boucher with his gold medal proudly in hand.

And when the phone rang once more, and it was Hockey Canada again, Quinn proudly took the helm of Canada's World Junior team in 2009. It was just months after Jean Quinn had passed, at eighty-six, like Jack—she had missed the life of song they shared, had missed it since he left. Despite criticism that he couldn't coach a young man's game, Quinn dove proudly into his role as the World Junior coach. In fact, he leapt right out of a helicopter with those boys during a team-building exercise.

Playing in Ottawa, looking for a fifth straight gold in the tournament, Quinn quelled the boys' nerves with his calm confidence. When he spoke, no one else made a sound. They hung on every word, as obscure and odd as his references might seem.

"He's been through it all," John Tavares thought. Even while scolding, Quinn kept it light. He called out P.K. Subban for his "Sub-Bi-Doo" in-game spinoramas—"*No more Sub-Bi-Doos!*"—and told them to put away their "Ataris," knowing full well the gaming system was extinct. He laughed to Sandra about the confused looks on their faces. Quinn lifted the pressure of playing in the capital. "I have a lot more of a job to do outside hockey at this tournament," Quinn told Guy Boucher. The press would completely envelope him before and after games. Only his white tuft of hair could be seen above the crush of reporters as he deflected the pressure away from the boys.

But along with the laughs, he captivated and inspired his players—as he had done in so many locker rooms so many times before. In turn, they captivated the nation, beating the United States in a New Year's Eve shoot-out after tying the game with mere seconds to go, the moment falling into hockey history, before they went on to the final to defend the fifth on Canadian soil. The next decade of stars—Eberle, Subban, Tavares, Benn—beginning their moments of glory with Quinn, proving that the game hadn't moved past him.

There were whispers of a return—rumors of a general manager's job in Ottawa, a coaching job in Pittsburgh. After a three-year exile from the NHL, the return he did make, he'd regret. A deal in Edmonton, signed just a few months after guiding the juniors to gold, was never what he expected, not what he'd hoped. He had only a single season, with twenty-seven wins, before being replaced the following June and pushed into a "senior advisor" role. The axe wounded him. It was wielded by his close friend Steve Tambellini, whom he'd mentored from his days working media relations with the Canucks. Tambellini was just one of the many executives he'd developed who had made a name for himself in a league that seemed to be done with him. Quinn felt betrayed—he never had complete control, never had a chance to prove that the NHL game had not moved past him. It was all business, though. Quinn knew tough decisions. (And when it was Tambellini's turn to be fired, in April 2013, the first call he received was from Quinn. "Keep your head up high," he said.)

Quinn couldn't have known, really, just how many people believed they owed their opportunities in the game to him. Even working with his Vancouver Giants, he continued to incite determination. In 2011, a reporter nervously asked him for an interview. Quinn—difficult as his relations with the press could be—graciously obliged. Quinn didn't realize it then, but as a boy the reporter he spoke to that day had dreamed of one day being part of an NHL team. The dream seemed crushed when he realized that his cerebral palsy would prevent him from getting there. But that day, Pat Quinn took the time to give an interview to fifteen-year-old Dickson Liong. And he was so impressed with the young man's mind for the game and his pure determination to overcome his obstacles that he made sure the Giants hired him as their in-house reporter. "Don't listen to anything negative," Quinn advised him. "Don't take any bullshit."

Quinn was winding down now, against his wishes. Quinn was powerless to stop it. There was a bout with cancer, successfully fought, and then the liver complications. The weight fell rapidly from the Big Irishman's once-imposing frame. His suits hung from him. He swam in his dress shirts. His round face tightened. Pat Quinn was wasting away. But he never told a soul, didn't ask for help or pity. At every event he attended, every lunch meeting he kept, Quinn never discussed his ailment. It wasn't something to dwell on. It was just another obstacle to beat. He humbly accepted his Order of Canada in 2012, while posing for a photo in front of a portrait of the ever-elusive Lord Stanley. He fulfilled his duties on the board of the Hockey Hall of Fame and fulfilled his duties with the Vancouver Giants, remaining ever generous to the team's players and fans. He was named to the Vancouver Canucks Ring of Honour, forever enshrined with the team where he'd once been relegated to the press box as a player.

And in 2014, he returned for the Heritage Classic as they honored the '94 team, two decades on. There, at a private dinner in Rogers Arena, he told his boys how proud he was to know them—Linden, McLean, Bure, Babych, Odjick, and all. He spoke with passion, from the gut. He told them what it meant, what they'd done—how special it all was. How sweet it was for him. The room was silent. Quinn reminded them that they should have won that Cup; their names should be etched on silver. But he was so proud, so damn proud of what they did together. He was weak. He was fading, and they knew it. Tears rolled down their aging cheeks. They stood and clapped and cheered and cried for Quinn.

After dinner, the Canucks alumni went down to the locker room and put on their gear. They took to the ice and played once more. Quinn sat on the bench, and watched them pass by.

He found the strength to take his grandson fishing that summer. And from his hospital bed, as he grew weaker, he watched on his iPad as his sixteen-year-old granddaughter, Kate, played hockey. "I need to talk to her about how she's holding her stick," he told Sandra with pride. He was in the same hospital where, months earlier, he would regularly visit Gino Odjick, who was gravely ill with AL amyloidosis. Quinn had sat and talked with his old enforcer for hours, but despite his frailty, he never mentioned his own illness. Now Quinn was the one who needed company.

Others came to visit Quinn. Kirk McLean and Trevor Linden sat beside his bed making jokes about the Toronto Maple Leafs and sharing old stories. Linden, president of the franchise that had drafted him, hung a photo of his favorite coach behind his desk. They didn't really say goodbye—it was more like, "See you soon." Everyone still hoped the Mighty Quinn would find one more way to pull out the win.

Two days later, however, on November 23, 2014, Pat Quinn passed away from unexpected complications caused by his failing liver. He was seventy-one.

In Vancouver, hundreds from the fraternity of hockey gathered at Christ the Redeemer church to remember Quinn. The sanctuary was filled with faces from a lifetime in the game, from old teammates like Roger Bourbonnais to NHL commissioner Gary Bettman. Tough men cried as Quinn's casket was carried out to "Ave Maria"—the Big Irishman's favorite song.

They were just down the hill from the Quinn home, where every inch of the basement walls is lined with rows of photos of his former teams, and in the corner sits the lucky old pinball machine with Hugh Hefner's face on it, across the hall from his office, where he kept the notebooks he meticulously scribbled in and where his diplomas hung. He kept more memories in the garage: framed articles from Salt Lake City; a signed photo of Bobby Orr addressed "To my friend Pat ... to a true gentleman"; a painting of a tiny wartime house, where the stories poured out, distilled over time. The trees are painted high around it, and the leaves almost touch the two street signs at the corner. There's one for Glennie Avenue. And one for Pat Quinn Way.

Near the street now named for him, Quinn's childhood friends gathered at St. Eugene's in Hamilton to remember days long gone. Baseball games at Mahoney. Morning practices at Parkdale. The green house on Glennie, where big Paddy Quinn always seemed to be reaching for something more.

And in Toronto they remembered him too. How he tangled with Bobby Orr and where decades later he gave them something to hope for. A tribute played on the screen to "The Parting Glass," and Leafs circled the ice with shamrock patches marked with *PQ*.

On St. Patrick's Day 2015, they remembered him once more. Bagpipes sang through the arena, moving a sea of green-clad fans. Before the Canucks played, warming up in number 3 jerseys, they all stopped to remember. *"When Irish eyes are smiling, sure, they steal your heart away,"* the song went, and everyone sang along.

When the ceremony was through and the great game carried on, Quinn's dear friends gathered in a suite, celebrating St. Patrick's Day together. They were a collection of moments from his past—Orland Kurtenbach, Cliff Fletcher, Mike Tilleman, Bob Clarke, Brian Burke, Stan Smyl, Trevor Linden, George McPhee, Pavel Bure, Markus Naslund, the names went on. Dickson Liong, now nineteen, watched from the press box, having made it to the NHL, covering the Canucks for a national hockey site. Sandra Quinn and her daughters were there too, surrounded by them all.

The bagpipes started to play. Slowly the chatter faded until it was just the tune. Mark Donnelly, the Canucks' anthem singer, offered the first notes to the song Quinn loved to sing:

Oh Danny boy, the pipes, the pipes are calling
From glen to glen, and down the mountain side
The summer's gone, and all the flowers are dying
'Tis you, 'tis you must go and I must bide.

But come ye back when summer's in the meadow
Or when the valley's hushed and white with snow
'Tis I'll be here in sunshine or in shadow
Oh Danny boy, oh Danny boy, I love you so.

The game whirled behind them as the rink glittered green and Irish. Outside, it rained faintly on the new Pat Quinn Way, officially named in front of the arena.

And I will hear
Though soft your tread above me
And o'er my grave
Will warmer sweeter be

And remembering his way, they sang on ...

And you will bend
And tell me that you love me
And I will sleep
In peace until you come to me.

... softly, but proudly, like a Quinn.

Notes

1. Glennie Avenue

Much of the information in this chapter and others was told to me by Pat Quinn's brothers and sister, who generously gave hours of their time to regale me with stories of their childhood. Barry Quinn is the unofficial historian of the family, and has taken a keen interest in his family ancestry and can tell you which navy destroyer his father boarded or what English town his Irish grandparents emigrated from (Liverpool). I shared several cups of coffee with Carol Quinn at the house on Glennie Avenue. Guy Quinn and I connected by phone. All three were incredibly kind and helpful in sharing stories about their big brother.

p. 7: Barry Quinn kept a 1915 clipping from the *Hamilton Spectator* announcing that Snooze would be joining the 205th Battalion.

p. 9: Rev. Earl Talbot of St. Basil's Parish in Brantford, Ontario, an old friend of Pat from St. Helen Elementary School, told me about how Pat would get in tussles with the Protestant kids who blocked his shortcut to school through a grape field.

2. Mahoney

p. 14: Johnny Walker, a friend who lived across the street from the Quinns, filled me in on many of the traditions and horseplay of Mahoney Park, including all the colorful characters who'd come to play each day. Former Hamilton mayor Bob Bratina, who played against Quinn at Glennie, was also a big help.

3. Mentors and Toothpicks

p. 23: Pat's mentor, Sam Hart, still lives in Hamilton, just down the street from his old house. He kindly talked to me about his one-on-one coaching sessions with a young Pat Quinn. While Quinn had always considered Hart to be one of the most influential forces in his life, Hart himself is a modest guy. When he talked, I was struck by how grateful he was that Pat had gotten him and his family tickets to a Maple Leafs game and taken him into the dressing room to meet the players. "I was just a neighborhood man," says Hart.

Hart wrote this poem for Pat after he died. It was read at the memorial service at the family's longtime church in Hamilton, St. Eugene's.

> Born in Hamilton's east end
> You were more than a friend
> Mahoney Park, Hamilton Place minor
> All your coaches, it was an honour
> In the NHL you played nine years
> Some memorable, some with tears
> Achievement in coaching gave you fame
> John Brian Patrick Quinn is your name
> You were someone I met, but someone I won't forget.
> Thanks for everything.

p. 27: Quinn would always contend that neither he nor his parents ever signed the C-form.

p. 29: Sandra Quinn thought that it was Bob Pallante who told Pat about Michigan Tech. Pallante can't recall, but doesn't dispute that he did. He did hang out with Pat on campus at Michigan Tech and fondly remembers traveling with Pat to football games when they were both at St. Mike's.

p. 30: On February 1, 1959, Quinn was part of a game between the Tiger Cubs and the St. Michael's Majors at Maple Leaf Gardens, where he faced his future teammate Dave Keon.

4. "Go for the Education"

p. 32: Frank Orr is a legendary Canadian sports journalist who wrote for the *Toronto Star*. He was kind enough to sit down with me one afternoon to share his insightful perspective on Quinn's life, having covered both his playing and coaching days. I consulted his work often while researching and writing this book, including his 1980 feature "Hamilton boys front and centre," which talked about the accomplishments of steeltown's Quinn, Glen Sonmor, and North Stars assistant coach Murray Oliver.

p. 38: Don and Doreen Hunt provided a copy of the eulogy Quinn wrote and read at Kay Knox's funeral. Don Hunt and his brother Swede Knox told me stories about living with Pat when he boarded with the family.

5. "They're Not Tough … They're Just Dirty"

p. 44: Former Philadelphia Flyers right-winger Gary Dornhoefer told me about when Pat Quinn knocked him out cold during the 1963 Memorial. The hit put him in a cast from his toes to his groin. The pair would play together again when they were both in the NHL and cross paths later in life when Pat was coaching the Leafs and Dornhoefer was working with *Hockey Night in Canada*. "With Pat, the reason so many players respected him [is that] it's so easy to hit when you're in your own building. But how many guys do it on the road? Quinn did that, he played the same way on the road as he did at home," Dornhoefer told me.

The history of how the Niagara Falls Flyers got to the Memorial Cup came from an old souvenir program given to me by Gregg Pilling, the old Oil Kings winger. Bert Marshall, another Oil Kings teammate, also provided accounts of the 1963 Oil Kings.

p. 44: Roger Bourbonnais, the Oil Kings' captain, recounted for me how coach Buster Brayshaw rallied his players in the locker room when they were behind. Quotes Brayshaw made to the media at the time came from various newspaper reports such as this May 7, 1963, *Toronto Daily Star* article: "Flyers fall again to Oil Kings."

p. 47: Announcer Wes Montgomery's breathless play-by-play of the win was printed in a 1963 *Globe and Mail* article, "Oil Kings win first Memorial Cup." A recording by Montgomery also told of the shower Leo LeClerc was forced to take after the win. The recording was provided by Gregg Pilling.

6. The Policeman

In this chapter, I borrowed heavily from the words of Pat Quinn himself. In 2010, Quinn did several interviews with journalist, statistician, and hockey executive Jason Farris, and the lengthy discussion between the two hockey buffs touches on just about every notable moment in Quinn's career. Farris interviewed Quinn for his expansive book on the inside world of NHL general managers, *Behind the Moves: NHL Manager Tell How Winners Are Built*. You can find it at nhlgms.com. When Farris found out I was writing this book he was generous enough to give me the transcript of that interview, and I have used it throughout the book. In this chapter, Pat recalls the time he met Gordie Howe, the problems with his "C" form, and his run-in with assistant coach Jimmy Skinner. Also, how he got loaned to Tulsa (including its farm team in Memphis), and his educational pursuits at the time. I am immensely grateful to Farris for allowing me to use this interview.

pp. 54, 58: Ray Miron told me about the conversations he had with Johnstown Jets GM John Mitchell about Quinn.

p. 57: Sandra Quinn told me of the kindness Ray and Rowena Miron showed to her young family.

p. 59: Guy Quinn told me all about the makeshift wooden trailer used to move the Quinns' belongings.

p. 60: The story of Quinn's dust-up at a downtown Winnipeg cocktail lounge and his night in jail comes from a small story in the *Winnipeg Free Press* from November 24, 1964.

7. One More Shot

p. 68: Serge Savard shared the story of Quinn attempting to shave Bill McCreary with Jason Farris, who passed the interview along to me.

pp. 67–71: Between Quinn's interviews with Jason Farris and my interviews with Sandra Quinn, I was able to piece together Quinn's gamble with Montreal and their moves to Houston, then Seattle, and finally back to Tulsa.

p. 71: Ray Miron helped me fill in the gaps on how he got Quinn back to Tulsa. As well, how Quinn's cerebral thinking of the game developed. Miron and former Leafs and Rangers player Jim Dorey helped explain how Quinn became an affable leader off the ice (including refereeing a fight between two teammates).

p. 71: The story of how Quinn turned Monday nights into a full-tackle Oilers football league comes from former Oilers teammate Jim Keon.

p. 73: The story of how Quinn saved teammate Mike Pelyk's ass comes from Pelyk himself.

8. Blue and White

p. 76: Researcher Paul Patkou, an incomparably knowledgeable hockey historian who was a lifeline while I was writing this book, helped me understand how the Leafs were affected by expansion and the moves Punch Imlach was making at the time.

p. 78: After all that moving, Sandra Quinn remembered her husband's first game in the NHL, in Pittsburgh on November 27, 1968. I should note that an old NHL game sheet found by Jason Farris from a match with Detroit a month earlier—October 13, 1968—lists Pat Quinn, 23. But Sandra Quinn has no recollection of the game and says Pat was always puzzled why his name was on the score sheet.

p. 78: Barry Quinn shared the story of Pat meeting Foster Hewitt.

p. 79: Guy Quinn, with a laugh, shared the story of his arrest before Pat's first game at Maple Leaf Gardens.

p. 81: Here's an interesting read by *Sportsnet Magazine*'s Brett Popplewell on "Greatest Maple Leafs: No. 6 Frank Mahovlich" that touched on the players' relationship with Punch Imlach: www.sportsnet. ca/hockey/24-7/greatest-maple-leafs-no-6-frank-mahovlich/

p. 83: That Dick Beddoes interview with Quinn referenced in the chapter appeared in the *Globe and Mail* on January 9, 1969. The detail about the souvenir puck Quinn received from the Leafs to commemorate his first goal came from a January 8, 1969, *Globe and Mail* article written by sportswriter Louis Cauz.

p. 84: In his interview with Jason Farris, Quinn recalled Punch Imlach's not-so-subtle instructions to put a stop to Howie Young. A March 3, 1969, *Globe and Mail* article by Rex MacLeod, "Howie Young subdued by Leafs' Quinn," added additional color.

p. 85: Paul Henderson and Dave Keon recalled the story of the more established players' fruitless initiation attempt on the rookies and lessons learned by Quinn.

p. 87: Former veteran Leafs forward Bob Pulford told me about the fight to get more rights for players.

p. 87: Sandra Quinn told me about her family's relationship with the Hortons. The information about the conversation about Pilote's salary that Quinn and Horton accidentally heard came from Quinn's interview with Jason Farris.

p. 88: A September 3, 1969, *Toronto Daily Star* article by Red Burnett gives a good overview of the salary demands made by Horton.

p. 88: Marcel Pronovost talks about his responsibility to mentor young players in another Red Burnett *Toronto Daily Star* article, "Pronovost helps to hinder self," printed on January 17, 1969.

9. "We Want Quinn!"

p. 91: The information about Quinn's dustup with the Bruins' Brent Casselman and Bobby Orr came from an interview I did with Casselman.

p. 93: The information about the violent series with Boston (including the Bobby Orr hit) came from several newspaper sources. Most notably, Quinn's jeers from the Boston crowd were recorded in a March 18, 1969, *Boston Globe* article, "Bruins bomb Leafs. Tie two scoring marks." The Irishman's St. Patrick's Day smack talk was reported in a March 18, 1969, *Globe and Mail* article by Louis Cauz, "Can't turn your back, Quinn says of Bruins." Again, two weeks later, Quinn was egging the other side on in another piece by Cauz, "Mixed emotions among Maple Leafs on eve of Bruins series." Rex MacLeod of the *Globe and Mail* wrote an April 3, 1969, story, "Bruins 10, Leafs 0, in wild playoff home-opener." In another *Boston Globe* piece, "Espo, Bruins crush Toronto in wild opener," writer Tom Fitzgerald went after Quinn for what appeared to be a "premeditated" hit. Bruins president Weston Adams Jr. warned against playing Quinn in another story by Cauz, "'Don't use Pat Quinn again in Boston games.'" And Orr's comments post-hit were recorded in an April 4, 1969, *Globe and Mail* article, "Imlach can't explain Leaf's ineptness."

p. 93: The documentary "The Mighty Quinn," on Leafs TV, shows video clips of the Orr hit and its aftermath.

p. 95: Guy Quinn told me about his mother's reaction.

p. 97: Jim Dorey told me the story about how assistant manager King Clancy wanted to get out onto the ice with the players.

p. 97: George Ashley told me about the time he got punched in the face trying to prevent a fight during the chaos.

p. 100: Quinn told the story of his encounter at the Irish pub in Boston many times over the years. It was recounted to me, with different details, by many of Quinn's closest friends. The version used in this chapter, which offered the most colorful details, was printed in the *Vancouver Sun* in a story written by the excellent Canucks beat reporter Iain MacIntyre.

p. 101: *Toronto Daily Star* reporter Milt Dunnell chronicled Punch Imlach's firing from the Leafs in an April 7, 1969 article, "Punch departs in a limousine."

10. Figures and Shillelaghs

p. 103: If you're interesting in learning more about power skating, here's a good 2014 *Hamilton Spectator* feature by Steve Milton: www.thespec.com/sports-story/4305871-milton-the-birth-of-power-skating/.

p. 103: Former figure skater Judy Williams talked to me about what it was like teaching Pat Quinn.

p. 105: Quinn's comments during the Leafs' training camp came from a September 30, 1969, article by Red Burnett at the *Toronto Daily Star*, "Pat Quinn remains a hold out but he will play for the Leafs."

p. 105: Quinn's longtime friend and colleague Rick Ley told me about their skirmishes in practice and the wisdom Quinn would impart while the pair carpooled to work.

p. 108: The information about Quinn's return to Boston Garden comes from a February 2, 1970, *Globe and Mail* article by Dan Proudfoot, "Bruins move on to win after second-period brawl."

p. 111: The information about the Pacific Coast Hockey League and the Canucks' early years came from a fabulous book by Norm Jewison that I've consulted often while writing this book: *Vancouver Canucks: The First Twenty Years* (Vancouver: Polestar Press, 1989).

11. "It's Been a Great Life"

p. 115: That interview with *The Province*'s Tom Watt, quoted throughout the chapter, ran in 1971 with the headline, "'It's been a great life.'" (The story was posted online after Quinn's death, but did not provide the original publication date.)

p. 117: Orland Kurtenbach, the Canucks franchise's first-ever captain, talked about the team's punishing travel schedules in those early days.

p. 117: Broadcaster Jim Robson told me about the time Quinn and Kurtenbach fought. Kurtenbach added to the story by talking about the 220-yard race the men ran to settle the score.

p. 119: Sandra Quinn filled me in on how the family fared in Vancouver, and Kalli Quinn told me about the summers she spent with her grandparents in Hamilton. The story about the Quinns shutting off power in a good portion of Hamilton comes from Barry Quinn.

p. 123: Much of the information about the fledgling hockey team in Atlanta comes from Bernard Geoffrion's thoroughly entertaining memoir, *Boom-Boom: The Life and Times of Bernard Geoffrion*, by Bernard Geoffrion and Stan Fischler (Toronto: McGraw-Hill Ryerson, 1997), as well as an interview I did with Cliff Fletcher.

12. Rejects and Has-Beens

p. 127: Frank Orr's 1975 profile of Quinn in the *Toronto Star*, "A case for the defense," is one of the best features I've read on Quinn. In it, Orr explains how Quinn became an NHL success story and gets the player's thoughts on everything from going to school to playing in Atlanta. I've quoted from the profile throughout.

p. 129: Phil Myre and Mike Pelyk talked about how the team came together on and off the ice.

p. 129: The Omni was a great arena in which to watch hockey, but it was outdated as a source of ancillary revenue. It had fifteen thousand seats but no standing room and only four private boxes. "It was doomed before it even started," Cliff Fletcher told me.

p. 129: Geoffrion's memoir talks about the buzz in that arena during those first games. Interviews with Phil Myre and Cliff Fletcher added key details.

p. 131: That Jim Huber profile on Quinn is also a great read. It ran in the 1973 *Atlanta Journal* with the headline, "Pat Quinn—Flames enforcer."

p. 132: Kalli Quinn told me about her childhood in Atlanta.

p. 135: Pat Quinn recalled his extraordinary—and unlikely—goal against the California Golden Seals in a 1985 interview with *Hockey Digest*'s Matt Carlson, "The game I'll never forget." Cliff Fletcher added a little color for good measure.

p. 135: Quinn's thoughts on how Cliff Fletcher ran the team and what he thought of his own role as captain come from his interviews with Jason Farris.

p. 137: Cliff Fletcher and Frank Orr, who I also interviewed for this book, helped me to understand how Quinn had developed and improved as a player over the years.

p. 138: The story of Geoffrion's resignation comes from his memoir.

p. 138: The story of how Pat Quinn broke his ankle has been told to me by many, but I took Kalli Quinn's account since she watched it happen.

p. 139: Ray Miron recounted how the Colorado Rockies passed on Quinn, much to Miron's disappointment.

13. Coach Quinn

p. 143: Brian Burke told me the story about how Quinn, a rookie coach, risked his own skin to tell his prospective players the truth.

p. 145: Quinn told Jason Farris all about his one-on-one meetings with Shero, the little nuggets of advice he'd receive in the coach's tiny office, and his perception on what worked and didn't work when it came to coaches dealing with management.

p. 146: Sandra Quinn told me about how Pat began keeping notebooks early in his coaching career. She still has them at her home in Vancouver.

p. 147: Quinn's thoughts on Keith Allen came from an interview Pat did with Barry Bloom (titled "The Goal: Interview") in *Goal* magazine, volume 8, issue 14. I also found some interesting details about the Flyers' computer system in a Keith Bellows piece in *Hockey Magazine*, spring 1980: "Take a new coach, some classy rookies, space-age scouting and a gang of recharged veterans and what do you have? The best team in the NHL."

p. 148: Frank Orr helped me understand what happened after Shero's departure with his *Toronto Star* story from January 1982, "Flyers coach just fell into the job."

p. 149: Sports broadcaster Mike Emrick, then just starting his career, remembered the relationship Quinn had with his minor players in Maine, the time Quinn tore onto the ice in Moncton to protect his player, and the day he packed his belongings in boxes to take his first head coaching position in the NHL.

p. 150: A 1978 *Hockey News* feature, "With playbook, fundamental rules, Flyers' Shero revolutionized coaching in the NHL," gave me a good sense of Fred Shero's coaching systems.

p. 151: Quinn's first interview as an NHL coach was with *The Philadelphia Enquirer*'s Bill Fleischmann. "Rebuild confidence Quinn's first move," read the headline. *Hockey Illustrated*'s Mark Brown also gave a solid overview of what hockey on the Flyers was like under Quinn with his 1980 feature, "Quinn's Flyers get back to basics."

p. 153: Bob Clarke told me how he came to be the Flyers' assistant coach.

p. 154: Quinn's thoughts on the Flyers' home opener were recorded by Dick Irvin in his book *Behind the Bench: Coaches Talk about Life in the NHL* (Toronto: McClelland & Stewart, 1993). The book is an oral history from some of the best coaches of our time. It's a fabulous read, even today.

14. The Streak

p. 155: Sandra and Kalli Quinn showed me the Playboy pinball machine, which sits in the basement of their home in West Vancouver.

p. 157: The Ice Capades anecdote and Quinn's thoughts on getting his team moving came from the Keith Bellows *Hockey Magazine* piece referenced in Chapter 13. Bob Clarke offered his thoughts on Quinn's strategies as well.

p. 159: Quinn's thoughts on Reggie Leach came from a Bill Fleischmann story, "Quinn's Flyers, patience works wonders," in *The Hockey News*.

p. 160: In interviews, Bill Barber and Paul Holmgren talked about the influence Pat had on them as players.

p. 161: Phil Myre remembered how the Flyers never discussed their streak, for fear of jinxing it.

p. 165: The story of St. Patrick's Day comes from Bob Butera, the former Flyers president and Quinn's friend.

p. 166: Quinn's thoughts on the Flyers' streak, including calls made by the refs, were also recorded in Irvin's *Behind the Bench*.

p. 172: Quinn complained about the refereeing to Jason Farris.

15. Finding an Edge

p. 176: Pat Croce, Wayne Halliwell, and Julie Anthony both told me about their work with the Flyers. And the *Toronto Star*'s Rex MacLeod recorded Quinn's thinking on why he started working with the psychologists in a 1992 article, "Quinn thought of better way."

p. 180: Kalli Quinn recounted the time she told her swimming coach to "fuck off" and memories from vacations in Hilton Head, South Carolina.

p. 184: The *Toronto Star*'s Jon Marks wrote of the surprise of Pat Quinn's firing in a March 2, 1982, article, "Floundering Flyers fire Coach Quinn."

p. 186: Here's a biography of Esther Clark, dean of Widener University: http://articles.philly.com/2002-03-02/news/25341117_1_public-defender-law-degree-law-review. Bob Curran, former US Attorney in Philadelphia and friend of Quinn, introduced him to Clark. Curran remembers Quinn would give her tickets to hockey games.

p. 187: Quinn's experience at law school was captured in a November 1982 feature by Jay Greenberg of *Hockey News*, "School days a challenge for Quinn."

p. 188: Bob Butera remembered how his friend stopped going to Flyers games after he was fired.

16. The Right Direction

p. 192: Frank Orr's November 3, 1984, *Toronto Star* story, "Quinn chose Kings' court after putting law on hold," helped clarify Rogie Vachon's courtship of Quinn and Quinn's thought process regarding the deal. Bill Fleischmann's July 15, 1984, *Hockey News* story, "Pat Quinn's approach," helped me understand the state of the LA Kings before Quinn came on board.

p. 194: I spoke with Dick Babush, Quinn's longtime lawyer, who negotiated all his major contracts. He took me through the deal with LA. Quinn's comments upon accepting the position in LA come from a May 30, 1994, *Globe and Mail* article, "Quinn agrees to coach Kings."

p. 197: It was also Frank Orr who got Quinn's position on tans on the record.

p. 200: Mike Murphy told me about his and Quinn's trip to Russia.

17. Quinngate

p. 202: Frank Griffiths's purchase of the Canucks and how the team fared in its first decade is detailed in Jewison's book on the Canucks' first twenty years.

p. 203: In an interview, Arthur Griffiths told me about why his family wanted Pat Quinn and how they went about securing him, including his cloak-and-dagger meeting with Dick Babush in a Georgia hotel, to the meeting he had with Quinn and his father in a San Diego beach resort, to the decision to pass one hundred thousand dollars in an envelope to Quinn through a Canucks trainer.

p. 203: Similarly, Dick Babush took me through what happened on his end, from the initial overtures to what, in hindsight, went wrong.

p. 204: The timeline of Quinn's negotiations and deal with Vancouver came from the NHL's official "Order and decision: Pertinent facts—order of expulsion," released January 30, 1987. There are a series of events explained in this release that all sides appear to have agreed on.

Also, from the appeal in the British Columbia Supreme Court, which says the fines were drastically reduced: *Vancouver Hockey Club Ltd. v. 8 Hockey Ventures Inc.*, 1987 2461 (BC SC).

p. 207: Canucks' former broadcaster Tom Larscheid told me about breaking the story that Quinn was coming to Vancouver, though, like any respectable journalist, he refused to divulge his source. Larscheid also told me about interviewing Quinn after his firing and seeing him from his hotel window get into a beat-up station wagon taxi and head off.

p. 208: Stein talked about how he'd recommended Quinn to Keith Allen a decade earlier during a press scrum to address Quinngate, which was broadcast on *Hockey Night in Canada*.

p. 208: Rogie Vachon spoke with me to share his reflections on Pat and Quinngate.

p. 211: The comments Quinn made outside his LA home came from a January 23, 1987, article by Rick Sadowski in *The Hockey News*, "Quinn expulsion an NHL shocker."

p. 212: Reaction from Kings fans comes from *Hockey Night in Canada* clips.

p. 213: The information about the loophole of not having a contract filed with the league (a precedent set by Jacques Demers) came from an October 10, 1987, *Globe and Mail* article, "Ziegler denies he was influenced by Eagleson." Eagleson's comments come from a January 17, 1986, *Globe and Mail* article, "Eagleson says Quinn wrong."

p. 213: Sandra Quinn told me the details about how Pat Quinn finished law school.

p. 214: Quinn's belief that he'd been "led down a garden path" with the Kings and his commitment to not renege on the deal with Vancouver came from a n October 9, 1987, Canadian Press article, "Rejected lucrative Kings bid: Quinn."

p. 215: Quinn's remarks that close out the chapter, about how tough the experience was on him, come from Irvin's *Behind the Bench*.

18. Selling Hope

p. 216: Brian Burke told me about the late-night talk he had with Pat Quinn that brought him to Vancouver. (The information about how Keith Allen told Burke he'd have a better chance in law is from a December 17, 1987, *Boston Globe* story, "Burke now seeing other side of coin.")

p. 219: Glen Ringdal, Arthur Griffiths, Brian Burke, and Pat Quinn (in his interviews with Jason Farris) talked about the state of the Vancouver Canucks upon Quinn's arrival and what the management team did in those early days to "sell hope."

p. 219: Again, Jewison's book on the Canucks' first twenty years came in handy when trying to explain major trades and game history.

p. 222: Trevor Linden told me about the first time he sat in Pat Quinn's living room. (Quinn told Jason Farris that Linden was a "hell of a kid.") A large photo of Quinn in his Canucks practice gear hangs behind Linden's desk in his office at Rogers Arena, where we chatted for an hour one afternoon about what Quinn had meant to him.

p. 222: A good rundown of all the roadblocks with the Bure draft can be found in a May 14, 1988, *Vancouver Sun* story by Mike Beamish, "Canucks make bid to Soviets."

p. 225: Vancouver scout Mike Penny told me about how he figured out Pavel Bure was eligible. Brian Burke and Bure's agent Ron Salcer also filled in the details.

p. 227: The information about the punishing Russian bootcamps came from a 2015 guest article in *The Players' Tribune* written by Igor Larionov. "We would practice on the ice for four hours a day and then lift weights, run, and do off-ice training for another five to six hours," Larionov wrote. www.theplayerstribune.com/miracle-on-ice-hockey-russia/.

p. 227: Other articles that helped flesh out the negotiations with the Soviets, including Pat Quinn's public comments, are the following three *Vancouver Sun* articles: "Larionov wants to play for the Canucks,"

January 26, 1989; "Soviets still a question mark for Quinn," June 28, 1989; and "Quinn off to Moscow in effort to sign Krutov," September 2, 1989.

p. 231: Brian Burke told me about when NHL commissioner John Ziegler told him and Quinn that the Canucks' claim to Bure was legitimate.

p. 232: The information about the Canucks' soured relationship with Vladimir Krutov came from the following articles: "Krutov: Speaking out at last," Elliott Pap, *Vancouver Sun*, September 20, 1990; "Canucks deem pudgy Krutov unfit to play," Grant Kerr, Canadian Press, October 3, 1990; "Krutov gone, but parting isn't settled," Elliott Pap, *Vancouver Sun*, October 3, 1990; "Quinn gears for Krutov arbitration: Russian great wants his $$$," Tony Gallagher, June 16, 1994.

19. Superboss

p. 234: The information about the plane crash at LAX comes from an interview with former Canucks player Garry Valk and a *Los Angeles Times* article by Steve Springer, "Canucks had close-up view of fatal airline crash at LAX," from February 4, 1991.

p. 236: Quinn's trades for Geoff Courtnall, Cliff Ronning, and others were summed up in a January 15, 1992, *Ottawa Citizen* article by Dave Molinari, "They're CANucks now."

p. 240: Many of the details of the messy matter of releasing Pavel Bure from the Red Army came from my interview with Brian Burke. Mike Penny also provided some details. Some information was gleaned from an October 1991 *Sports Illustrated* article, "The Russian Moscow-born right wing Pavel Bure is having a blast in Vancouver." I also spoke with Ron Salcer, Bure's agent who shared the story of Bure's first experience with the Canucks and his respect for Quinn.

p. 243: The story of Quinn's assault on the Gatorade jug was told to me by several players in the room, including Kirk McLean and Trevor Linden. Glen Ringdel shared the story Quinn snapping at him after the Canucks loss to the Jets.

p. 244: The information about the death of Pat Quinn's youngest brother Phillip comes from his siblings as well as Sandra and Kalli Quinn.

p. 246: Quinn's thoughts on losing his right-hand man, Brian Burke, and how that strained his workload came from a May 27, 1992, article by *The Province*'s Jim Jamieson, "Way too much work, even for Mighty Quinn."

p. 247: The challenges associated with re-signing Igor Larionov came from several articles, including Jim Jamieson's May 14, 1992, story in *The Province*, "Tough decisions await Quinn." The *Vancouver Sun*'s Iain MacIntyre wrote a May 30, 1992, article, "Larionov caught in middle of pact clause" (which includes the quote from Larionov about feeling like a "hostage"); *Vancouver Sun* reporter Elliott Pap wrote a June 18, 1992, piece, "Quinn completes NHL awards hat trick" (which includes the quote from Quinn about the "public relations nightmare" not coming home with Larionov would have caused); Tony Gallagher at *The Province* wrote a June 14, 1992, article, "Battle of egos could be costly," which offered more details about negotiation strategies; Pap also wrote a July 29, 1992, article, "Larionov keeping door ajar for return to Canucks someday"; both MacIntyre and Pap covered the result with MacIntyre's July 15, 1992, story, "Losing Larionov: Talented Russian signs deal to play in Switzerland," and Pap's "Larionov keeping door ajar for return to Canucks someday," which ran on July 29, 1992.

p. 249: Trevor Linden told me about his take on Quinn's coaching style in an interview. This chapter also uses information from interviews with Pavel Bure, Gary Valk, and Tom Larscheid.

p. 251: Criticisms of Quinn's coaching were summed up in two articles, the *Vancouver Sun*'s Elliott Pap's May 14, 1993, piece, "Canucks post-mortem must start with man of many hats"; and a May 18, 1993, story in the *Toronto Star*, "Quinn urged to hire coach."

20. Dreamland

p. 252: Vancouver's rocky start to the 1993–94 season was recorded in *Vancouver Sun* reporter Elliott Pap's October 4, 1993, story, "Just remember, the playoffs don't start until next April."

p. 252: Petr Nedved's problems with Pat Quinn and displeasure with the negotiations were put on the record in Tony Gallagher's October 12, 1993, *The Province* story, "Less bite for new Sharks."

p. 253: Elliott Pap's December 3, 1993, story in the *Vancouver Sun*, "Will Quinn do something before more seats become vacant," addressed the increasing scrutiny Quinn was under after losing Nedved and Larionov, as well as his failure to recruit any new stars in the draft.

p. 254: The story behind Quinn's trade for defenseman Jeff Brown and others was told by Iain MacIntyre in a March 22, 1994, *Vancouver Sun* story, "Quinn makes best of bad situation, acquiring trio in 'grade B movie plot.'"

p. 255: Broadcaster Jim Robson told me about the time Quinn canceled practice and annihilated his stick on the boards. Cliff Ronning added the story about the time he once kicked a garbage can so hard he broke his toe.

p. 256: Pat Quinn told Jason Farris about his affinity for Frank Griffiths (a sentiment that was echoed by many family and friends I spoke to while researching this book). The information about the players wearing "2 pts for FG" patches came from an April 8, 1994, *Vancouver Sun* article by Iain MacIntyre, "Canucks give Griffiths two points: Bure dazzles against Sharks."

p. 258: Quinn's attempts to spark a physical series with Calgary came from an April 15, 1994, *Calgary Herald* story by Mike Board, "Quinn's singing old song."

p. 259: Quinn's remarks about the heated series to both Tom Larscheid and George McPhee were recounted in interviews with both men.

p. 261: Kirk McLean told me how Quinn came up to him and said "you did it" after he saved the series against Calgary.

p. 261: The fans' elation after Bure's winning goal was captured in an article by Paul Chapman in *The Province*, "Canucks fans whoop it up," May 1, 1994.

p. 262: George McPhee told me the story about the birth of Sergio Momesso's child. He also told me about the team's use of hyperbaric chambers.

p. 264: Quinn's comments about the upcoming series with Toronto and his friend Cliff Fletcher's retort come from a May 16, 1994, story by Iain MacIntyre in the *Vancouver Sun*, "Bring on the Leafs: Quinn fires opening shots."

p. 265: Barry Quinn told me the story of his and Jack's Ireland trip and the family's reaction to the series win.

p. 266: Quinn's comments about the refereeing in the series with New York are from the Iain MacIntyre story of June 4, 1994, in the *Vancouver Sun*, "In this round the hombre in the black hat is Graves."

p. 267: Ellen Ley told me about her lucky spareribs. George McPhee told me about Quinn's lucky tie.

p. 268: Pat Quinn's comments about headlines declaring the Canucks were out of the Cup running were from a June 11, 1994, *Ottawa Citizen* article by Roy MacGregor, "Stop the presses! It's not over."

21. The End of an Era

p. 276: The information about Quinn's relationship with Bure and the rumor about Bure attempting to blackmail the Canucks into siging a contract comes from clips of Cherry and Quinn on *Hockey Night in Canada*.

Tony Gallagher wrote about Bure's rocky relationship with the Canucks brass in the *Vancouver Province* on January 20, 1999, citing an exclusive interview with Bure following his trade to Florida, after he sat out most of the season demanding to be moved. In a brief interview with Bure, he told me about his respect for Pat and that he always thought of him as a man he could trust. Ron Salcer, Bure's agent, cleared the air about the relationship he and his client had with Quinn in a subsequent interview with me.

This section also cites details from a story by Greg Douglas in the *Vancouver Sun* from April 12, 2013, about Quinn's remarks on Bure at the time. "Pavel Bure was—and is—the best player to ever wear a Canucks uniform," Quinn said.

p. 278: A decent overview of key dates in the ownership history of the Vancouver Grizzlies and Canucks can be found in a January 21, 2000, Canadian Press article, "Grizzlies chronology." In an interview, Arthur Griffiths talked about his struggles to keep hold of the franchise.

p. 279: Arthur Griffiths and Mike Penny told me about the fight Quinn had in his office with Stan McCammon. Penny told me about their perceptions of the new Orca Bay management.

p. 280: Rick Ley told me about how Quinn, his longtime friend, fired him.

p. 281: The story of the Canucks' botched attempt to bring Wayne Gretzky to Vancouver comes from interviews with Wayne Gretzky, Mike Barnett, Arthur Griffiths, George McPhee, and a series of exclusive interviews Jason Farris did with Quinn in 2010.

p. 284: Quinn's feelings about ownership's decision to go around management on the Messier deal come from his interviews with Jason Farris. Other details about the Canucks pursuit of Messier come from a *New York Times* article, "In Signing Messier, Canucks' Persistence Paid Off," by Jason Diamos on July 31, 1997.

p. 285: The story about Pat Quinn's plan to fire coach Tom Renney and his subsequent firing comes from Mike Penny. Trevor Linden told me about his reaction and Tom Larscheid told me about his interview in Quinn's hotel room, and how he saw the newly fired coach leaving that day in a beat-up taxi.

22. Back to Where It Began

p. 289: Dick Babush told me about the lump-sum agreement with the Canucks.

p. 290: Quinn told Jason Farris about how he considered moving on from hockey after being fired by the Canucks, and about how the job with the Leafs slowly piqued his interest.

p. 293: Pat Quinn's early plans to turn Toronto into a winning team were captured in a *Toronto Star* article by Paul Hunter, "The Mighty Quinn."

p. 296: Todd Warriner and Gary Valk both told me about their experiences with Quinn.

p. 298: Tom Anselmi told me the story of working with Quinn in Vancouver and ordering the special ventilation system for Quinn's new office at the Air Canada Centre.

p. 299: Reid Mitchell filled me in on his role with the Leafs as their video coach. He also told me the story about the time Bill Watters inadvertently ate a stick of Pat Quinn's lucky gum.

p. 304: Wayne Gretzky and Bob Nicholson told me how it came to be that Pat Quinn was selected as head coach of Canada's Olympic team.

23. Glitter and Gold

p. 306: The story of how Pat Quinn would sit on a bench outside the Canadian quarters came from a January 26, 2006, *Toronto Star* story by the great Randy Starkman, "Joys of being benched."

p. 308: Ken Hitchcock told me how the management and coaching staff for the Olympic team began planning. Andrew Podnieks' *Canadian Gold 2002: Making Hockey History* (Bolton, ON: Fenn Publishing, 2002) helped fill in some of the blanks.

p. 312: The story of how Ed Belfour came to the team was told to me by Wayne Gretzky.

p. 313: While Keith Hammond told me about the beer run, Quinn's comments to the press after the loss to Sweden and the win against Germany come from Podnieks' *Canadian Gold 2002: Making Hockey History*.

p. 316: Gretzky's comments about the Hamrlik hit were also recorded in Podnieks' *Canadian Gold 2002: Making Hockey History*. Gretzky told me about Quinn's can of "whoop-ass."

p. 318: Ken Hitchcock told me what Quinn said to the players the night before the gold medal game.

p. 318: Sandra Quinn, Kalli Quinn, and Barry Quinn filled me in on where the family was and how they reacted to the win. Barry Quinn provided home footage of the family's reactions during the gold-medal game.

p. 322: Bob Nicholson told me about the scene in the locker room after Canada took home the gold.

24. Last Dance

p. 323: Curtis Joseph, D'arcy Tucker, and Shayne Corson all told me about their experiences with Quinn.

p. 325: Quinn's grumblings to the press came from a *Toronto Star* article by Rosie DiManno, "Crusty Quinn is back in form: He's gruff, growling and not about to give up coach's job."

p. 326: Rick Ley and Mike Penny told me about their friend's cigar habit and commitment to get healthy.

p. 327: The information about the death of Pat's father, Jack Quinn, came from the family.

p. 330: Quinn's comments about Steve Stavro were made to Jason Farris in their 2010 interviews.

p. 332: Reid Mitchell told me about how Pat Quinn would often conjure up the image of Hamilton shift workers in his pregame talks.

p. 336: Quinn talked about his relationship with John Ferguson in his interviews with Jason Farris. Ron Toigo and Mike Penny also talked about Quinn's perspective on the young general manager being brought aboard.

p. 339: The story of St. Patrick's Day comes from Mike Penny.

p. 340: The politics of Quinn's firing from the Leafs were laid out in an April 21, 2006, *Globe and Mail* story by Tim Wharnsby, "Leafs fire Quinn."

25. A Song for Paddy Quinn

p. 341: Jim Robson, Trevor Linden, Kirk McLean, Cliff Ronning, and Gerald Diduck all told me the story of Quinn's appearance and speech at the Heritage Classic.

p. 342: Perspectives on Quinn and the Olympics in Turin come from Wayne Gretzky, Ken Hitchcock, and Bob Nicholson.

p. 343: Stories about the U-18 and World Junior tournaments come from interviews with Guy Boucher, Jesse Wallin, Matt Duchene, P.K. Subban, John Tavares, Thomas Hickey, and Dustin Tokarski.

p. 345: Steve Tambellini told me about Quinn's brief tenure time in Edmonton.

p. 345: Dickson Liong told me the story of his relationship with Quinn.

p. 345: Stories of Quinn's illness come from various family members and friends.

p. 347: Carol Quinn told me about the memorial service for Pat at St. Eugene's in Hamilton.

p. 347: Sandra Quinn and others shared details about Pat's funeral and memorial in Vancouver.

p. 347: Sandra Quinn was kind enough to invite me to her home to learn more about Pat and to check out his incredible collection hockey memories.

p 348: I attended the St. Patrick's celebration of Pat Quinn in Vancouver and interviewed others who were there.

Acknowledgments

I never had the privilege of meeting Pat Quinn. The closest I came was at the Hockey Hall of Fame in Toronto. Quinn stood near a vault in the elegant old bank where the ghosts of the game live. He looked like a statue, tall and broad, in a three-piece suit. The Great Hall was full of reporters covering the induction of the 2011 class—Doug Gilmour, Ed Belfour, Joe Nieuwendyk, and Mark Howe. Quinn towered over everyone. He was chairman of the board at the Hall of Fame, the proud custodian of hockey tradition. But he was *more* than that, really. Quinn and Gordie Howe—who was there with his family—filled the room with their presence. They *were* hockey history. Legends, both. But of course Quinn became a legend in such a different way. At the time, I didn't really know his story beyond the early 1990s, when I was still a kid who watched *Hockey Night* on Saturdays with my dad and would fall asleep dreaming about the game. In my hockey life, Quinn was always one of the revered greats. But I didn't know, then, how hard he worked to become that.

I was too timid to speak to Pat Quinn that day. I'm not the type to approach legends with small talk (a real weakness in my profession).

Knowing what I know now about Pat Quinn, I wish I had.

Four years later, I sat in an Irish pub with Nick Garrison from Penguin Random House Canada, sipping Jamieson, when he asked me to embark on the most important and intimidating project of my career. He wanted me to tell the story of hockey's Big Irishman.

The request was such an honor, but also such a risk. I worried that I'd be crushed beneath the mass of Quinn's life. That night, I called my father—as I always did when a huge decision needed to be made. "Son, I don't know how you'll do it," he said. "But I know you will."

And so, as he always had, my dad encouraged me with his faith and support to face a wild unknown.

He is the first person I need to thank. But there are so many others, so I'll get moving:

Sandra Quinn, having lost her love of more than fifty years, was kind enough to open her door to me to share the moments of their life together. This book was almost unbearably painful for her to be part of. Sandra, thank your for being so gracious, patient, and strong—this could never have happened without you. I hope these pages honor the legacy of the love you shared.

Along with Sandra, the Quinn family were tremendous through this process. Kalli Quinn shared beautiful stories of Pat Quinn as a dad. Carol Davis-Quinn, Guy Quinn, and Barry Quinn took me on delightful tours of life on Glennie, and brought Captain Jack and Jean Quinn to life. I'm so grateful for your help. (Barry, I look forward to sharing a Guinness with you again soon.)

The truth is, Pat Quinn told his story better than anyone. He was a vibrant, colorful storyteller who would have filled volumes. Thankfully, he left so many of his great stories with his friends. I can't possibly thank them all here. More than a hundred people were interviewed over the course of a few months. They took the time because Pat had meant so much to them. I hope this book reflects the man you knew, respected, and loved.

The Philadelphia Flyers, Vancouver Canucks, and Toronto Maple Leafs were a tremendous help in tracking down key interviews and providing me with original content that helped bring his story to life. Thank you for your support.

Each of the interviews for this book were transcribed word for word. Nick Faris, editor-in-chief of the *Queen's Journal* and Sean Sutherland, the *Journal*'s features editor, generously spent hours on end listening to my scattershot interviews, typing every word. You guys are amazing. Thank you.

Researcher Paul Patskou worked tirelessly to provide every article, magazine feature, and video clip of Pat Quinn available. His vast knowledge of hockey history and invaluable contacts made this book possible. His meticulous fact checking spared me from a great deal of embarrassment. Paul, it was such a pleasure to work with you.

Jason Farris was also an invaluable help throughout this process. He provided me with transcriptions of his exclusive interviews with Pat Quinn from 2011, which are sourced heavily throughout. Jason also proofread the manuscript and suggested key changes. I can't possibly repay you for your time and input. Thank you, Jason.

My mentor and friend Gare Joyce generously combed through the manuscript with his critical eye. As always, his advice led to enormous improvements in the final draft. Thanks for passing on your craft.

Thank you to Nick Garrison and Penguin Random House Canada for giving me this opportunity. Nick, you were patient and supportive from beginning to end. When things felt like they were going to fall apart, your calm confidence held it together. I can't thank you enough. Laurel Sparrow, thanks for all of your hard work carefully copy-editing the manuscript. (I apologize for keeping you so busy.) Sandra Tooze, thank you for your patience, understanding, and diligence in getting this book to print.

This biography wouldn't have been possible without John Intini, who graciously granted me a lengthy leave from *Sportsnet* and was understanding when circumstances required that I extend my absence even further.

Rick Broadhead, my friend, thank you for working so hard to help me pursue my dreams. I'd be lost in this industry without you. You've done more for me than any agent should ever have to do. Thank you for believing in me.

There are so many people who have shown me love and support through this process. Friends and family, thank you so much. John Poisson, thank you for lending me your meticulous eye in proofreading the manuscript. Mom, Jai, and Jenna—I know that nothing in my life could be done without the people around me propping me up. Love you.

To Jayme Poisson: I owe you everything. Each time I fell to pieces, you were there to fix me. You transcribed interviews. You fixed my sloppy writing and navigated my confusing chapter structures. You researched endlessly. You learned about Fred Shero's sixteen-rule system and the frustrating contract negotiations with Russian players. And you did it all while being an award-winning investigative journalist at the *Toronto Star* and a much better reporter than I'll ever be. You made this happen for me, and I adore you for it. And I will, forever.

And, the hardest part.

In late May, with deadlines looming, I found myself overwhelmed with anxiety—afraid that I was going to let down everyone who had put their faith in me. It was a Tuesday afternoon. I wasn't able to type. My mind had locked up, fixated on failure.

I called him right away. I always did when things fell apart. Just the sound of his voice when he answered the phone "Hello, son" was enough to bring me back. He was on a business trip in Calgary. We spoke for about ten minutes as he drove to a meeting.

I don't know if he understood just how much I needed him that day. But he certainly knew what to say. Before we hung up, my dad repeated what he'd told me back at the beginning when I was about to step into this great unknown.

"I don't know how you'll do it, son," he said. "But you will. You always do."

It felt warm, like a hug. After we hung up, I turned back to the screen on the desk my dad had built for me, and I continued to type.

It was then—I can remember it clearly—that I decided to dedicate this book to my best friend, Rick Robson.

I didn't get the chance to tell him. He died suddenly a few days later, a week before his sixtieth birthday.

Those words still haven't settled. The last two months have been a wretched blur. I'm not sure how the world makes any sense without him in it. It will, I think. It must. What I do know, though, is that today I am exactly where he said I'd be.

I don't know how we did it, Dad. But we did. We always do.

It's finished. And every word is for you.

Index